Arthur Underhill

A Concise Manual of the Law

relating to private trusts and trustees

Arthur Underhill

A Concise Manual of the Law
relating to private trusts and trustees

ISBN/EAN: 9783337367916

Printed in Europe, USA, Canada, Australia, Japan

Cover: Foto ©Suzi / pixelio.de

More available books at **www.hansebooks.com**

Concise Manual

OF THE LAW RELATING TO PRIVATE

TRUSTS AND TRUSTEES.

BY

ARTHUR UNDERHILL, M.A.

OF LINCOLN'S INN, AND THE CHANCERY BAR, BARRISTER-AT-LAW.

LONDON:

BUTTERWORTHS, 7, FLEET STREET,

Law Publishers to the Queen's most excellent Majesty.

DUBLIN: HODGES, FOSTER & CO.
EDINBURGH: T. & T. CLARK; BELL & BRADFUTE.
CALCUTTA: THACKER, SPINK & CO. BOMBAY: THACKER, VINING & CO.
MELBOURNE: GEORGE ROBERTSON.

1878.

TO

THE RIGHT HONORABLE

SIR GEORGE JESSEL,

MASTER OF THE ROLLS,

THE

𝔉𝔬𝔩𝔩𝔬𝔴𝔦𝔫𝔤 𝔚𝔬𝔯𝔨

IS,

BY EXPRESS PERMISSION,

MOST RESPECTFULLY DEDICATED.

PREFACE.

EVERY person who has had practical experience as a lawyer, divides his professional knowledge into two distinct heads, namely:—first, his habitual knowledge— that knowledge of the rules of law which is laid up in his memory, so that whenever he has reason to apply those rules they are accurately recalled without external aid; and secondly, his knowledge of the storehouses, so to speak, where he can get the actual knowledge of any branch of law of which he is uncertain. Now of storehouses of law we have an ample supply. Putting aside the various digests, no works could well be more complete and detailed than Mr. Dart's Book on Vendors and Purchasers, Mr. Jarman's on Wills, Mr. Chitty's on Contracts, Mr. Addison's on Torts, Mr. Justice Lindley's on Partnership, and last, but far from least, Mr. Lewin's Model Treatise on Trusts. Again, we have smaller but singularly complete summaries of case law in Mr. Roscoe's Nisi Prius Evidence, and Mr. Watson's excellent Compendium of Equity, a book which ought to be in the hands of every practical lawyer.

But although the law libraries are rich in great works of reference, such as those above referred to, they are comparatively poor in manuals giving a systematic view of those *principles* of the law—the oases in "the wilderness of single instances"—with which every lawyer ought to be mentally furnished.

As has been well said by our most eminent living jurist (*a*), "it becomes obvious, that if a lawyer is to have anything better than a familiarity with indexes, he must gain his knowledge in some other way than from existing books on the subject. No doubt such knowledge is to be gained. Experience gives by degrees, in favourable cases, a comprehensive acquaintance with the principles of the law with which a practitioner is conversant. *He gets to see that it is shorter and simpler than it looks*, and to understand that the innumerable cases which at first sight appear to constitute the law, are really no more than illustrations of a comparatively small number of principles."

The want above indicated has been of late years somewhat met by the publication of such works as Sir Fitzjames Stephens' Digests of Evidence and the Criminal Law, Mr. Vaughan Hawkins' handy treatise on Wills, Mr. Farwell's work on Powers, and Mr. Pollock's on Partnership; the writers of which have with success and ability presented to their readers the *principles* of those several branches of the law in a distinct and accurate manner.

(*a*) Sir Fitzjames Stephens, Dig. Evidence, VI.

It has been my endeavour in this volume to perform in a humble way the same task in relation to the Law of Private Trusts. Every student has now-a-days to show himself acquainted with the subject, and has to depend upon those manuals of general equity, which are necessarily very elementary, and do not appear to me to draw a sufficient distinction between principle and illustration.

Again, the law of Trusts is the one branch of Equity, of the principles of which a solicitor ought to have an habitual and accurate knowledge; for not only is he continually called upon to give off-hand advice to trustees, but he is frequently a trustee himself. So far as I know, there is no work of moderate size which will give him an accurate knowledge of the principles which ought to guide him; and I fancy, that in the heat and worry of general practice but few have the time or the inclination to *study* (not merely read) a large volume on this one of the many branches of law upon which they have to advise their clients. A person of ordinary industry and capacity may easily learn the 76 Articles of this Work, and may, without great effort, remember the main facts of such of the illustrative cases as are what may be called "leading;" and when he has done so I feel no doubt that he will possess such a knowledge of the principles upon which the court acts with regard to Private Trusts, as will enable him to answer without hesitation all such questions as occur in the every-day experience of a general practitioner.

With regard to the typography I would mention that the words printed in heavy type (or clarendon) are those which are the key to the nature of the example in which they occur, so that by casting the eye over a page in search of an example, it may by this means be readily found.

ARTHUR UNDERHILL.

23, SOUTHAMPTON BUILDINGS,
   CHANCERY LANE.
     July 20*th*, 1878.

TABLE OF CONTENTS.

DIVISION II. – CONSTRUCTIVE TRUSTS.

DIVISION III.—THE ADMINISTRATION OF A TRUST.

SUB-DIVISION I.—PRELIMINARY.

SUB-DIVISION II.—THE ESTATE OF THE TRUSTEE AND ITS INCIDENTS.

SUB-DIVISION III.—THE DUTIES OF A TRUSTEE.

TABLE OF CASES CITED.

H.

I.

J.

A

Concise Manual

OF THE LAW RELATING TO

PRIVATE TRUSTS.

ART. 1.—*Definitions.*

In this manual, the following terms are used with the meanings assigned to them in the subsequent paragraphs, namely:—

A trust means an obligation under which some person is bound, or has bound himself, to deal with the beneficial interest in real or personal property which is vested in him, in a particular manner and for a particular purpose, either wholly in favour of another or others, or partially in favour of another or others conjointly with himself (*a*).

(*a*) I can cite no authority for this definition. Mr. Lewin adopts Lord Coke's definition of a use, namely, "A confidence reposed in some other, not issuing out of the land, but as a thing collateral, annexed in privity to the estate of the land, for which cestui que trust has no remedy but by subpœna in chancery." Co. Lit. 272 b. This definition would seem to be applicable to real estate only, and certainly not to trusts of choses in action, the equities attaching to which are, generally speaking, not merely collateral. The expression "some other," is also apt to mislead, and to convey the impression that the trustee must be some other than either the settlor or the cestui que trust, whereas, as will be seen further on, such an impression would be incorrect. Then, so far as the remedy is concerned, the definition is obsolete. The Court of Chancery no longer exists, and all branches of the High Court take cognizance of equitable rights, although the

U.T.   B

duty to perform, except to convey to the cestuis que trust.

An executive trustee is the trustee appointed to carry out a special trust.

In relation to their inception, trusts are divisible into two classes (*f*).

α. **A declared or express trust** means a trust created by words either expressly or impliedly evincing an intention to create a trust in respect of certain property, for a particular purpose.

β. **A constructive trust** means a trust which is not created by any words either expressly or impliedly evincing a direct intention to create a trust, but by the construction of equity, in order to satisfy the demands of justice (*g*).

In relation to their construction and enforcement, trusts are divisible into two classes.

α. **An executed trust** means a trust in which the limitations of the estate of the trustee and the cestuis que trust are perfected and declared by the settlor (*h*).

β. **An executory trust** means a trust in which the limitations of the estate of the trustee or of the cestui que trust are not perfected and declared by the settlor, but only certain instructions or heads of settlement declared by him, from which the trustee is subsequently to model, perfect and declare the trust (*i*).

A trust based upon value means a trust created by

(*f*) This classification seems to me to be preferable to that usually adopted of express, implied, and constructive trusts. Independently of the fact that it is generally immaterial by what name you call a trust, I have ventured to disregard the usual classification, because implied trusts, properly so called, are in reality constructive trusts, and implied trusts, loosely so called (as, for instance, trusts created by precatory words), are in reality declared trusts.

(*g*) Smith's Eq. Man. 11th ed. 178.

(*h*) See *Stanley* v. *Lennard*, 1 Eden, 95.

(*i*) See *Austen* v. *Taylor*, 1 Eden, 366; *Lord Glenorchy* v. *Bosville*, For. 3; and *Stanley* v. *Lennard, sup.;* and see per Cairns, L. C., in *Sackville West* v. *Holmesdale*, L. R., 4 H. L. 543.

the settlor, upon such consideration as would support a contract at law.

ILLUST.—1. A trust of leasehold property to which liabilities are attached is always based upon value, inasmuch as the cestui que trust thereby takes upon himself the primary discharge of those liabilities (k).

2. Where there are mutual promises, each is a valuable consideration for the other. Thus it is settled, that if husband and wife, *each of them having interests*, no matter how much, or of what degree or of what quality, come to an agreement which is afterwards embodied in a settlement, that is a bargain between husband and wife, which is not a transaction without valuable consideration (l).

A voluntary trust means a trust created by the settlor either *ex mero motu* or in consideration of a mere moral obligation or natural love and affection (m), or a trust made to take effect by way of remainder, after satisfaction of a trust based upon value and not coming within the scope of the contract (n) upon which the latter was founded.

ILLUST.—1. In general, in a marriage settlement by an intended husband, where there are the usual life estates to himself and wife with remainder to the issue and in default of issue to the settlor's next of kin, the latter limitation is voluntary, because it cannot be presumed that the benefit of the husband's next of kin out of *his* property was within the scope of the bargain for the settlement made between him and the wife (o).

(k) *Price* v. *Jenkins*, L. R., 5 Ch. Div. 619.

(l) *Teasdale* v. *Braithwaite*, L. R., 4 Ch. Div. 90; aff., L. R., 5 Ch. Div. 630; *Re Foster & Lister*, L. R., 6 Ch. Div. 87.

(m) See *Eastwood* v. *Kenyon*, 11 A. & E. 447; *Beaumont* v. *Reeve*, 8 Q. B. 483; *Tweddle* v. *Atkinson*, 1 B. & S. 393; *Jeffry* v. *Jeffry*, 1 Cr. & Ph. 138; and *Moore* v. *Crofton*, 3 J. & Lat. 43.

(n) *Osgood* v. *Strode*, 2 P. W. 245 (overruling *Jenkins* v. *Kemesh*, 2 P. W. 252, and *Hale* v. *Lambe*, 2 Ed. 292); *Johnson* v. *Legard*, 3 Mad. 283, and T. & R. 66, 281; *Stackpoole* v. *Stackpoole*, 4 Dr. & War. 320; *Smith* v. *Cherril*, L. R., 4 Eq. 390; *Wollaston* v. *Tribe*, L. R., 9 Eq. 44.

(o) See Dart, V. & P. 891.

2. But where the presumption can naturally arise that the ultimate limitation was part of the marriage bargain, it is apprehended (in spite of some authorities to the contrary (*p*)) that it is not then voluntary. Thus, in *Clarke* v. *Wright* (*q*), Blackburn, J., said, "It seems to me, that though in general it may be supposed that on a marriage treaty, after the interest of the intended husband and wife and the issue of the marriage is provided for, the remainder of the estate is left to be disposed of as the party to whom that would revert pleases; yet that when we find the interests of the husband, wife, and issue so much affected by the settlement, we must take it that it was agreed by all parties, *as part of the marriage bargain*, that the estate should be thus settled—that the wife agreed to marry the husband on the terms that this settlement should be thus made. If this be so, the question comes to be, if a limitation in favour of a third person, not merely inserted in the marriage settlement, but *appearing from its nature to have been made one of the terms of the marriage bargain*, is to be considered voluntary, or is to be considered as made for the valuable consideration of marriage? In my opinion the case would have been the same if the plaintiff had been some distant relation of the wife's first husband, or even a stranger in blood. The husband got the enjoyment of some part of the wife's property, which he could not have had if the marriage had not taken place. He may have got this on cheaper terms; he may have been allowed to take a larger portion of her personal estate than he would have been permitted to take if this settlement had not been made; or he may have been allowed to keep free a greater portion of his own property than he would otherwise have done, and in consideration of these substantial benefits to himself he may have become a party to a contract for this limitation. . . . .

(*p*) *Wollaston* v. *Tribe*, L. R., 9 Eq. 44; *Johnson* v. *Legard*, T. & R. 66, 281; *Smith* v. *Cherril*, L. R., 4 Eq. 390.
(*q*) 30 L. J., Ex. (Ex. Ch.) 113, and 6 H. & N. 849.

It seems to me, that as on every marriage settlement there are reciprocal considerations between husband and wife, we ought not to hold a limitation, which is not merely included in the marriage settlement, but appears from its nature to have been really one of the terms of the marriage bargain, to be voluntary."

3. And so where a widow or widower on a second marriage makes provision for the children of a first marriage, as well as for those of the second marriage, it is presumed to be within the scope and object of the marriage bargain, and therefore based upon value (*r*).

4. And so generally, it is laid down by Mr. Dart (*s*), in a passage approved of by the present Lord Blackburn and the late Mr. Justice Willes (*t*), that where the limitations over are in favour of the collateral relatives, not of the settlor but of the other party, the settlement may be considered primâ facie evidence of such other party having stipulated for their insertion. And so where on a settlement of an intended wife's estate, the limitations over are in favour of her own collateral relatives, in derogation of the husband's marital rights. But where in other cases the limitations over are in favour of the collateral relatives of the *settlor*, such presumption cannot so readily arise; but it might be proved that the other parties stipulated for their insertion. If such a stipulation cannot be presumed or proved, the limitations over must, it is conceived, be considered voluntary.

A breach of trust means any act or neglect on the part of a trustee, which is not authorized or excused, either by the settlement or by the doctrines of judicial equity.

(*r*) *Newstead* v. *Scarles*, 1 Atk. 265; *Ithell* v. *Beane*, 1 Ves. Sen. 216; *Gale* v. *Gale*, L. R., 6 Ch. Div. 144.
(*s*) Dart's V. & P. 894.
(*t*) *Clarke* v. *Wright, sup.*

Division I.
DECLARED TRUSTS.

Sub-div. I.—Introduction.
Art. 2. *Analysis of a declared Trust.*

Sub-div. II.—The creation of declared Trusts.
Art. 3. *Language declaratory of a Trust.*
„ 4. *Illusory Trusts.*
„ 5. *Formalities immaterial where Trust based on Value.*
„ 6. *Formalities material where Trust voluntary.*
„ 7. *The Trust Property.*
„ 8. *The expressed Object of the Trust.*
„ 9. *Necessity of writing.*

Sub-div. III.—Validity of declared Trusts.
Art. 10. *Who may be a Settlor.*
„ 11. *Who may be a Cestui que trust.*
„ 12. *Validity as between Settlor and Cestui que trust.*
„ 13. *Validity as against Creditors.*
„ 14. *Validity as against Trustee in Bankruptcy.*
„ 15. *Validity as against subsequent Purchasers.*

Sub-div. IV.—Construction of declared Trusts.
Art. 16. *Executed Trusts construed strictly, and Executory liberally.*

INTRODUCTION.

ART. 2.—*Analysis of a declared Trust.*

WHERE a person has used language from which it can be gathered that he intended to create a trust (*a*), and such intention is not negatived by the surrounding circumstances (*b*), and the settlor has done such things as are necessary in equity to bind himself not to recede from that intention (*c*), and the trust property is of such a nature as to be legally capable of being settled (*d*), and the object of the trust is lawful (*e*), and the settlor has complied with the provisions of the law as to evidence (*f*), a good and valid declaration of trust has (primâ facie) been made. But a trust primâ facie valid, may yet be impeachable from incapacity of the settlor (*g*), or of the cestui que trust (*h*), or from some mistake or fraud attendant upon its creation (*i*); or again it may be valid as between the parties, and yet invalid as against the settlor's creditors (*k*), trustee in bankruptcy (*l*), or as against subsequent purchasers (*m*); and lastly, the circumstances under which the trust was created, may be such as to necessitate a very liberal construction being given to the language in which it was declared, so as to give effect to the manifest intentions of the settlor (*n*). In the following articles, these several matters will be treated of separately, and in the order in which they have been above referred to.

(*a*) Art. 3.	(*f*) Art. 9.	(*k*) Art. 13.
(*b*) Art. 4.	(*g*) Art. 10.	(*l*) Art. 14.
(*c*) Arts. 5, 6.	(*h*) Art. 11.	(*m*) Art. 15.
(*d*) Art. 7.	(*i*) Art. 12.	(*n*) Art. 16.
(*e*) Art. 8.		

SUB-DIVISION II.

THE CREATION OF DECLARED TRUSTS.

ART. 3.—*Language declaratory of a Trust.*

No technical expressions are necessary in order to raise a trust (*a*) ; any will suffice, from which it is clear that the settlor intended to create a trust, or to confer a benefit best carried out by means of a trust, *provided that the objects, the property, and the way it shall go, are clearly pointed out* (*b*). And subject to this proviso, the following principles are of importance in construing a settlor's intentions:—

α. Words of confidence, direction, subjection (*c*), or proviso (*d*), in general raise a trust;

β. Where a settlor *empowers* a person to dispose of property in favour of another in a particular event (*e*), or among a class, or some of a class, and there is no gift over in default of appointment, a general intention to benefit such individual or class will be presumed and the power will be construed as a trust (*f*).

γ. When property is given to one, who is by the donor recommended or requested to dispose of it in favour of another, these words create a trust. Subject to this, that if the donee was to have a

----

(*a*) *Dipple* v. *Corles*, 11 Ha. 184 ; *Cox* v. *Page*, 10 Ha. 163.

(*b*) *Knight* v. *Knight*, 3 B. 148.

(*c*) *Wright* v. *Wilkin*, 2 B. & S. 232.

(*d*) *Cox* v. *Page*, *sup.*

(*e*) See *Tweedale* v. *Tweedale*, L. R., 7 Ch. Div. 633; *Wheeler* v. *Warner*, 1 S. & S. 304.

(*f*) *Burrough* v. *Philcox*, 5 My. & C. 72; *Greiveson* v. *Kirsopp*, 2 Ke. 653; *Brown* v. *Higgs*, 4 Ves. 708.

discretion, or if there are expressions in the settlement inconsistent with the words being imperative,
or if they were merely explanatory of the donor's
motive, or words of mere expectation, or if it is
otherwise collected, that they were not intended to
be imperative, no trust will be created (*g*).

ILLUST.—1. A. gives property to B., and **directs** him to
apply it for the benefit of C.; B. is held to be a mere
trustee for C. (*h*).

2. If an estate be given to A., **he paying** the testator's
debts within twelve months from the testator's death, the
words of subjection or condition are not construed to
impose a legal forfeiture on breach, but are viewed as
declaratory of trusts (*i*). Where, however, the words are
merely declaratory of a legal obligation which would
attach in their absence, they do not, it is apprehended,
raise any trust. For instance, if a house be devised to A.
for life, "he keeping the same in repair," no trust is
created, for it is merely an informal affirmation of the
common law obligation not to suffer permissive waste (*k*).

3. If a testator **direct** his realty to be sold, or charge it
with debts and legacies (*l*), or a particular legacy (*m*), the
legal estate may descend to the heir, or it may descend
to the devisee; but the court will view the direction as a
declaration of trust, and will force the legal owner to carry
it into execution (*n*).

4. The leading illustration of the class of cases coming
under the principle contained in Sub-article β is *Burrough*
v. *Philcox* (*o*). There a testator directed that certain stock
should stand in his name, and certain real estates remain

(*g*) See per Lord Langdale,
M. R., in *Knight* v. *Knight*, *sup.*,
and *Harding* v. *Glyn*, 1 At. 469.
(*h*) *White* v. *Briggs*, 2 Ph. 583.
(*i*) *Wright* v. *Wilkin*, 2 B. &
S. 232; *Re Skingly*, 2 M. & C.
224; *Gregg* v. *Coates*, 23 B. 33.

(*k*) *Kingham* v. *Lee*, 15 Sim.
396; 11 Jur. 4.
(*l*) *Pitt* v. *Pelham*, 2 Freem.
134; *Cook* v. *Fountain*, 3 Sw.
592.
(*m*) *Wigg* v. *Wigg*, 1 Atk. 382.
(*n*) Lewin, 123.
(*o*) 5 My. & C. 72.

unalienated, "until the following contingencies are completed." He then proceeded to give life estates to his children with remainder to their issue, and declared that if his children should both die without issue, the properties should be disposed of as after mentioned,—namely, the survivor of his children **should have power** to dispose by will of the said real and personal estate amongst the testator's nephews and nieces, or their children, either all to one of them, or to as many of them as his, the testator's, surviving child should think proper. It was held that a trust was created in favour of the testator's nephews and nieces, and their children, subject only to a power of selection and distribution; Lord Cottenham saying, "Where there appears a general intention in favour of a class, and a particular intention in favour of individuals of a class to be selected by another person, and the particular intention fails from that selection not being made, the court will carry into effect the general intention in favour of the class."

5. And so where a testator gave personalty to his widow for life, and to be at her disposal by her will, "therewith to apply part for charity, the remainder to be at her **disposal among** my relations, in such proportions as she may be pleased to direct," and the widow died without so disposing of the property, it was held that half the property was in trust for charitable purposes, and the residue for the testator's relatives, according to the Statutes of Distribution (*p*).

6. A testator gives his trustees **power**, if his daughter marries with their consent, to appoint part of her fortune, on her death, to her husband. This power is equivalent to a trust in favour of a husband who marries the daughter with the trustees' consent (*q*).

(*p*) *Salisbury* v. *Denton*, 3 K. & J. 529; *Little* v. *Neil*, 10 W. R. 592; *Gough* v. *Butt*, 16 Sim. 45.

(*q*) *Tweedale* v. *Tweedale*, L. R., 7 Ch. Div. 633.

7. A testator bequeaths property to A., and states, either that he "**hopes** and doubts not" (*r*), "**entreats**" (*s*), "**recommends**" (*t*), "**desires**" (*u*), "**requests**" (*r*), or "**well knows**" (*w*), that it will be applied for the benefit of B. In such case a trust would be created in favour of B., unless the property, or the mode of its application for B.'s benefit, were ambiguously or insufficiently stated, or unless a discretion were given to A. whether he should or should not apply it for B.'s benefit, or unless it were expressed to be given to A. "absolutely," or accompanied by words to that effect.

8. But where there are other **inconsistent expressions**, the precatory words will not be construed as imperative. Thus in *Green* v. *Marsden* (*x*), a testator gave certain shares of freehold and leasehold houses to his wife for *her sole use and benefit*, begging and requesting that at her death she would give and bequeath the same in such shares as she should think proper, and unto such members of her own family as she should think most deserving of the same. He also gave her all his moneys in the funds, and all the money he might be entitled to, for her *sole use and benefit* (*y*), begging and requesting that at her death she would give and bequeath *what should be remaining*, in such shares as she should think proper, unto such members of her own and his family that she should think most deserving. It was held, that both as to the freeholds and leaseholds, and also the money, there was no trust created,

(*r*) *Paul* v. *Compton*, 8 Ves. 380.

(*s*) *Prevost* v. *Clark*, 2 Mad. 458.

(*t*) *Tibbits* v. *Tibbits*, 19 Ves. 656.

(*u*) *Birch* v. *Wade*, 3 V. & B. 198.

(*v*) *Foley* v. *Barry*, 2 M. & K. 138.

(*w*) *Briggs* v. *Penny*, 3 M. & G. 546; but see *Stead* v. *Mellor*, L.

R., 5 Ch. Div. 225.

(*x*) 1 Dr. 646; and see *Cole* v. *Hawes*, L. R., 4 Ch. Div. 238.

(*y*) See also *McCulloch* v. *McCulloch*, 11 W. R. 504; *Johnston* v. *Rowlands*, 2 De Gex & S. 356; *Meredith* v. *Heneage*, 1 Sim. 542; *Wood* v. *Cox*, 2 M. & C. 684; *Webb* v. *Wools*, 2 Sim., N. S. 267; *Abraham* v. *Abraham*, 1 Russ. 509; *Reeves* v. *Baker*, 18 B. 373.

but the wife took absolutely. The Vice-Chancellor said: " He gives it her for her sole use; that does not mean her separate use in the technical sense, but it means that she should have the absolute use and enjoyment,—that the property should be for the benefit of her, and of no other person than her. . . . In the bequest of the specific portion, he uses the words " which shall be remaining at her death." What does that mean? What he means is this,— the widow is to have it for her own sole use and benefit, that she may do as she pleases with it, that she may spend it, or give it away, or bequeath it; but he expresses his wish, *not imperatively*, but desiring that she may know his wish, as to what she should do with what remains."

9. The case of *Lechmere* v. *Lavie* (*z*) exemplifies the last clause of the article now under consideration as regards the words being **merely expectant,** and also the rules as to **certainty** in the property. There a testatrix said in her will : " I hope none of my children will accuse me of partiality in having left the largest share of my property to my two eldest daughters, my sole motive for which is to enable them to keep house so long as they remain single ; but in case of their marrying, I have divided it amongst all my children. If they die single, *of course they will leave what they have amongst their brothers and sisters, or their children.*" The eldest of the two daughters died leaving all her property to the second. The second died leaving her property otherwise than in accordance with her mother's will. Upon this state of facts, Sir J. Leach, M. R., said : " I consider the words of this codicil as words expressing *the expectation* of the testatrix, but not as words of *recommendation,* or as intended to create an obligation upon the two eldest daughters. The words apply, not simply to the property given by the testatrix, but to all property which the daughters might happen to possess at their deaths,

(*z*) 2 M. & K. 197.

leaving what she gives by her will at their disposition during their lives, and extending to property which might never have belonged to her, and *wanting altogether certainty of amount.*"

10. So in the leading case of *Knight* v. *Knight* (*a*), the words were: "I trust to the liberality of my successors to reward any others of my old servants and tenants according to their deserts, and to their justice in continuing the estates in the male succession, according to the will of the founder of the family, my grandfather." Lord Langdale, M. R., held, that these words were **not sufficiently imperative,** and that the *subject* intended to be affected, and the interests intended to be enjoyed by the objects, were not sufficiently defined to create trusts, either in favour of the servants and tenants or of the male line (*b*).

11. In *McCormick* v. *Grogan* (*c*), C. made a will leaving the whole of his property to G., whom he also appointed his executor. When about to die, C. sent for G., and in a private interview told him of the will, and on G.'s asking whether that was right, said he would not have it otherwise. C. then told G. where the will was to be found, and that with it would be found a letter. This was all that was known to have passed between the parties. The letter named a great many persons to whom C. wished sums of money to be given, and annuities to be paid, but it contained several expressions as to G. carrying into effect the intentions of the testator as he "**might think best,**" and also this sentence, "I do not wish you to act strictly on the foregoing instructions, but leave it entirely to your own good judgment to do as you think I would if living, and as the parties are deserving; and as it is not my wish

(*a*) 3 B. 148; and see also *Stead* v. *Mellor*, L. R., 5 Ch. Div. 225.

(*b*) For instances of trusts held void for uncertainty as to the property, see *Bardswell* v. *Bards-*well, 9 Sim. 319; *Winch* v. *Brutton*, 14 Sim. 379; *Fox* v. *Fox*, 27 B. 301; *Palmer* v. *Simmonds*, 2 Dr. 221; *Cowman* v. *Harrison*, 10 Ha. 234.

(*c*) L. R., 4 H. L. 82.

that you should say anything about this document, there
cannot be any fault found with you by any of the parties,
should you not act in strict accordance with it." G. paid
the money to some of the persons mentioned in the letter,
but not to others, who accordingly sued him; but it was
held that there was no trust created binding on G.

12. A legacy is given to a father " **the better to enable
him** to bring up his children." No trust is thereby
created, for such words are not imperative, but only
explanatory of the donor's motive (*d*). But where, on the
other hand, there is a bequest of income to A., "that he may
use it for the benefit of himself, and the maintenance and
education of his children," it has been held that a trust
was intended to be imposed upon A. to maintain and
educate his children (*e*). It is, however, apprehended, that
the courts would not in these days hold that such words
constitute a trust, as the current of modern decisions tends
against construing mere precatory words as imperative (*f*).

OBS.—In order to obviate any confusion in the reader's
mind, I think it well at this place to draw his attention to
the fact that he must carefully distinguish between cases
in which (as in the foregoing) it has been held that the
precatory words are not imperative, and raise no trusts at
all, and cases in which the words actually used, or the
surrounding circumstances, make it clear that although
the donor has not sufficiently specified the property, the
objects and the way it shall go, yet he never meant the
donee to take the entire beneficial interest. In such cases,
which are treated of in Division II., a constructive trust
is created in favour of the donor or his representatives.

(*d*) *Brown* v. *Casamajor*, 4 Ves.
498.

(*e*) *Woods* v. *Woods*, 1 M. & C.
401; *Crockett* v. *Crockett*, 2 Ph.
553; and see *Bird* v. *Maybery*, 33
B. 351; *Hora* v. *Hora*, 33 B. 88;

Castle v. *Castle*, 1 De G. & J.
352.

(*f*) See *Lambe* v. *Eames*, L. R.,
6 Ch. 597; see also *Wilson* v. *Bell*,
L. R., 4 Ch. 581, and *Hutchinson* v. *Tennant*, W. N. 1878, p.
110.

Cases of precatory words, must also be carefully distinguished from those constructive trusts which arise out of the fraud of those to whom a settlor communicates a disposition which he has formally made in their favour, but at the same time tells them that he has a purpose to answer, which he has not expressed in the formal instrument, but which he depends upon them to carry into effect, and to which they assent.

Art. 4.—*Of illusory Trusts.*

Where persons are, by the form of the settlement, apparently cestuis que trust, but the object of the settlor, as gathered from the whole settlement, does not appear to have been to make the settlement for their benefit, they will not in general be considered as cestuis que trust, and cannot call upon the trustee to execute the settlement in their favour.

Illust.—1. Thus, where a person who is indebted makes provision for **payment of his debts** by vesting property in trustees upon trust to pay them, but does so behind the backs of the creditors and without communicating with them, the trustees do not become trustees for the creditors. The arrangement is one supposed to be made by the debtor for his own convenience only; it is as if he had put a sum of money into the hands of an agent with directions to apply it in paying certain specified debts. In such a case there is no privity between the agent and the creditor (a), and the trust is revocable by the settlor at any time before the money is paid to the creditors. The case is, however, different where the creditor is a party to the arrangement; the presumption then is, that the deed was intended to create a trust in his favour, which he therefore is entitled to

(a) *Walwyn* v. *Coutts,* 3 Sim. 14; *Garrard* v. *Lauderdale,* 3 Sim. 1; *Acton* v. *Woodgate,* 2 My. & K. 495; *Bell* v. *Cureton, ibid.* 511; *Gibbs* v. *Glamis,* 11 Sim. 584; *Henriquez* v. *Bensusan,* 20 W. R. 350; *Johns* v. *James,* W. N. 1878, p. 110.

C

call on the trustee to execute (b); and so, even though he be
not made a party, if the debtor has given him notice of the
existence of the deed, and has expressly or impliedly told
him that he may look to the trust property for payment of
his demand, the creditor may become a cestui que trust (c)
if he has been thereby induced to a forbearance in respect
of his claims, which he would not otherwise have exercised (d), or if he has assented to the deed, and has actively,
and not merely passively, acquiesced in it, or acted under
its provisions and complied with its terms, and the other
side expresses no dissatisfaction, but not otherwise (e).

2. So, where there was an assignment of property to trustees upon trust to **pay all costs**, charges, and expenses of the
deed, and other incidental charges and expenses of the trust,
and to reimburse themselves, and then to pay over the residue
to third parties, it was held, that a solicitor who had prepared the deed, and had acted as solicitor to the trustees,
was not a cestui que trust. It was not that the trust did
not provide for the costs, or that they were not to be paid,
but simply that the solicitor was not a cestui que trust
under the trust for the payment of them; the trust might
of course be enforced, but not by the solicitor (f). It is
obvious that the principle also excludes from the benefit
of a trust all persons who are merely auxiliary to the real
object of the trust, as for instance, auctioneers, valuers,
solicitors, and other persons carrying out a sale, although
the trust instrument contains a trust for payment of costs
and expenses.

(b) *Mackinnon* v. *Stewart*, 1
Sim., N. S. 88; *Le Touche* v. *Earl
of Lucan*, 7 C. & F. 772; *Montefiore* v. *Brown*, 7 H. L. C. 241.

(c) Lord Cranworth in *Synnot*
v. *Simpson*, 5 H. L. C. 121.

(d) Per Sir John Leach in
Acton v. *Woodgate*, *sup.*

(e) Per Lord St. Leonards in
Field v. *Donoughmore*, 1 Dru. &

War. 227; see also *Nicholson* v.
Tuttin, 2 K. & J. 23; *Kirwan* v.
Daniel, 5 Ha. 499; *Griffith* v.
Ricketts, 7 Ha. 307; *Cornthwaite*
v. *Frith*, 4 De G. & S. 552; *Sigger*
v. *Evans*, 5 Ell. & B. 367; *Gould*
v. *Robertson*, 4 De G. & S. 509.

(f) *Worral* v. *Harford*, 8 Ves.
4; see also *Ex parte Percy*, L. R.,
9 Ch. 33.

3. But where there is a **positive direction** to the trustees
to employ a particular person and to allow him a salary, a
trust is created in his favour (*g*); a mere recommendation
or expression of desire is, however, not sufficient (*h*) for
this purpose.

ART. 5.—*Formalities immaterial where Trust s based on
Value or declared by Will.*

Where a trust is based upon value, or is created by
will (*a*), it is immaterial whether it is in its nature
complete and executed, or merely rests in contract,
and whether the settlor has declared himself or
another a trustee, or has omitted to appoint any
trustee; for equity will never allow a trust to fail
for want of a trustee, but will, if the settlor has
used language sufficiently explicit to enable the
court to gather his intentions, fasten the trust upon
the estate, and will hold the person in whom it
becomes vested to be bound in conscience to perform the trust, unless he be a purchaser for value
and without notice (*b*).

ILLUST.—1. Thus where a marriage settlement contains
a **covenant** by the intended husband that he will duly vest
in, and transfer to, the trustees, any property which may
accrue to him in right of his wife during the marriage,
upon any property so becoming vested in him, he immediately becomes a trustee of it, in the first place, upon
trust to transfer it to the trustees, and until that is done
he himself holds it upon the trust declared in the settlement (*c*); so that, not only is there an action for breach of

(*g*) *Williams* v. *Corbett*, 8 Sim.
349; *Hibbert* v. *Hibbert*, 3 Mer.
681.
(*h*) *Shaw* v. *Lawless*, 1 Dr. &
Walsh, 512.
(*a*) See Lew. 60, 114, 678; *Lee*
v. *Lee*, L. R., 4 Ch. Div. 175;
Re Michell, L. R., 6 Ch. Div. 618.

(*b*) See Art. 75.
(*c*) See *Lewis* v. *Maddocks*, 8
V. 150; and see *Wellesley* v. *Wellesley*, 4 M. & C. 561; *Lyster* v.
Burroughs, 1 Dr. & W. 149;
Stock v. *Moyse*, 12 Ir. Ch. Rep.
246.

covenant maintainable against him, but the actual property
is burdened and charged with the executory trust (*d*), and
any volunteer taking it would take it burdened with that
trust; and so would a purchaser if he had notice of the
trust, as will be seen hereafter.

2. And so if lands be devised (*e*), or money bequeathed (*f*), to a married woman for her **separate use**,
the property vests at law in the husband; but in equity he
holds it upon trust for the separate use of the wife.

3. So if the **trustee appointed, fails**, either by death (*g*),
or disclaimer (*h*), or incapacity (*i*), or otherwise (*k*), the
trust does not fail, but fastens upon the conscience of any
person (other than a purchaser for value without notice)
into whose hands the property comes (*l*).

4. Again, if a testator direct a sale of lands for *certain
purposes*, but **names no person** to sell, the heir is a trustee
for that purpose (*m*).

Art. 6.—*Formalities material where Trust is voluntary.*

Where a trust is voluntary, and is not created by
will, the court will not enforce it, unless the settlor
has done everything in his power which, according
to the nature of the property, is necessary to be
done in order to establish a complete and *executed*
trust (*a*), either—

(*d*) *Lewis* v. *Maddocks, sup.;
Hastie* v. *Hastie*, L. R., 2 Ch.
Div. 304; *Agar* v. *George, ibid.*
706; *Cornmell* v. *Keith*, L. R., 3
Ch. Div. 767.

(*e*) *Bennet* v. *Davis*, 2 P. W.
216; *Major* v. *Lansley*, 2 R. & M.
355.

(*f*) *Rolf* v. *Budder*, Bunb. 187;
Tappenden v. *Walsh*, 1 Ph. 352;
Pritchard v. *Ames*, Tur. & Rus.
222; *Parker* v. *Brook*, 9 Ves. 583;
and see Lew. 679; *Green* v. *Car-
lill*, L. R., 4 Ch. Div. 882.

(*g*) *Moggridge* v. *Thackwell*, 3
B. C. C. 528; *Attorney-General* v.

Downing, Amb. 552; *Tempest* v.
Lord Camoys, 35 Beav. 201.

(*h*) *Backhouse* v. *Backhouse*,
quoted by Lew. 678.

(*i*) *Sarley* v. *Clockmakers' Co.*,
1 B. C. C. 81.

(*k*) *Attorney-General* v. *Stephens*,
3 M. & K. 347.

(*l*) See per Wilmot, C. J., in
Attorney-General v. *Lady Downing*, Wil. 21, 22.

(*m*) *Pitt* v. *Pelham*, Fre. 134.

(*a*) Story, § 793; *Ellison* v. *Ellison*, 1 L. C. 245; *Milroy* v. *Lord*,
4 De G., F. & J. 261.

α. By actually declaring that he himself holds it for the purposes of the trust (*b*);

β. By plainly evincing an intention (as distinguished from an expressed declaration) to constitute himself a trustee *in præsenti*, and not merely an intention to create a trust *in futuro;* which intention may be inferred by looking at the nature of the transaction, the whole of the transaction, and any other evidence tending to show that he considered that he actually was a trustee of the property, and adopted that character, as distinguished from evidence tending to show that he considered that he had made an actual gift of the property (*c*); or

γ. By transferring his entire interest, legal or equitable, in the property to a trustee, or doing all in his power to transfer it to a trustee for the purposes of the settlement (*d*).

ILLUST.—1. In *Jeffries* v. *Jeffries* (*e*), a father voluntarily conveyed freeholds to trustees upon certain trusts in favour of his daughters, and also **covenanted to surrender** copyholds to the use of the trustees, to be held by them upon the trusts of the settlement. The settlor afterwards died without surrendering the copyholds, having devised certain portions of both freeholds and copyholds to his wife. Upon a suit by the daughters to have a settlement enforced, it was held, that the court would carry out the settlement of the freeholds, for with respect to them the trust was executed, the title of the daughters complete, and the property actually transferred to the trustees; but that it would not decree a surrender of the copyholds, for with respect to them the settlor had neither declared himself a trustee

---

(*b*) See judgment of the Master of the Rolls in *Richards* v. *Delbridge*, L. R., 18 Eq. 11; and *Ex parte Pye*, 18 Ves. 140.

(*c*) See per Wigram, V.-C., *Hughes* v. *Hughes;* and see also *Dipple* v. *Corles*, 11 Ha. 184; and

per Master of the Rolls, *Antrobus* v. *Smith*, 12 Ves. 39.

(*d*) *Milroy* v. *Lord, sup.;* and *Richards* v. *Delbridge, sup.*

(*e*) Cr. & Ph. 138; and see also *Bizzey* v. *Flight*, 24 W. R. 957.

nor had he transferred them to the trustees, but had merely entered into a voluntary contract to transfer them, which, being a nudum pactum, was of no greater validity in equity than at law. It will be borne in mind, that not only was there no evidence that the settlor considered that he had constituted himself a trustee, but the fact that he assumed to deal with the property in his will was of itself strong evidence to the contrary.

2. In *Gilbert* v. *Overton* (*f*), A., having an agreement for a lease, executed a voluntary settlement, **assigning all his interest** in the agreement to trustees, upon certain trusts. It was objected that he had not declared himself a trustee, nor intended to declare himself one, and had not conveyed the leasehold premises to the trustees; but Vice-Chancellor Wood said: "In the inception of this transaction, there is nothing to show that the settlor had the power of obtaining a lease, before the time when he did so, after the execution of the settlement. There is, therefore, nothing to show that the settlor did not by the settlement *do all that it was in his power to do* to pass the property."

3. In *Kekewich* v. *Manning* (*g*), residuary personal estate was bequeathed to a mother for life, with remainder to her daughter absolutely. The daughter on her marriage **assigned all her interest** under the will to trustees upon certain trusts, not material to be stated, with a final trust in favour of her nieces. Assuming that, quâ the nieces, the settlement was voluntary, it was held that it was good, on the ground that the daughter had done all she could do to divest herself of her interest under the will; for she had a mere equitable remainder, and the only way in which she could transfer that was by assignment. If she had been the legal owner of the funds, it would have been necessary for her to transfer it in the proper way in the

books of the bank; but not being the legal owner, she did all that she could do (h).

4. In *Jones* v. *Lock* (i), the facts were as follows:—The alleged settlor had children by a first wife, and one son, an infant, by a second wife. One day returning from a journey, the infant's nurse said, "You have come back from Birmingham, and have not brought baby anything;" upon which the alleged settlor said, "Oh! I gave him a pair of boots, and now I will give him a handsome present." He then went up stairs and brought down a cheque which he had received for 900*l.*, and said, "Look you here, I give this to baby; it is for himself; I am going to put it away for him, and will give him a great deal more with it; it is his own, and he may do what he likes with it." He then put the cheque away. He had previously told his solicitor that he intended adding 100*l.* to the cheque, and investing it for the infant's benefit. A few days after the above, he suddenly died, leaving the child penniless. The child's mother contended, that the settlor had made a valid declaration of trust in favour of the child, but Lord Cranworth said, "I regret to say that I cannot bring myself to think, either on principle or authority, there has been any gift or any valid declaration of trust. No doubt a gift may be made by any person, sui juris and compos mentis, by conveyance of real estate, or by delivery of a chattel, and there is no doubt also that, by some decisions, a parol declaration of trust of personalty may be perfectly valid, even when voluntary. If I give any chattel, that of course passes by delivery; and if I say, expressly or impliedly, that I constitute myself a trustee of personalty, that is a trust executed and capable of being enforced without consideration. The cases all turn upon the question whether what has been said was a declaration of

(h) See also *Donaldson* v. *Donaldson*, Kay, 711.

(i) L. R., 1 Ch. 25; and see also *Marlow* v. *Tommas*, L. R., 17 Eq. 8.

trust or **an imperfect gift.** In the latter case the parties
would receive no aid from a court of equity if they claimed
as volunteers. But when there has been a declaration
of trust, then it will be enforced, whether there has been
consideration or not."

5. In *Antrobus* v. *Smith* (k), the alleged settlor made the
following endorsement on a share held by him in a public
company : "I do hereby assign to my daughter B. all my
right, title and interest of and in the enclosed call, and all
other calls, in the F. and C. Navigation." The share was
not handed over to the daughter, and the endorsement did
not operate as a valid assignment of the share ; but it was
attempted to enforce the assignment by contending that the
endorsement operated as a valid declaration of trust. The
court, however, rejected this view, the Master of the Rolls
saying : "Mr. Crawfurd (the alleged settlor) was not in
form declared a trustee, nor was that mode of doing what
he proposed in his contemplation. . . . . He meant a gift,
and there is no case in which a party has been compelled
to perfect a gift which in the mode of making it he has
left imperfect (l).

Obs.—In *Richardson* v. *Richardson* (m), Vice-Chancellor
Wood (afterwards Lord Hatherley), and in *Morgan* v.
Malleson (n), Lord Romilly, did not follow the principle
contained in the last sentence, and the former very
learned judge said : "An instrument executed as a present
and complete assignment, not being a mere covenant to

(k) 12 Ves. 39.

(l) It would seem that there is
an exception, or a seeming exception, to this principle in the
case of husband and wife. In
Grant v. *Grant*, 34 B. 623, the
Master of the Rolls said : "I
apprehend the fact of the transaction taking place between husband and wife instead of between
strangers makes no difference
further than this, that in the
case of a gift of chattels from
one stranger to another, there
must be a delivery of the chattels
in order to make the gift complete, whereas in the case of husband and wife there cannot be a
delivery, because, assuming they
are given to the wife, they still
remain in the legal custody of
the husband.

(m) L. R., 3 Eq. 686.

(n) L. R., 10 Eq. 475.

assign on a future day, *is equivalent to a declaration of trust;* the real distinction that should be made is between an agreement to do something when called upon, something distinctly expressed to be future in the instrument, and an instrument which affects to pass everything, independently of the legal estate. . . . The expression used by the Lord Justice in *Kekewich* v. *Manning* is this: 'A declaration of trust is not confined to any express form of words, but may be indicated by the character of the instrument.' Reliance is often placed on the circumstance that the assignor has done all that he can—that there is nothing more for him to do; and it is contended that he must in that case only, be taken to have made a complete and effectual assignment. But that is not the sound doctrine on which the case rests, for *if there be an actual declaration of trust,* although the assignor has not done all he could do—for example, although he has not given notice to the assignee, yet the interest is held to have effectually passed as between the donor and the donee. The difference must rest on this—*aye or no, has he constituted himself a trustee?"* It will be perceived that the learned Vice-Chancellor did not dissent from or add to the recognized rule stated in Article 6. Where he differed from the previous authorities was in deciding that an instrument, purporting to be an assignment, although void as such, was nevertheless good as a declaration of trust. This view has been expressly dissented from by Vice-Chancellor Bacon in *Warriner* v. *Rogers* (*o*), and by Sir George Jessel, M. R., in *Richards* v. *Delbridge* (*p*). In the latter case his lordship relied upon the judgment of Lord Justice Turner in *Milroy* v. *Lord,* in which the learned Lord Justice said: "If the settlement is intended to be effectuated by one of the modes to which I have referred, the court will not give effect to it by applying another of those modes. If it is intended to take effect by transfer,

(*o*) L. R., 16 Eq. 340. (*p*) L. R., 18 Eq. 11.

*the court will not hold the intended transfer to operate as a
declaration of trust"* (*q*). The decision also seems to be
inconsistent with Lord Cranworth's judgment in *Jones* v.
Lock (*r*), and it is respectfully submitted that, both on
principle and authority, the law as laid down by the Master
of the Rolls in *Richards* v. *Delbridge* is accurate.

6. In *Ex parte Dubose* (*s*), the alleged settlor wrote to
an agent in Paris, authorizing him to purchase, and
the agent accordingly did purchase, an annuity **for the
benefit of a lady whom he named,** but as the lady was
married, and also deranged, the annuity was purchased in
the name of the settlor. The settlor then sent the agent a
power of attorney, authorizing him to transfer the annuity
to the lady, which he did not do till after the settlor's
death. It was nevertheless held, that the settlor had
considered himself a mere trustee for the lady, and had
never intended the annuity for himself, but for her, and
that therefore the trust was good.

7. On the other hand, in *Smith* v. *Ward* (*t*), letters,
which would have raised a declaration of trust, were
held to have been explained away by the **acts of the settlor,**
those acts showing that down to his death he considered
the property as his own.

———

Art. 7.—*The Trust Property.*

All property, real or personal, legal or equitable, at
home or abroad (*a*), and whether in possession or
action, remainder, reversion, or expectancy, may be
made the subject of a trust, unless the policy of
the law, or any statutory enactment, prohibits the

(*q*) Compare *Edwards* v. *Jones*,
1 My. & Cr. 226; and *Pearson* v.
Amicable Assurance Co., 27 B.
229; and *Fortescue* v. *Burnett*, 3
My. & K. 36.

(*r*) *Supra.*
(*s*) 18 Ves. 140.
(*t*) 15 Sim. 56. See further on
this subject *Paterson* v. *Murphy*,

Hare, 88; and *Vanderberg* v. *Palmer*, 4 Kay & Johns. 204; and
Stock v. *McElroy*, L. R., 15 Eq. 55.

(*a*) But in the case of real property abroad, the trust must not
be such as to create an estate not
recognized by the law of the land:
see *Nelson* v. *Bridport*, 8 Beav. 547;
and *infra*, Validity of Trusts.

settlor from parting with the beneficial interest in such property.

ILLUST.—1. In *Gilbert* v. *Overton* (*b*), a settlor, holding an agreement for a lease, assigned all his interest under such agreement to trustees upon certain trusts. The legal estate was never assigned to trustees. Held, that the settlement was complete, and ought to be carried into execution. V.-C. Page Wood, in giving judgment, said: "It appears to me that there are several reasons for upholding the settlement. In the first place, it contains a declaration of trust, and that is all that is wanted to make any settlement effectual. The settlor conveys his **equitable interest**, and directs the trustees to hold it upon the trusts thereby declared " (*c*).

2. In *Shafto* v. *Adams* (*d*), the plaintiff had settled upon his wife and children certain real estate, to which, under the will of his uncle, he was entitled in **reversion.** Held good.

3. In *Wethered* v. *Wethered* (*e*), an agreement was entered

(*b*) 2 H. & M. 110; and see also *Knight* v. *Bowyer*, 23 Beav. 635.

(*c*) Prior to the Judicature Act, 1873, debts, and other legal choses in action, were not assignable at law, on the ground (as put by Lord Coke) that it "would be the occasion of multiplying of contentions and suits, of great oppression of the people, and the subversion of the due and equal execution of justice" (10 Co. 48). But even at law, negotiable instruments (as debentures, bills of exchange and promissory notes made negotiable) were exceptions to the rule; and so were all contracts where a novation took place, that is to say, where both parties to the original contract assented to the transfer of the interest of one of them (*Buron* v. *Husband*, 4 B. & Ad. 611). Equity, however, almost always, from its earliest days, disregarded the legal doctrine, and freely enforced contracts for the sale of chose in action; and now, by 8 & 9 Vict. c. 106, s. 6, contingent and future interests and possibilities, *coupled with an interest in real estate*, may be granted or assigned at law. By 30 & 31 Vict. c. 144, policies of life assurance may be legally assigned, and by 31 & 32 Vict. c. 86, a similar relaxation of the law was introduced in favour of marine policies; and finally, by the 6th section of the Judicature Act, 1873, debts and other legal choses in action may be assigned at law, where the assignment is absolute and not by way of charge only.

(*d*) 4 Giff. 492.

(*e*) 2 Sim. 183.

into between two sons, to divide equally whatever **property they might receive** from their father in his lifetime, or become entitled to under his will, or by descent, or otherwise. It was held that this agreement was binding, although made in respect of a mere possibility, and V.-C. Shadwell said: "It is clear that if the testator meant that his devisee should have the *personal* enjoyment of his bounty, he might so devise as to stint the enjoyment of the devisee, and restrain him from alienating the subject of the gift; but that if the testator did not so devise, it must be intended that he meant that his devisee should not be so stinted, but should have the full enjoyment of the property, and that it should be liable to all his antecedent debts and all his antecedent contracts; and, therefore, that where there was a general devise the property was liable to be encumbered *in any way that the devisee might think proper, either before* or after he took it" (*f*).

4. As an instance of property not assignable on the ground of public policy, may be mentioned **salaries or pensions** given for the purpose of enabling persons to perform duties connected with the public service, or to enable them to be in a fit state of preparation to perform those duties. In *Grenfell* v. *Dean and Canons of Windsor* (*g*) the Master of the Rolls explained the true reasons for this doctrine. In that case a canon of Windsor had assigned the canonry and the profits to the plaintiffs to secure a sum of money. There was no cure of souls, and the only duties were residence within the castle and attendance in the chapel for twenty-one days a-year. In giving judgment for the plaintiffs and upholding the assignment, the Master of the Rolls said: "If he (the Canon) had made out that the duty to be performed by him was a public duty, or in any way connected with the public service, I should have thought it right to attend very seriously to

(*f*) See also *Beckley* v. *New-land*, 2 P. W. 182; and *Harwood* v. *Tooke*, 2 Sim. 192.
(*g*) 2 Beav. 554.

that argument, because there are various cases in which
public duties are concerned in which it may be against
public policy that the income arising from the performance
of those duties should be assigned; and for this simple
reason, because the public is interested not only in the performance from time to time of the duties, but also in the
fit state of preparation of the party having to perform
them. Such is the reason in the cases of half-pay, where
there is a sort of retainer, and where the payments which
are made to officers from time to time are the means by
which they—being liable to be called into public service—
are enabled to keep themselves in a state of preparation
for performing their duties." So, in *Davis* v. *Duke of
Marlborough* (h), the Lord Chancellor said: "A pension
for past services may be aliened, but a pension for sup-
porting the grantee in the performance of future duties is
inalienable."

5. Some classes of property are expressly made **inalienable by statute.** Thus, in *Davis* v. *Duke of Marlborough*,
a pension was granted by statute to the duke and his
successors in the title "for the more honourable support
of the dignities." It was held, that the object of parliament being, that "it should be kept in mind that it was
for a memento and a perpetual memorial of national
gratitude for public services," it was inalienable.

6. **Pay**, pensions, relief, or allowance payable to any
officer of her Majesty's forces, or to his widow, or to any
person on the compassionate list, are made unassignable by
statute (i). As also is the pay of seamen in the navy (j),
and of half-pay in the marine forces (k); but it would
seem that the right to pay actually due at the date of
the assignment is assignable (l). Salaries or pensions,

(h) 1 Sw. 74.
(i) 47 Geo. 3, sess. 2, c. 25,
ss. 1—14.
(j) 1 Geo. 2, c. 14, s. 7.

(k) 11 Geo. 4 & 1 Will. 4,
c. 20, s. 47.
(l) *Ib.* s. 54.

not given in respect of public services, are freely assignable (*m*).

_____

ART. 8.—*The Expressed Object of the Trust.*

α. The expressed object of a trust must be such as is consistent with the *policy* of the law (as distinguished from mere technical rules of pleading or tenure) (*a*), and must be such as is not opposed to any statutory enactment. Where a trust contravenes these principles, it will not vitiate other trusts or provisions in the settlement unconnected with such illegal object (*b*), but will itself be wholly void.

β. The chief cases in which trusts have been held invalid on account of their expressed objects being contrary to the policy of the law, are where those objects have been unreasonable accumulations (*c*), or perpetuities; the continued *personal* enjoyment of property in derogation of the rights of creditors under the bankruptcy laws (*d*); restrictions upon that power of alienation which the law has annexed to the ownership of property (*e*); the promotion or encouragement of immorality (*f*), fraud, or dishonesty, and general restraint of marriage (*g*)

(*m*) *Feistel* v. *St. John's College*, 10 B. 491; and for other cases bearing on assignments of salaries and pensions, see *Stone* v. *Lidderdale*, 2 Aust. 533; *Arbuthnot* v. *Norton*, 5 Moore, P. C. C. 219; *Carew* v. *Cooper*, 10 Jur., N. S. 429; *Alexander* v. *Duke of Wellington*, 2 Russ. & My. 35.

(*a*) Lew. 74; *Att.-Gen.* v. *Sands*, Hard. 494; *Parlett* v. *Att.-Gen.* ib. 469; *Burgess* v. *Wheate*, 1 Ed. 595; *Duke of Norfolk's case*, 3 Ch. Cas. 35.

(*b*) *H.* v. *W.* 3 K. & J. 382; *Cartwright* v. *Cartwright*, 3 D. M. & G. 982; *Merryweather* v.

Jones, 4 Giff. 509; *Cocksedge* v. *Cocksedge*, 14 Sim. 244.

(*c*) *Cadell* v. *Palmer*, L. C. Conv. 360; *Griffiths* v. *Vere*, ib. 430.

(*d*) *Graves* v. *Dolphin*, 1 Sim. 66; *Snowdon* v. *Dales*, 6 Sim. 524; *Brandon* v. *Robinson*, 18 Ves. 429.

(*e*) *Floyer* v. *Banks*, L. R., 8 Eq. 115; *Sykes* v. *Sykes*, L. R., 13 Eq. 56.

(*f*) *Bladwell* v. *Edwards*, Cro. Eliz. 509.

(*g*) See per Wilmot, L. C. J., in *Low* v. *Peers*, Wil. Op. & Jud. 375; *Morley* v. *Rennoldson*, 2 Ha. 570; *Lloyd* v. *Lloyd*, 2 Sim., N. S. 255; Story, § 283.

(unless of a second marriage) (*h*). The objects forbidden by statute are too numerous to mention, but those which chiefly arise with reference to trusts are such as are simoniacal or in derogation of the Mortmain Acts.

ILLUST.—1. At common law a fee simple estate could not (except by executory devise) be made to **shift** from one person to another, but before the Statute of Uses the same object was gained by means of shifting uses, which were then mere equitable interests; and by means of that statute it was rendered allowable at law.

2. So, again, a **chattel** cannot at law be limited to one for life, with remainder to another absolutely. But the same object can nevertheless be attained through the medium of a trust (*i*).

3. At law the freehold must always be in some person in esse, which is often expressed by saying, that a remainder requires a **particular estate** to support it. This is, however, a rule of tenure, the reasons for which do not now apply, and a trust imposed upon the legal owner to deal with the equitable freehold in a particular way, would be perfectly valid, although it provided for a period of suspended vesting—as, for instance, a trust to accumulate the rents and profits (*k*).

4. But if the trust directed the trustee to accumulate the income for a period exceeding a life or lives in being, and twenty-one years afterwards, then, since such a trust would be contrary to the *policy* of the common law, which discountenances such **unreasonable accumulations**, the whole trust would be void (*l*).

(*h*) *Marples* v. *Bainbridge*, 1 Mad. 590; *Lloyd* v. *Lloyd, sup.; Craven* v. *Brady*, L. R., 4 Ch. 296; and, as to second marriage of a man, *Allen* v. *Jackson*, L. R., 1 Ch. Div. 399.

(*i*) Lew. 75.

(*k*) And see also as to trusts which would, if legal estates, be void as contrary to the custom of a manor, *Allen* v. *Bewsey*, L. R., 7 Ch. Div. 453.

(*l*) *Cadell* v. *Palmer, sup.; Marshall* v. *Holloway*, 2 Sw. 450.

5. By the **Thellusson Act** (*m*) the common law period was further restricted to the life or lives of the grantor or grantors, settlor or settlors; *or* (not *and*) twenty-one years from the death of any grantor, settlor, devisor, or testator; *or* during the minorities of any persons who shall be living, or en ventre sa mere, at the time of the death of the grantor, settlor, devisor, or testator; *or* during the minorities of any persons who, under the instrument directing the accumulation, would for the time being, if of full age, be entitled to the income directed to be accumulated. The statute, however, does not extend to any provision for payment of debts, or for raising portions for the children of the settlor, grantor, or devisor, or of any person taking any interest under the instrument directing such accumulations, nor to any direction as to the produce of timber upon any lands. It might perhaps be thought that by analogy to the action of the courts, with regard to trusts which transgress the common law period, a trust which endeavoured to go beyond the period allowed by the statute would be wholly void; but this is not so. The statute is merely *prohibitory* of accumulations going beyond the period prescribed by it, and being in derogation of a common law right, is construed strictly; and therefore, as accumulations which exceed that period, but are within the common law period, are not contrary to public policy as defined by common law, such a trust is good pro tanto (*n*).

6. A trust, with a proviso that the interest of the cestui que trust shall not be liable to the **claims of creditors,** is void, so far as the proviso is concerned; and if it can be only ascertained that the cestui que trust was intended to take a vested interest, the mode in which, or the time when, he was to reap the benefit, is immaterial, and the entire interest may either be disposed

(*m*) 39 & 40 Geo. 3, c. 98.
(*n*) See *Griffiths* v. *Vere, sup.*;
Longdon v. *Simpson*, 12 Ves. 295;
Haley v. *Bannister*, 4 Mad. 275;

Shaw v. *Rhodes*, 1 M. & C. 135;
Crawley v. *Crawley*, 7 Sim. 427;
Att.-Gen. v. *Poulden*, 3 Ha. 555.

of by the act of the cestui que trust, or may enure for the benefit of his creditors, under the operation of the bankruptcy law (o). The question generally depends upon whether, on the decease of the cestui que trust, his executors would have a right to call upon the trustees retrospectively to account for the arrears (p). Of course, however, a trust to A. until he becomes bankrupt, or aliens the property, and *then over* to B., is good (q); but a man cannot make a *voluntary* settlement upon himself until bankruptcy, and then over (r). although he can do so by an antenuptial marriage settlement, where it would be presumed to be part of the wife's terms of the marriage bargain.

7. Trusts, framed with the object of preventing the **barring of entails,** or imposing restrictions on alienation of property, are contrary to the policy of the law, and are therefore void (s), with the single exception that trusts limiting the power of married women to alienate their separate property *during coverture,* are regarded as valid.

8. Where a man *by deed* creates a trust in favour of **future illegitimate children** (putting aside the objection as to want of certainty in the cestui que trust), the trust will be void as being contrary to public policy, and conducive to immorality (t).

9. Similarly, a trust **by will,** in favour of the future illegitimate children *of another,* would clearly be a direct

(o) Lew. 87. For example, see *Younghusband* v. *Gisborne*, 1 Coll. 400; *Green* v. *Spicer*, 1 R. & M. 395: *Graves* v. *Dolphin*, 1 Sim. 66; *Piercy* v. *Roberts*, 1 M. & K. 4: *Snowdon* v. *Dales*, 6 Sim. 524.
(p) See *Re Saunderson's Trusts*, 3 K. & J. 497.
(q) See *Billson* v. *Crofts*, L. R., 15 Eq. 314; *Re Alwyn's Trusts*, L. R., 16 Eq. 585, and cases therein cited.
(r) *Higginbottom* v. *Holme*, 19 Ves. 88; *Ex parte Hodgson, ib.* 208; *Knight* v. *Brown*, 7 Jur., N. S. 894; *Brooker* v. *Pearson*, 77

Beav. 181; *Re Pearson*, L. R., 3 Ch. Div. 807.
(s) *Floyer* v. *Banks*, L. R., 8 Eq. 115: *Sykes* v. *Sykes*, L. R., 13 Eq. 56; and as to alienation, *Snowdon* v. *Dales*, 6 Sim. 524; *Green* v. *Spicer*, 1 R. & M. 395; *Graves* v. *Dolphin*, 1 Sim. 66; *Brandon* v. *Robinson*, 18 Ves. 429; *Ware* v. *Cann*, 10 B. & C. 433; *Hood* v. *Oglander*, 34 B. 513.
(t) *Bladwell* v. *Edwards*, Cro. Eliz. 509; Moo. 430; and see per Mellish, L. J., in *Occleston* v. *Fullalove*, L. R., 9 Ch. 147.

encouragement to such other to continue his illicit intercourse after the testator's death, and would be therefore
void (u).

10. But, in *Occleston* v. *Fullalove* (r), a testator by his
will gave a share of the proceeds of his residuary estate to
his reputed children, Catherine and Edith, "and all other
children which I may have, or be reputed to have, by the
said M. L., now born, or **hereafter to be born.**" This gift
in favour of future-born children was held valid, and Lord
Justice James said: "If there be any inducement to wrong,
the law can and does deal with it. If there be a covenant
for a turpis causa, the covenant is void. If there be an
illicit condition, precedent or subsequent, to a gift, it either
avoids the gift or becomes itself void. If the gift requires
or implies the continuation of wrong-doing, that is in substance a condition of the gift, and falls within the rule of ·
the condition. But how can that apply to an instrument
like a will, with reference to gifts taking effect at the death
in favour of persons then in existence?" And Lord Justice
Mellish said: "In the present case, the will being the will
of the putative father himself, it is impossible that it can
encourage an immoral intercourse after his death. If the
bequest is to be held to be contrary to public policy, it
must be because it tended to promote an immoral intercourse in his lifetime. There was no evidence that M. L.
knew that the will was made; and if she did know it, she
must also have known that it could be revoked at any
moment. Then, can it be said that the testator himself
would be encouraged in immorality by having the power
to make a will in favour of his future children. I cannot
see that he would; or, at any rate, I think that this is too
uncertain to be made a ground of decision. I am of
opinion that a will no more comes into operation for the
purpose of promoting immorality, or for effecting some-

(u) *Metham* v. *Duke of Devon*,
1 P. W. 529; and see per Mel-
lish, L.J., *Occleston* v. *Fullalove, sup.*
(r) *Sup.*

thing contrary to public policy during a testator's lifetime, than it does for any other purpose."

11. A trust to take effect upon the **future separation** of a husband and wife is void, as being contrary to public morals (*x*); but a trust in reference to an immediate separation, *already agreed upon*, is good and enforceable (*y*). If, however, the separation does not in fact take place, the trust becomes wholly void (*z*). The reason of all this is at once obvious, when we consider that a provision for husband or wife, to take effect upon a future separation, is a direct encouragement to misconduct, which may eventuate in a separation; whereas, when a separation is actually agreed on—when both parties have decided that they will no longer remain together—there can be no encouragement to marital misconduct in agreeing to the distribution of their income in a particular manner and for their mutual benefit and advantage.

12. Where property is settled in trust for a woman until she marry a man with an income of not less than 500*l*. a-year (*a*), or until she marry any person of a particular trade (*b*), and then over in trust for another, the latter trust is bad, as its object, as gathered from its probable result (*c*), is to **restrain marriage** altogether.

13. If, however, the trust over is to take effect only upon the first cestui que trust **marrying a particular person**, it would be good, as it would not be in general restraint of marriage (*d*).

14. So where (*e*) a person by her will gave her residuary estate to trustees, upon trust to pay the income to her

(*x*) *Westmeath* v. *Westmeath*, 1 Dow., N. S. 519; *Proctor* v. *Robinson*, 15 W. R. 138.

(*y*) *Wilson* v. *Wilson*, 1 H. L. Cas. 538; 5 H. L. Cas. 40; *Vansittart* v. *Vansittart*, 2 D. & J. 249; *Jodrell* v. *Jodrell*, 9 B. 45; and see 14 B. 397.

(*z*) *Bindley* v. *Mulloney*, L. R., 7 Eq. 343.

(*a*) Sm. R. & P. Prop. 80; Story, 280—283.

(*b*) *Ib.*

(*c*) *Ib.*; and Story, 274—283; *Lloyd* v. *Lloyd*, 2 Sim. N. S. 255.

(*d*) Sm. R. & P. Prop. 81—107.

(*e*) *Allen* v. *Jackson*, L. R., 1 Ch. Div. 399.

nephew and his wife (the testatrix's niece) for their joint
lives and the life of the survivor, with a gift over (in the
event of the nephew surviving and **marrying again**) in
trust for the children of her said niece, and in default of
such children, for the children of the testatrix's sister, it
was held that the gift over was good; and Mellish, L. J.,
in delivering his judgment, said: "It has been said with
respect to this rule against restraint of marriage that it
has no foundation on any principle; that it has nothing to
do with public policy, but that it is a positive rule of law,
adopted nobody can tell why; and that, because it is a
positive rule of law, adopted nobody can tell for what
reason, and without any regard to public policy, therefore
it is impossible to make an exception to it, and that the
court can do nothing with it but carry it out. I cannot
agree with that. It may be, no doubt, that in these
modern times we should not for the first time establish
such a rule of public policy, but of course if a rule has
been established as a rule of law because it was thought
agreeable to public policy and to the interests of the nation
at the time it was established, it may be that the court
cannot alter it because circumstances have altered. . . . If
then there was such a rule of public policy, we are to consider how does that rule apply to second marriages? It
has never been decided that it applies to second marriages.
. . . It appears to me very obvious that, if it is regarded
as a matter of policy, there may be very essential distinc-
tions between a first and a second marriage; at any rate
there is this, that in the case of a second marriage, whether
of a man or a woman, the person who makes the gift may
have been influenced by his friendship towards the wife in
the one case, and towards the husband in the other case;
that is to say, regarding the case of some member of the
husband's family, he may make a gift to the husband for
life, and then make a gift to the wife because she is the
wife of that particular husband, and because he thinks it

is more for the benefit of the children that the wife should
have the money while the children are young rather than
that the children should have it."

Art. 9.—*Necessity or otherwise of Writing and Signature.*

α. All declarations of trust of freehold, copyhold (*a*),
or leasehold (*b*) lands, tenements, or hereditaments,
must be manifested and proved by some writing,
or by a last will, showing clearly what the intended
trust is, or referring to some other document which
shows clearly what the trust is; and the declaration
of trust (but not necessarily any other writing referred to thereby) must be signed by the party who
is by law enabled to declare the trust, or else it is
wholly void (*c*) : Provided that the rule does not
apply where it would operate so as to effectuate a
fraud (*d*). Where the legal estate is vested in a
trustee for an absolute beneficial owner, the latter
is the proper party to declare the trust (*e*).

β. Declarations of trust of personalty, other than
chattels real, may be made by word of mouth (*f*).

Illust.—1. In *Foster* v. *Hale*, a gentleman named Burdon
had a share in a colliery, and the suit was for the purpose
of fixing a trust upon his share for the benefit of his partners in a bank, in which he was also concerned. Lord
Alvanley, after commenting upon the conduct of the
plaintiffs, said: "But it is insisted, that though their
names do not appear upon the lease, nor that they pub-
licly, even by inquiry, ever busied themselves about the

(*a*) *Withers* v. *Withers*, Amb. 152.
(*b*) *Foster* v. *Hale*, 3 Ves. 696.
(*c*) Statute of Frauds, 29 Car. 2, c. 3, s. 7.
(*d*) See per Lord Westbury in *M'Cormick* v. *Grogan*, L. R., 4 H. L. 82; *Strickland* v. *Aldridge*, 9 V. 219.

(*e*) *Kronheim* v. *Johnson*, L. R., 7 Ch. Div. 60: *Tierney* v. *Wood*, 19 B. 330; *Rudkin* v. *Dolman*, 35 L. T. 791.
(*f*) *McFadden* v. *Jenkins*, 1 Ph. 157: *Hawkins* v. *Gardner*, 2 Sm. & G. 451; *Benbow* v. *Townsend*, 1 M. & K. 506: *Middleton* v. *Pollock*, L. R., 4 Ch. Div. 49.

colliery; yet in fact an agreement took place that he, Burdon, should be a trustee as to his share for them (the plaintiffs) and himself, in equal shares. They say they can make it out satisfactorily to the court and within the Statute of Frauds, and that not by any formal declaration of trust, but by letters under his, Burdon's, *hand, and signed by him*, in which they allege he admitted himself such trustee, and that, under the true meaning of the statute, it is sufficient if it appears in writing under the hand of a person having a right to declare himself a trustee, and that is a formal declaration of trust. It was contended for the defendants that there is great danger in taking a declaration of trust arising from letters loosely speaking of trusts, which might or might not be actually and definitely settled between the parties with such expressions as ' our,' ' your,' &c., intimating some intention of a trust; that upon such grounds the court may be called upon to execute a trust in a manner very different from that intended, and that it is absolutely necessary that it should be clear from the declaration what the trust is. *That I certainly admit.* The question, therefore, is, whether sufficient appears to prove that Burdon *did admit and acknowledge himself a trustee, and whether the terms and conditions on which he was a trustee sufficiently appear. I do not admit that it is absolutely necessary that he should have been a trustee from the first. It is not required by the statute that a trust should be created by a writing . . . . but that it shall be manifested and proved by writing;* plainly meaning that there should be evidence in writing, proving that there was such a trust. Therefore, unquestionably, it is not necessarily to be created by writing, but it must be evidenced by writing, and then the statute is complied with. I admit that it must be proved in toto, not only that there was a gift, but what that gift was."

2. In *Smith* v. *Matthews(g)* the husband of one Mrs.

(g) 3 De G., F. & J. 139.

Matthews, being a person of dissolute habits, got into difficulties; and thereupon, one Clark, the brother of Mrs. Matthews, entered into an arrangement with Matthews, whereby the latter conveyed to him certain real property, and a certain business, in consideration of his undertaking to pay off all his, Matthew's, debts. Clark entered into possession, and carried on the business for the benefit of his said sister and her children. There was no explicit and formal declaration of trust by Clark, but from several letters it appeared that Clark considered that he held the property "for the benefit of Mrs. Matthews and her family;" and by a memorandum given to the mortgagee, upon paying off the mortgage on the property, it was expressly stated that the title deeds had been handed over to Clark "as the trustee of the real and personal estate of Mrs. Matthews." Clark having died intestate, the lands descended at law to Mrs. Matthews as his heir-at-law, and thereupon her husband tried to get possession of them jure mariti. In order to resist this attempt, it was contended that Clark had constituted himself a trustee for Mrs. Matthews and her children, and that the property therefore devolved, burdened with the trust. Lord Justice Turner, however, held that the trust was not expressed with sufficient certainty in any of the documents, and said, " it must be **manifested and proved by writing**, signed as required, what the trust is; . . . the main reliance was placed on the memorandum; . . . . . but I think it by no means improbable that, in speaking of himself as trustee in that memorandum, Clark may have meant no more than that he considered himself a trustee with reference to the duty which he had undertaken for the payment of Matthews' debts; and at all events the memorandum does not show what was the trust to which it refers, and I think, therefore, that no trust in favour of Mrs. Matthews can be founded upon it."

   3. In *Kilpin* v. *Kilpin* (*h*) a person transferred stock into

(*h*) 1 M. & K. 521.

the name of an illegitimate daughter and her husband and their two eldest children, and by **parol declaration**, confirmed by an *unsigned* entry in a memorandum book, declared that such investments were to be for the benefit of *all* his daughter's children. Held a good declaration of trust, as the stock was mere personalty.

4. So in *McFadden* v. *Jenkins* (i) a creditor **desired his debtor** to hold the debt in trust for A. The debtor acquiesced, and paid over part of the money to A.; and it was held that the creditor had made a valid declaration of trust, and had constituted the debtor a trustee of the debt for A.

5. But where a father is **induced not to make a will** by statements of his heir presumptive, that the latter would make suitable provision for his immediate relatives, the court considers that that is a fraud, and, notwithstanding the statute, will oblige the heir to make a provision in conformity with his implied obligation (k). For, as was said by Lord Westbury, in *McCormick* v. *Grogan* (l), "the court has from a very early period decided that even an act of parliament shall not be used as an instrument of fraud; and if in the machinery of effectuating a fraud an act of parliament intervenes, a court of equity, it is true, does not set aside the act of parliament, but it fastens upon the individual who gets a title under that act, and imposes upon him a personal obligation, because he applies the act as an instrument for accomplishing a fraud. In this way a court of equity has dealt with the Statute of Frauds, and in this manner also it deals with the Statute of Wills; and if an individual on his deathbed, or at any other time, is persuaded by his heir-at-law or next of kin to abstain from making a will, or if the same individual, having made a will, communicates the disposition to the person on the face of the will benefited by that disposition, but at the

(i) 1 Ph. 153.

(k) *Sellack* v. *Harris*, 5 Vin. Ab. 521; *Strickland* v. *Aldridge*,

9 V. 219.

(l) L. R., 4 H. L. 82.

same time says to that individual that he has a purpose to answer which he has not expressed in the will, but which he depends upon the disponee to carry into effect, and the disponee assents to it, either expressly or by any mode of action which the disponee knows must give to the testator the impression and belief that he fully assents to the request, then undoubtedly the heir-at-law in one case, and the disponee in the other, will be converted into trustees, simply on the principle that an individual shall not be benefited by his own personal fraud."

SUB-DIVISION III.

VALIDITY OF DECLARED TRUSTS.

Art. 10.—*Who may be a Settlor.*

Every person who can hold or dispose of any legal or equitable (*a*) estate or interest in property may create a trust in respect of such estate or interest.

Illust.—1. Practically speaking, **an infant** cannot now effectually dispose of property so as to bind himself; and, therefore, cannot in general make an irrevocable settlement. However, males over the age of twenty and females over the age of seventeen years can now upon marriage, with the approbation of the High Court (acting in pursuance of the power given to it by the statute 18 & 19 Vict. c. 43, explained by 23 & 24 Vict. c. 83), make binding settlements of real and personal estate belonging to them in possession, reversion, remainder, or expectancy.

2. **A married woman** cannot in general dispose of her property without the consent and joinder of her husband, and in accordance with the provisions of the Fines and Recoveries Abolition Act. But with regard to property which is her separate property in equity, either under a settlement or the Married Women's Property Act, 1870, she is considered a feme sole, and may therefore either dispose of it or settle it (unless restrained from anticipating it) (*b*). So, again, she may dispose of property over which she has a general power of appointment, and her husband's concurrence is not necessary (*c*); and as she can

(*a*) *Gilbert* v. *Overton,* 2 H. & M. 110; *Kekewich* v. *Manning,* 1 Hare, 464; *Donaldson* v. *Donaldson,* Kay, 711.

(*b*) See judgment in *Noble* v. *Willock,* L. R., 8 Ch. 787.

(*c*) *Burnet* v. *Mann,* 1 Vez. 156; *Wright* v. *Lord Cadogan,* 2 Eden, 239; *Doe* d. *Blomfield* v. *Eyre,* 5 C. B. 713; *Lady Travel's case,* cit. 3 Atk. 711.

dispose of it, so also, in accordance with the rule, she can create a trust in respect of it (*y*).

3. A **convict** while such (*i. e.* until he has worked out his sentence or been pardoned) is incapable of disposing of his property; and, consequently, cannot create a valid trust in respect of it (*z*).

ART. 11.—*Who may be a Cestui que trust.*

Every person who can hold property may lawfully be a cestui que trust of it (*a*); but a cestui que trust must be a human being or beings (*b*).

ILLUST.—1. A **corporation** cannot be cestui que trust of lands without licence under the Mortmain Acts (*c*), for without such licence it cannot hold lands, and therefore cannot take through the medium of a trust.

2. Similarly, before the act 33 Vict. c. 14, **an alien**, as he could hold property against everyone except the crown, could also be cestui que trust of land as against everyone except the crown (*d*); but as he could not take a legal estate by operation of law, so likewise he could not be a cestui que trust by act of law (*e*). As the above act is not retrospective, it would seem that aliens who acquired lands anterior to the passing of the act are not protected by it, and that the crown is entitled to all lands of which they are cestui que trust (*f*).

3. A trust for keeping up **family tombs** is void, because there would be no human cestui que trust (*g*). A trust, on the other hand, for keeping up a church might be valid as

---

(*y*) See judgment of Westbury, L. C., in *Taylor* v. *Meads*, 34 L. J., Ch. 203; 13 W. R. 394.
(*z*) 33 & 34 Vict. c. 23.
(*a*) Lew. 39.
(*b*) *Rickard* v. *Robson*, 31 B. 244; *Lloyd* v. *Lloyd*, 2 Sim., N. S. 255; *Thompson* v. *Shakespeare*, Johns. 612; *Fowler* v. *Fowler*, 33 B. 616; *Fisk* v. *Att.-Gen.* L. R., 4 Eq. 521; *Hunter* v. *Bullock*,

L. R., 14 Eq. 45; *Dawson* v. *Small*, L. R., 18 Eq. 104.
(*c*) Lew. 40.
(*d*) *Barrow* v. *Wadkin*, 24 B. 1; *Ritson* v. *Stordy*, 3 Sm. & Giff. 230; *Sharp* v. *St. Saveur*, L. R., 7 Ch. 351.
(*e*) *Calvin's case*, 7 Rep. 49.
(*f*) *Sharp* v. *St. Saveur, sup.*
(*g*) *Rickard* v. *Robson*, 31 B. 244.

a charity, as it would be in reality a trust for the benefit of the congregation (*h*).

ART. 12.—*Validity as between Settlor and Cestui que trust.*

A settlor cannot revoke or vary a voluntary trust (*a*) (and, à fortiori, a trust based upon valuable consideration), unless there has been some fraud or undue influence exercised to induce him to create the trust (*b*), or unless he executed the settlement in ignorance of its legal effect (*c*) ; and not even then, if he has acquiesced in or acted upon the settlement after the influence has ceased or after he has become aware of the legal effect of the settlement (*d*). And unless there is at least a meritorious consideration, it will in general, and particularly where the cestui que trust stood in the relation of parent (*e*), guardian, counsel, solicitor, doctor, priest, or trustee (*f*) to the settlor, be incumbent upon the cestui que trust to prove that all the provisions are proper and usual, or if there are any unusual provisions that they were brought to the knowledge of and were understood by the settlor (*g*). No general rule can be laid down as to what are proper and usual provisions, but a power of revocation is not essential (*g*).

ILLUST.—1. A father transferred a sum of stock into the joint names of his son and of a banker, and told the latter

(*h*) *Hoare* v. *Osborne*, L. R., 1 Eq. 585; *Re Rigley's Trusts*, 1 W. R. 342.

(*a*) *Crabbe* v. *Crabbe*, 1 M. & K. 506; *Sidmouth* v. *Sidmouth*, 2 B. 455.

(*b*) *Osmond* v. *Fitzroy*, 3 P. W. 129; *Huguenin* v. *Baseley*, 14 V. 273; *Dent* v. *Bennett*, 4 M. & C. 277; *Hoghton* v. *Hoghton*, 15 B. 299; *Cooke* v. *Lamotte*, 15 B. 234.

(*c*) *Phillips* v. *Mullings*, L. R., 7 Ch. 244; *Fanshawe* v. *Welsby*, 30 B. 343; and see as to mistake

where a provision for daughters was omitted by the engrossing clerk, *Re Daniell*, L. R., 1 Ch. Div. 375; and see *Clarke* v. *Girdwood*, L. R., 7 Ch. Div. 9.

(*d*) *Davies* v. *Davies*, L. R., 9 Eq. 468, and cases cited.

(*e*) *Davies* v. *Davies*, *sup.*

(*f*) *Hylton* v. *Hylton*, 2 Vez. 547; *Hunter* v. *Atkins*, 3 M. & K. 113 ; *Tate* v. *Williamson*, L. R., 2 Ch. 55.

(*g*) *Phillips* v. *Mullings*, *sup.*

to carry the dividends to the son's account ; the father subsequently made a codicil to his will, attempting to qualify
the trust thus declared. The Master of the Rolls, however,
said : " If the transfer is not ambiguous, but a clear and
unequivocal act, I must take it on the authorities, that **for
explanation there is plainly no place.** If, then, it cannot
be admitted to explain, still less can it be allowed to qualify
the operation of the previous act, the transfer being held
an advancement, nothing contained in the codicil, nor any
other matter ex post facto, can ever be allowed to alter what
has been already done " (*i*).

2. In *Phillips* v. *Mullings* (*k*) the facts were these : A
young man of improvident habits, being entitled to a sum
of money, was induced by the trustee of the money and by
a solicitor to execute a settlement, by which he assigned a
part of the money to trustees upon trust to invest and to
pay him during his life the income thereof as they should
think fit, and after his death upon trust for his wife and
children (if any), and in default thereof and subject thereto
upon trust for certain of his cousins. There was no power
of revocation or of appointment, nor a power to nominate
new trustees ; the deed was, however, fully explained to
him before its execution, and his attention called to the
particular clauses. Some years afterwards he attempted to
upset this deed, but the court held that it was **irrevocable,**
Lord Hatherley saying : " It is clear that anyone taking
any advantage under a voluntary deed and setting it up
against the donor must show that he thoroughly understood
what he was doing ; it cannot, however, be laid down that
such a deed would be voidable unless it contained a power
of revocation " (*l*). This case would seem to greatly
modify the decisions in *Coutts* v. *Acworth* (*m*), *Wollaston* v.
Tribe (*n*), and *Everitt* v. *Everitt* (*o*), the latter of which

(*i*) *Crabbe* v. *Crabbe, sup.*
(*k*) *Sup.*
(*l*) See also *Hoghton* v. *Hoghton*, 15 B. 278 ; and *Hall* v. *Hall*,
L. R., 8 Ch. 329.
(*m*) L. R., 8 Eq. 558.
(*n*) L. R., 9 Eq. 44.
(*o*) L. R., 10 Eq. 405.

would seem to have been practically overruled, the circumstances being the same as in *Phillips* v. *Mullings* (with the exception that the settlor was a young and inexperienced girl instead of a dissolute young man), and the decision exactly opposite.

3. On the other hand, in the leading case of *Huguenin* v. *Baseley* (*p*), where a widow lady, very much under the **influence of a clergyman**, made a voluntary settlement in his favour, it was held to be invalid.

4. So, where a **father induced a young son**, who was still under his roof, and subject to his influence, to make a settlement in favour of his step-brothers and sisters, it was held, that if the son had applied promptly, the court would have set it aside; but that as he had remained quiescent for some years, and had made no objection to the course which he had been persuaded to follow, he was not entitled to relief; on the ground that by so doing, he had in his maturer years practically confirmed that which he had done in his early youth (*q*). Nor will the court interfere where the settlor subsequently acts under the deed, or does something which shows that he recognizes its validity (*r*), unless indeed he was ignorant of the effect of the settlement at the date of such recognition (*s*).

5. Where a person, apparently at the point of death, signed a settlement of which he recollected nothing, which was never read to him, and in which a power of revocation was purposely omitted by the solicitor on the ground that he knew the variable character of the settlor, and there was also evidence that **the settlor thought** that he was executing the settlement **in place of a will**, it was held that the settlement was revocable (*t*).

(*p*) 14 V. 273; and 2 L. C. 556.
(*q*) *Turner* v. *Collins*, L. R., 7 Ch. 329.
(*r*) *Jarratt* v. *Aldon*, L. R., 9 Eq. 463; *Motz* v. *Moreau*, 13 M. P. C. 376; *Wright* v. *Vanderplank*, 2 K. & J. 1; *Milner* v. *Lord Hare-*
wood, 18 V. 259; *Davies* v. *Davies*, L. R., 9 Eq. 468.
(*s*) *Lister* v. *Hodgson*, L. R., 4 Eq. 30.
(*t*) *Fanshaw* v. *Welsby*, 30 B. 243.

6. Where a settlor has been **induced by fraud** to make a settlement, whether voluntary or based upon value, it will not be enforced; as, for instance, where a wife induces her husband to execute a deed of separation, in *contemplation* of a renewal of illicit intercourse (*u*). Where, however, it is not in her contemplation at the time, but she does in fact subsequently commit adultery, then, as there was no original fraud, the subsequent adultery will not avoid the settlement (*v*).

7. Even where there is **valuable consideration** given, but the settlor is **infirm and ignorant**, and there is reason to suppose that he did not fully understand the transaction, it will be set aside, unless it be proved that full value was given (*w*).

8. As an example of the action of the court where the settlor has **mistaken the effect** of the settlement, the case of *Nanney* v. *Williams* (*x*) may be referred to. There the settlor made an irrevocable voluntary settlement in favour of a relation who also acted as his solicitor. The court considered from the evidence, that the settlor had intended to reserve to himself a power of revocation, and held, that although the deed was otherwise unobjectionable, and would have been valid if the settlor had died intestate and without having revoked it, yet that he having devised the property by his will, had exercised the power of revocation which ought to have been inserted, and that the settlement was consequently avoided.

Art. 13.—*Validity as against Creditors.*

Every settlement of freehold, copyhold (*a*), or leasehold lands or hereditaments, corporeal or incorpo-

(*u*) *Brown* v. *Brown*, L. R., 7 Eq. 185; and see *Evans* v. *Carrington*, 2 D. F. & J. 481; and *Evans* v. *Edmonds*, 13 C. B. 777.

(*v*) *Seagrave* v. *Seagrave*, 13 V. 443.

(*w*) *Baker* v. *Monk*, 33 B. 419;

Clark v. *Malpas*, 31 B. 80; *Linquate* v. *Ledger*, 2 Giff. 137; and see *O'Rorke* v. *Bolingbroke*, L. R., 2 Ap. Cas. 814.

(*x*) 22 B. 452.

(*a*) Formerly not included (*Matthews* v. *Feaver*, 1 Cox, 272), but

real, or of such kinds of goods and chattels as are
capable of being taken in execution (*b*), is void as
against existing and future creditors of the settlor,
in the following cases :—

α. If there is *direct and positive* evidence of an
intention to defeat or delay such creditors, independently of the consequences which may have followed, or which might have been expected to follow
the settlement (*c*).

β. If (although there is no direct proof of
such intention) the settlement is voluntary, *and* the
circumstances are such that the settlement must
necessarily have the effect of defeating or delaying
such creditors, and whether some of the debts
existing at the date of the settlement still remain
unpaid (*d*) or not (*e*). The mere fact that such a
settlement has in the event defeated or delayed
creditors is not sufficient unless that was its probable result (*semble*).

Such settlements are, however, valid in the hands of
persons who are bonâ fide purchasers for valuable
consideration (*f*), whether from the settlor or from
the persons claiming under such settlements.

now included by effect of 1 & 2
Vict. c. 110, s. 11.

(*b*) *Rider* v. *Kidder*, 10 V. 360.
As to what goods come under this
description, see *Barrack* v. *McCul-
lock*, 3 K. & J. 110: *Stokoe* v.
Cowan, 29 B. 637. And as to
choses in action, *Norcut* v. *Dodd*,
Cr. & Ph. 100: and 1 & 2 Vict.
c. 110.

(*c*) *Freeman* v. *Pope*, L. R., 5
Ch. 540; *Spirett* v. *Willows*, 11
Jur., N. S. 70; *Harman* v. *Richards*, 10 Ha. 89; *Strong* v. *Strong*,
18 B. 511: *Columbine* v. *Penhall*,
1 Sm. & G. 228; *Bott* v. *Smith*,
21 B. 511; *Reese River Co.* v.
Attwell, L. R., 7 Eq. 347: *Bar-
ling* v. *Bishop*, 29 B. 417 ; *Re
Pearson*, L. R., 3 Ch. Div. 807.

(*d*) *Freeman* v. *Pope*, *sup.; Lush*
v. *Wilkinson*, 5 V. 384 ; *Holmes*
v. *Penney*, 3 K. & J. 99 ; *Scarf* v.
Soulby, 1 M. & G. 375; *Thompson*
v. *Webster*, 7 Jur., N. S. 531.

(*e*) *Taylor* v. *Coenen*, L. R., 1
Ch. Div. 636; but see *Kidney* v.
Coussmaker, 12 V. 136; *Townsend* v.
Westacott, 4 B. 58; *Richardson* v.
Smallwood, Jac. 558; *Jenkyn* v.
Vaughan, 3 Dr. 419; *Freeman* v.
Pope, sup.

(*f*) *George* v. *Milbanke*, 9 V.
189; *Dauheney* v. *Cockburn*, 1 Mer.
638. And where the consideration
was marriage, and the intended
wife knew nothing of the fraudulent intention, the settlement was
held good quâ her and her children
(*Kevan* v. *Crawford*, L. R., 6 Ch.
Div. 29).

Obs.—In the above rule I have attempted to digest the decisions upon the construction of the statute **13 Eliz. c. 5,** passed "for the avoiding of feigned, convinous, and fraudulent feoffments, &c., contrived of malice, fraud, covin, collusion, or guile, to delay, hinder, or defraud creditors or others," by which it was enacted, that "all and every feoffment, gift, grant, alienation, bargain, and conveyance of lands, tenements, hereditaments, goods, chattels, or any of them, by writing or otherwise, and all and every bond, suit, judgment, and execution to and for any intent or purpose *before declared* and expressed, shall be deemed and taken only as against that person or persons, his or their heirs, successors, executors, administrators and assigns whose action, suits, debts, accounts, damages, penalties, forfeitures, heriots, mortuaries and reliefs by such guileful, covinous or fraudulent devices and practices as is aforesaid are, shall, or might be in any ways disturbed, delayed or defrauded, to be clearly and utterly void, frustrate and of none effect; any pretence, colour, feigned consideration, or any other matter or thing to the contrary notwithstanding. By the fifth section it was provided that the act should not extend to any estate or interest in lands, &c., or goods, &c., assured upon good consideration and bonâ fide to any person not having at the time of such assurance any notice or knowledge of such covin, fraud or collusion.

ILLUST.—1. In **Twynne's case** *(g)* one Pierce was indebted to Twynne in 40*l.* and to C. in 200*l.* C. brought an action for his debt, and pending the result Pierce conveyed all his goods, to the value of 300*l.*, to Twynne in satisfaction of his debt; but Pierce continued in possession of them. Here the court held that there was direct evidence of an intention on the part of Pierce to hinder and delay C. And although Twynne had given valuable consideration for the goods, yet he was privy to the fraud, and consequently

(g) 1 Sm. L. C. 1.

could not avail himself of the proviso in sec. 5. Stress was laid upon the fact that Pierce was allowed to remain in possession of the goods, although the conveyance purported to be not a mere mortgage, but an absolute alienation. Had it been a mortgage, of course the mere fact of the mortgagor retaining possession would have been no badge of fraud, as it is one of the usual incidents of a mortgage(h). The main and substantial point, however, which the court decided was, that it was obvious, for divers reasons, that the conveyance was a mere fraudulent arrangement between Twynne and Pierce to shelter the latter from the just demands of his creditors, and was therefore void under the statute.

2. So, again, where a director of a company was sued by the company, and **fearing that a judgment** would be given against him, made a voluntary assignment to his daughter of all his property, it was held that the fraudulent intention was manifest, and that the settlement was void as against the company, although they were not creditors at the time, and it did not appear that there were any creditors at the time (i). Even though the daughter was no party to the fraud, yet she was not protected, because she had not given valuable consideration.

3. And so again, in *Spirrett v. Willows* (j), the settlor being solvent at the time, but having contracted a considerable debt which would fall due in the course of a few weeks, made a voluntary settlement, by which he withdrew a large portion of his property from the payment of debts, after which he collected the rest of his assets and spent them in the most reckless way, thus depriving the expectant creditor of the means of being paid. In that case there was clear and plain evidence of an **actual intention to defeat creditors**, and accordingly the settlement was set aside.

(h) *Edwards v. Harben*, 2 T. R. 587.

(i) *Reese River Co. v. Attwell*, L. R., 7 Eq. 347.
(j) 3 D. J. & S. 293.

4. And again, where one made a voluntary settlement **upon himself until bankruptcy**, and then over, it was so clearly intended to defraud creditors that it was held void (k).

5. But where value is *boná fide* given by a person for an assignment, even although he may know that the *effect* of the assignment will be to hinder or defeat the assignor's creditors, or expectant creditors, yet if the transaction be a boná fide purchase, and **not a mere collusive arrangement** between the parties with the *intention* of causing such hindrance or delay, it will be upheld (l).

6. In **Freeman** *v.* **Pope** (m) the circumstances, so far as they are material as illustrating the principle laid down in paragraph 3 of this article, were as follows:—The settlor was a clergyman, with a life income of about 1,000l. a year; but at the date of the settlement in question his creditors were pressing him, and he had to borrow from his housekeeper a sum wherewith to pay pressing creditors; and he handed over to her as security the only property he had in the world and a policy of insurance for 1,000l. upon his own life. The security to the housekeeper exceeded in value her debt by about 200l.; but the settlor also owed a debt of 339l. to his bankers, which was subsequently increased at the date of the settlement to 489l. under an arrangement that he would allow his solicitor to receive part of his income, and out of it pay 100l. a year towards liquidating the 489l., and would pay the residue into the banker's bank upon a current account. There was no bargain, however, that the bankers would not sue. Being in these circumstances, he executed a voluntary settlement of the life policy in favour of a Mrs. Pope, and having done so, was consequently in this position, that he had nothing wherewithal to pay, or to give secu-

(k) *Re Pearson*, L.R., 3 Ch. Div. 807.

(l) See *Darville* v. *Terry*, 6 H. & N. 807; *Hale* v. *Saloon Omnibus*

Co., 4 Dr. 492; and see judgment in *Harman* v. *Richards*, 10 Ha. 89.

(m) L. R., 5 Ch. 540.

rity for the debt of 489*l.*, except the surplus value of the furniture, and he was clearly and completely insolvent the moment he executed the settlement. Upon these facts, a subsequent creditor instituted a suit to set aside the settlement, on the ground that although there was no actual fraud, yet the effect of the settlement was to defraud creditors, and that as there were creditors antecedent to the settlement still unpaid (*n*), he could ask for it to be set aside; and the court held that this was so, Lord Hatherley saying: " The principle on which the statute of Elizabeth proceeds is this, that persons must be just before they are generous, and that debts must be paid before gifts can be made. The difficulty the Vice-Chancellor seems to have felt in this case was, that if he, as a special juryman, had been asked whether there was actually any intention on the part of the settlor in this case to defeat, hinder or delay his creditors, he should have come to the conclusion that he had no such intention. It appears to me, that this does not put the question exactly on the right ground, for it would never be left to a special jury to find whether the settlor *intended* to hinder, delay or defeat his creditors, without a direction from the judge that if the **necessary effect of the instrument** was to defeat, hinder or delay creditors, that necessary effect was to be considered as evidencing an intention to do so. . . . . Of course there may be cases (of which *Spirett* v. *Willows* is an example) in which there is direct and positive evidence to defraud; . . . . but it is established by the authorities, that, in the absence of any such direct proof of intention, if a person owing debts makes a settlement which subtracts from the property which is the proper fund for the payment of those debts an amount without which the debts cannot be paid; then, since it is the necessary consequence of the settle-

---

(*n*) It has been since held that the fact of the existence of unpaid debts contracted antecedent to the settlement is immaterial. *Taylor* v. *Coenen*, L. R., 1 Ch. Div. 636.

ment (supposing it effectual) that some creditors must remain unpaid, it would be the duty of the judge to direct the jury that they must infer the intent of the settlor to have been to defeat or delay his creditors, and that the case is within the statute." And Lord Justice Giffard said: "There is one class of cases, no doubt, in which an actual and express intent is necessary to be proved, that is in such cases as *Holmes* v. *Penney* and *Lloyd* v. *Attwood*, where the instruments sought to be set aside were founded on valuable consideration; but where the settlement is voluntary, the intent may be inferred in a variety of ways. For instance, if, after deducting the property which is the subject of the voluntary settlement, sufficient available assets are not left for the payment of the settlor's debts, the law infers intent. Again, if at the date of the settlement the person making the settlement was not in a position actually to pay his creditors, the law would infer that he intended, by making the voluntary settlement, to defeat and delay them. . . . . . That being so, the appeal must be dismissed."

ART. 14.—*Validity as against Trustee in Bankruptcy of a Trader.*

α. A voluntary settlement by *a trader* (unless the trust property has accrued to him since marriage in right of his wife, and the trust is in favour of his wife or his children) is void as against the settlor's trustee in bankruptcy, if he become bankrupt within two years after the date of such settlement; and if the settlor become bankrupt within ten years it is void, unless it can be shown that he was solvent at the date of the settlement without the aid of the property comprised therein (a).

β. Any covenant or contract made by *a trader* in

(a) Bankruptcy Act, 1869 (32 & 33 Vict. c. 71, s. 91); *Ex parte Huxtable*, L. R., 2 Ch. Div. 54.

consideration of marriage, for the future settlement
upon or for his wife or children, of any money or
property wherein he had not at the date of his
marriage any estate or interest, whether vested or
contingent (z), in possession or remainder, and not
being money or property of or in right of his wife,
is, upon his becoming bankrupt before such property or money has been actually transferred or
paid pursuant to such contract or covenant, void
against his trustee in bankruptcy.

Obs.—It need scarcely be pointed out that these provisions are in addition to, and not in substitution for,
those heretofore contained with regard to fraudulent
settlements.

Art. 15.—*Validity as against subsequent Purchasers.*

Every settlement of freeholds, copyholds, or leaseholds (a), made with *intent* to deceive purchasers,
or made without *any* valuable consideration (b), *or*
containing a power of revocation (c) at the will, or
practically at the will (d), of the settlor, is void as
against subsequent bonâ fide purchasers for value
from, or mortgagees (e) or lessees (f) of, the settlor,
and it is immaterial that they have had notice of
the settlement (g) ; but where there is no actual
fraud, the settlement will be void so far only (h)

(z) See *Re Andrews*, L. R., 7
Ch. Div. 635.
(a) As to copyholds, see *Doe* v.
Bottriell, 5 B. & Ad. 131; *Currie*
v. *Nind*, 1 M. & C. 17; and as
to leaseholds, see last note to
Saunders v. *Dehew*, 2 Ver. 272;
but remember that a settlement
of leaseholds cannot in general be
voluntary. See " Definitions,"
and *Price* v. *Jenkins*, L. R., 5 Ch.
Div. 619.
(b) *Doe* v. *Manning*, 9 East, 59.
(c) 27 Eliz. c. 4, s. 5.

(d) *Standon* v. *Bullock*, cit. 3
Rep. 82 b; *Lavender* v. *Blackstone*,
3 Keb. 526; *Jenkins* v. *Kemiss*, 1
Lev. 150.
(e) *Doe* v. *Webber*, 1 A. & E.
733; *Dolphin* v. *Aylward*, L. R.,
4 H. L. 486; *Ede* v. *Knowles*, 2
Y. & C. C. 172.
(f) *Doe* v. *Moses*, 2 W. Bl.
1019.
(g) *Doe* v. *Manning, sup.*
(h) *Croker* v. *Martin*, 1 Bl., N.
S. 573; *Dolphin* v. *Aylward, sup.*

as may be necessary to give effect to such
subsequent transaction. A voluntary cestui que
trust has no equity to the purchase-money as
against the settlor (*i*). This article is, however,
subject to the proviso, that every such settlement is
valid in the hands of purchasers for value and bonâ
fide (*k*), whether claiming as cestuis que trust under
the settlement, or as purchasers from voluntary
cestuis que trust, and whether with or without
notice of the voluntary character of the settlement (*l*).

Obs.—In this article, I have attempted to digest the
effect of the decisions upon the Act **27 Eliz. c. 4**, whereby
all conveyances, &c. of land, tenements or hereditaments,
made with the intent to defraud purchasers, and also all
conveyances with any clause of revocation at the grantor's
pleasure, are made void against subsequent purchasers.
The principle upon which voluntary settlements have been
held void under this act seems to be, that by selling the
property afterwards for a valuable consideration, the vendor
so entirely repudiates the former voluntary settlement, and
shows his intention to sell, as that it shall be taken con-
clusively against him and the person to whom he conveyed
that such intention existed when he made the voluntary
conveyance, and consequently that it was made in order to
defeat the purchaser (*m*). This being the principle, the
statute can only apply to voluntary conveyances, when the
settlor and the subsequent vendor are the same person,
and does not apply where the latter is the heir, or a second
voluntary grantee of the former (*n*); unless indeed the
settlement was actually fraudulent (*o*).

It has been repeatedly held that a very small consideration

(*i*) *Dakin* v. *Whymper*, 26 B. 568.

(*k*) 27 Eliz. c. 4, s. 4.

(*l*) *Prodgers* v. *Langham*, Keb. 486; Sid. 133.

(*m*) Per Campbell, C. J., *Doe* v. *Rusham*, 17 Q. B. 723; 21 L. J., Q. B. 139.

(*n*) *Ibid.*; and see *Parker* v. *Carter*, 4 Ha. 409.

(*o*) *Burrell's case*, 6 Rep. 72.

is sufficient to take the case out of this statute (*p*); and in a recent case it was held, that the mere onus of performing covenants, attaching to the voluntary assignee of a lease, was a sufficient consideration (*q*).

ILLUST.—1. As an illustration of the principle, that the settlement is **void so far only** as is necessary to give effect to the subsequent transaction, the case of property subsequently mortgaged may be instanced. In such a case, the voluntary cestuis que trust will be entitled, subject to the mortgage; and if unsettled estates are included in the mortgage, the cestuis que trust are entitled to throw the mortgage on to the unsettled estates, if they are sufficient to answer it (*r*).

2. The subsequent purchase for value, must be bonâ fide. Thus where the **consideration is grossly inadequate**, the sale may be impeached by the voluntary cestui que trust, on the ground that the transaction is on the face of it a collusive arrangement between the settlor and the so-called purchaser, for the purpose of relieving the former from the settlement (*s*).

(*p*) *Bagspoole* v. *Collins*, L. R., 6 Ch. 228; *Townend* v. *Toker*, L. R., 1 Ch. 446.
(*q*) *Price* v. *Jenkins*, L. R., 5 Ch. Div. 619.

(*r*) *Hales* v. *Cox*, 32 B. 118.
(*s*) *Doe* v. *Routledge*, Cowp. 705; *Metcalfe* v. *Pulvertoft*, 1 V. & B. 184.

SUB-DIVISION IV.

CONSTRUCTION OF DECLARED TRUSTS.

ART. 16.—*Executed Trusts construed strictly, and Executory liberally.*

α. IN the construction of executed trusts, technical terms are construed in their legal and technical sense (*a*).

β. In the construction of executory trusts, the court is not confined to the language of the settlement itself; and where the words of the settlement are improper or informal (*b*), or would create an illegal trust (*c*), or would otherwise defeat the intention of the settlor as gathered from the motives which led to the settlement, and from its general object and purpose, or from other instruments to which it refers, or from any circumstances which may have influenced the settlor's mind (*d*), the court will not direct a conveyance according to the strict words of the settlement, but will order it to be made in a proper and legal manner so as best may answer to the intent of the parties (*e*).

ILLUST.—1. If an estate is vested in trustees and their heirs, in trust for A. for life without impeachment of waste, with remainder to trustees to preserve contingent remainders, with remainder in trust for the heirs of A.'s body, the trust being **an executed trust**, A., according to the rule in Shelley's case, which is a rule *of law* and not

(*a*) *Wright* v. *Pearson*, 1 Ed. 125; *Austen* v. *Taylor, ibid.* 367; *Brydges* v. *Brydges*, 3 Ves. jun. 125; *Jerroise* v. *Duke of Northumberland*, 1 J. & W. 571.

(*b*) See *Earl Stamford* v. *Sir John Hobart*, 3 Br. P. C. Tarl. ed. 31—33.

(*c*) *Humberston* v. *Humberston*, 1 P. W. 332.

(*d*) See per Lord Chelmsford in *Sackville West* v. *Holmesdale*, L. R., 4 H. L. 543.

(*e*) *Earl Stamford* v. *Sir John Hobart, sup.;* and see *Cogan* v. *Duffield*, L. R., 2 Ch. Div. 44.

merely of construction, will be held to take an estate tail (*f*). Of course, where the doctrine could not apply in law, owing to the life estate being equitable, and the remainder legal, or vice versâ, the rule will not apply in equity (*g*); nor where the word "heir" is used in the sense of persona designata (*h*), as where the ultimate limitation is "to the person who may *then* be the heir of A."

2. But in the leading case of *Lord Glenorchy* v. *Bosville* (*i*), where the settlor devised real estate to trustees upon trust, upon the happening of the marriage of his grand-daughter, **to convey** the estate to the use of her for life, with remainder to the use of her husband for life, with remainder to the issue of her body, with remainders over, it was held, that though the grand-daughter would have taken an estate tail had it been an executed trust, yet the trust, being executory, was to be executed in a more careful and accurate manner; and that as the testator's intention was to provide for the children of the marriage, that intention would be best carried out by a conveyance to the grand-daughter for life, with remainder to her husband for life, with remainder to her first and other sons in tail, with remainder to her daughters.

3. And so in **marriage articles**, a covenant to settle estates to the use of the husband for life, with remainder to wife for life, with remainder to their heirs male, and the heirs of such male, is always construed to mean that the settlement shall be so drawn as to give life estates only, to the husband and wife successively (*k*); for it is not to be

<hr>

(*f*) *Wright* v. *Pearson*, 1 Ed. 119; *Austen* v. *Taylor*, ibid. 361; *Jones* v. *Morgan*, 1 Bro. C. C. 206; *Jervoise* v. *Duke of Northumberland*, 1 J. & W. 559.

(*g*) *Collier* v. *M'Bean*, 34 Beav. 426.

(*h*) *Greaves* v. *Simpson*, 10 Jur., N. S. 609.

(*i*) 1 W. & T., L. C. 1.

(*k*) *Trevor* v. *Trevor*, 1 P. W. 622; *Streatfield* v. *Streatfield*, 1 W. & T. L. C. 333; *Jones* v. *Langton*, 1 Eq. C. Ab. 392; *Cusack* v. *Cusack*, 5 Bro. P. C. Tom. ed. 116; *Griffith* v. *Buckle*, 2 Vern. 13; *Stoner* v. *Curwen*, 5 Sim. 268; *Davies* v. *Davies*, 4 Beav. 54; *Lambert* v. *Peyton*, 8 H. L. Cas. 1.

presumed that the parties meant to put it in the power of
the husband to defeat the very object of the settlement,
which is to make a provision for the issue of the marriage (*l*).

4. So where in marriage articles **the word "issue"** is
used, it will not be confined to male issue, because that
would be inconsistent with the object of the articles, but
will be construed to mean sons successively in tail, with
remainder to daughters in tail, with cross remainders
over (*m*).

5. But where the articles show that the **parties understood the distinction**, as, for instance, where part of the
property is limited in strict settlement, and part not, the
trust will be construed strictly (*n*).

6. In **a will** it is obvious that the same presumption will
not arise as in the case of marriage articles; and, therefore,
where a testator gave 300*l*. to trustees, upon trust to lay it
out in the purchase of lands, and to settle such lands to the
only use of M. and her children, and if M. died without
issue, "the land to be divided between her brothers and
sisters then living," it was held that this gave M. an estate
tail (*o*).

7. There is, however, no difference between the construction to be put on an executory trust created by marriage articles, and on an executory trust created by will,
except so far as the former by its very nature furnishes
more emphatically the means of **ascertaining the intention**
of those who created the trust (*p*). In *Sackville West* v.

(*l*) Snell, 50.
(*m*) *Nandick* v. *Wilkes*, Gil. Eq.
Rep. 114; *Burton* v. *Hastings*,
ibid. 113; *Hart* v. *Middlehurst*,
3 Atk. 371; *Maguire* v. *Scully*, 2
Hy. 113; *Burnaby* v. *Griffin*, 3
Ves. 206; *Horne* v. *Barton*, 19
Ves. 398; *Phillips* v. *James*, 2 D.
& Sm. 404; *Re Daniel*, L. R., 1
Ch. Div. 375.

(*n*) *Howel* v. *Howel*, 2 Ves. 358;
Powel v. *Price*, 2 P. W. 535;
Chambers v. *Chambers*, 2 Eq. C. Ab.
35, c. 4; *Highway* v. *Banner*, 1
Bro. C. C. 584.
(*o*) *Sweetapple* v. *Bindon*, 2 Ver.
536.
(*p*) *Sackville West* v. *Holmesdale*, L. R., 4 H. L. 543.

Viscount Holmesdale, Lady A., by a codicil to her will, revoked certain uses declared therein, and declared her intentions to be, to give certain real and personal property to trustees, in trust to settle it as near as might be, with the limitations of the barony of Buckhurst, in such manner as the trustees should consider proper, or as their counsel should advise. The barony was limited to Lady De la Warr for life, with remainder to R., her second son, and the heirs male of his body, with remainder to the third, fourth, and other sons in like manner. It was held, that the property ought not to be settled upon R. in tail like the barony, but that it ought to be limited in a course of strict settlement to R. and other younger sons of Lady De la Warr for their respective lives, with remainder to their sons successively in tail male, in the order mentioned in the patent whereby the barony was created; and Lord Chelmsford said : " The best illustration of the object and purpose of an instrument furnishing an intention in the case of executory trusts, is to be found in the instance of marriage articles, where, the object of the settlement being to make a provision for the issue of the marriage, no words, however strong, which in the case of an executed trust would place the issue in the power of the father, will be allowed to prevail against the implied intention. So, as Sir W. Grant said, in *Blackburn* v. *Stables* (*q*), 'in the case of a will, if it can be clearly ascertained from anything in the will that the testator did not mean to use the expressions which he has employed in their strict technical sense, the court, in decreeing such settlement as he has directed, will depart from his words to execute his intention.' . . . There are cases of executory trusts in wills, where the words 'heirs of the body' have been made to bend to indications of intention that the estate should be strictly settled; and a direction in a will, that a settlement 'shall be made as

(*q*) 2 V. & B. 369.

counsel shall advise,' has been held sufficient to show that
the words were not intended to have their strict legal
effect (r). . . . It appears to me that the words of the
codicil express an intention that the barony and the estates
should go together to the same person, but not that the
limitations of the two should be identical. . . . The word
'correspond' does not mean that the limitations are to be
exactly the same, but that they are to be adapted to each
other so as to carry out the testatrix's intention that the
estate and title should go together. . . . If the settlement
were framed with a limitation in the words of the letters
patent, Lord Buckhurst would be able to defeat this intention, and, by converting his estate tail into a fee simple, to
separate the estate and the title for ever."

8. So again, where a testator bequeathed *money* to
trustees upon trust to purchase real estate, and settle it
upon A. for life without *impeachment of waste*, with
remainder to trustees to preserve contingent remainders,
with remainder to the heirs of A.'s body, and with a power
to jointure, and also devised *land* to A. upon exactly
similar uses, it was held, that the testator manifested an
intention to give A. a life estate only, and that consequently in the case of the executory trusts this intention
should be carried out; but that in the case of the devise,
that being executed, must be construed according to the
rule in Shelley's case (s). Where there was a devise to a
corporation in trust to convey to A. for life, and afterwards
upon the death of A. to his first son for life, and so to the
first son of that first son for life, with remainder in -
default of issue male of A. to B. for life, and to his sons
and their sons in like manner, Lord Cowper said, that
though the **attempt to create a perpetuity** was vain,
yet, so far as was consistent with the rules of law, the
devise ought to be complied with; and he directed, that

(r) *Bastard* v. *Proby*, 2 Cox, 6.   (s) *Papillon* v. *Voice*, 2 P. W.
571.

all the sons already born at the testator's death should take estates for life, with limitations to their unborn sons in tail (*t*).

9. As a last illustration may be quoted the recent case of *Willis* v. *Kymer* (*u*). There a testatrix had by her will, after requesting her sister Eliza to perform her wishes as therein expressed, bequeathed various legacies to her brothers and sisters and their children, including a legacy of 3,000*l.* to her brother John for life, "the principal to be divided at his death between his children John, Sophia, and Mary Ann." The testatrix subsequently made a codicil, whereby she bequeathed to Eliza, "all I possess," requesting at her death she "will leave the sums as I have directed heretofore." Eliza, by her will, appointed the shares of Sophia and Mary Ann to them to **their separate use,** and the question then arose whether she could do so; and Sir George Jessel, M. R., said, "I am of opinion that Eliza had power to attach a limitation to separate use. . . . The original will and codicil say nothing about separate use. They merely direct her to leave the money after her brother's death to his children, and nothing more. She is therefore bound not to make a different disposition. Well, she has conformed to that direction, by leaving the money to the children; and in doing so has taken care to dispose of it in such a manner that the shares of the daughters shall, in case of their marriage, still remain for their own benefit, *thus effectually carrying out her sister's intention.*"

(*t*) *Humberston* v. *Humberston*, 1 P. W. 332; *Williams* v. *Teale*, 6 Ha. 239; *Lyddon* v. *Ellison*, 17 Beav. 565; *Peard* v. *Kekewich*, 15 Beav. 173; but see *Blagrove* v. *Handcock*, 18 Sim. 378.

(*u*) L. R., 7 Ch. Div. 181.

Division II.

CONSTRUCTIVE TRUSTS.

ART. 17.—*Introductory Summary.*

CONSTRUCTIVE trusts arise, either (1) when the legal estate is given but the equitable interest is not, or is only partially disposed of; (2) when the equitable interest is disposed of in a manner which the law will not permit to be carried out; (3) when a purchase has been made in the name of some other person than the real purchaser (in each of which three cases the equitable interest may return, or, as it is technically called, "result" to the settlor or purchaser); (4) when some person holding a fiduciary position has made a profit out of the trust property; and (5) in all other cases where there is no express trust, but the legal and equitable estates in property are nevertheless not co-equal and united in the same individual.

ART. 18.—*Resulting Trust where Equitable Interest not wholly disposed of.*

When property is given to a person, and it is either expressed on the face of the instrument by which it was given, or, in the absence of such expression, it appears to have been the probable intention of the donor, extracted from the general scope of the instrument (*a*), that the donee was

---

(*a*) Per Lord Hardwicke, *Hill v. Bishop of London*, 1 Atk. 620;   *Walton v. Walton*, 14 V. 322; *King v. Denison*, 1 V. & B. 279.

not intended to take it beneficially, but the instrument is either silent as to the way in which the
beneficial interest is to be applied, or directs that it
shall be applied for a particular purpose (as distinguished from a mere subjection to such purpose (*b*)), which purpose turns out to be insufficient
to exhaust the property or cannot be carried into
effect (*c*), there will be a resulting trust in favour
of the donor or his representatives (*d*).   Where the
non-beneficial character of the gift appears on the
face of the instrument, no evidence to the contrary
is admissible (*e*); but where it is merely presumed
from the general scope of the instrument, parol
evidence is (at all events in the case of gifts inter
vivos) admissible, both in aid and in contradiction
of the presumption (*f*).

ILLUST.—1. Thus, where real estate was devised to "**my
trustees**," but no trusts were declared in relation to it, it
was held that the trustees must hold it in trust for the
testator's heir; for by the expression "trustees," unex-
plained by anything else in the instrument (*g*), all notion
of a beneficial interest in the gift to those individuals was
excluded (*h*).

2. And so where a testator *devised* and bequeathed all

(*b*) See 1 Jarm. 533; *Watson* v.
Hayes, 5 M. & C. 125; *Wood* v.
Cox, 2 M. & C. 684.

(*c*) *Stubbs* v. *Sargon*, 3 M. & C.
507; *Ackroyd* v. *Smithson*, 1 B.
C. C. 503.

(*d*) As to whether it results to
his residuary devisees, legatees,
or real or personal representatives, see Lewin, 182 *et seq.*

(*e*) See *Langham* v. *Sandford*,
17 V. 442; *Irvine* v. *Sullivan*,
L. R., 8 Eq. 673.

(*f*) 29 Car. II. c. 3, s. 8.
Gascoigne v. *Thwing*, 1 Ver. 366;
Willis v. *Willis*, 2 Atk. 71; *Cook*
v. *Hutchinson*, 1 Ke. 50. As to
parol evidence explanatory of a
testator's intention, see *Docksey* v.

Docksey, 2 Eq. C. A. 506; *North*
v. *Crompton*, 1 Ch. Ca. 196; *Walton*
v. *Walton*, 14 V. 322; *Langham*
v. *Sandford, sup.*; *Lynn* v. *Beaver*,
1 T. & R. 66; and Lewin, 52
et seq., and 130; and see *Biddulph*
v. *Williams*, L. R., 1 Ch. Div.
203.

(*g*) As, for instance, if the expression is used with reference to
one only of two separate funds.
Bateley v. *Windle*, 2 B. C. C. 31;
Pratt v. *Sladden*, 14 V. 193; *Gibbs*
v. *Rumsey*, 3 V. & B. 294.

(*h*) *Dawson* v. *Clark*, 18 V.
254; *Barrs* v. *Fewke*, 2 H. & M.
60; and see *Elcock* v. *Mapp*, 3
H. L. Cas. 492.

his estate and effects to A. and B., their heirs, executors, and administrators, *upon trust* to convert his *personal* estate, and to stand possessed of the proceeds and of the residue of his estate and effects, upon **trusts only applicable to personalty**, it was held that the real estate of the testator passed to the trustees by the use of the word "devise" in the gift, and the word "heirs" in the limitation; but that as the trusts were rigidly and exclusively applicable to personal property, and as the trustees had been designated by that name, and so could not take beneficially, there was a resulting trust of the real estate in favour of the settlor's heirs (*i*).

3. Where lands have been conveyed to a trustee, and the trusts have not been manifested and proved by a signed writing in accordance with the Statute of Frauds, there will be a resulting trust to the settlor (*j*).

4. So, if a declared trust is too **uncertain** or vague to be executed (*k*), or **fails by lapse** (*l*) or otherwise, then as it is expressed on the face of the instrument, that the trustee was not intended to take beneficially, there will be a resulting trust.

5. Where real property is granted to another, either **without any consideration** at all, or for a merely nominal one (*m*), then if no trust is declared of any part of it, and the grant *is to a stranger*, and no intention of passing the beneficial interest appears, either by the instrument or by parol or other evidence (*n*), the law presumes that the prob-

(*i*) *Loughley* v. *Loughley*, L. R., 13 Eq. 133; *Dunnage* v. *White*, 1 J. & W. 583; *Lloyd* v. *Lloyd*, L. R., 7 Eq. 458; comp. *D'Almaine* v. *Moseley*, 1 Dr. 629; *Coard* v. *Holderness*, 20 B. 147.

(*j*) *Rudkin* v. *Dolman*, 35 L. T. 791.

(*k*) *Stubbs* v. *Sargon*, 2 Ke. 255; *Morice* v. *Bishop of Durham*, 9 V. 399, and 10 V. 522; *Kendal* v. *Granger*, 5 B. 300.

(*l*) *Ackroyd* v. *Smithson*, 1 B. C. C. 503; *Spink* v. *Lewis*, 3 B. C. C. 355; or becomes in the event too remote, *Tregonwell* v. *Sydenham*, 3 Dow, 210.

(*m*) *Hayes* v. *Kingdome*, 1 Ver. 33; *Sculthorpe* v. *Burgess*, 1 V. jun. 92.

(*n*) *Cook* v. *Hutchinson*, 1 Ke. 50.

able intention of the grantor was not to confer a benefit (*o*), and accordingly looks upon the grantee as a trustee for the grantor or his representatives.

6. But where the **gift is of chattels**, it would seem that an intention to confer beneficially would be presumed, on the ground of the utter fatuity of the proceeding on any other supposition (*p*). But this presumption is, of course, rebuttable by evidence (*q*).

7. Where there is a devise to A. upon **trust to pay debts** or to answer an annuity, there is a resulting trust of what remains, after payment of the debts or satisfaction of the annuity (*r*).

8. But where (*s*) one made his will, and thereby gave 5*l.* to his brother (who was also his heir-at-law), and made and constituted his "dearly beloved wife" his "sole heiress and executrix" of all his lands and real and personal estate, to sell and dispose thereof at her pleasure, and to pay his debts and legacies, it was held, that the wife was entitled to the real estate for her own benefit, and that there was no resulting trust to the heir, on the ground that the direction that the wife should be sole heiress, did in every respect place her in the stead of the heir-at-law and not as trustee for him, and that this was "rendered plainer by reason of the language of tenderness and affection which must intend to her something beneficial, and not what would be a trouble only;" in addition to which the heir was not forgotten, but had 5*l.* left him.

9. And so under a devise to A., **charged with the payment** of debts and legacies (*t*), or charged with the payment of a contingent legacy (*u*) which does not take effect, there

---

(*o*) *Sculthorpe* v. *Burgess, sup.;* and see *Hutchins* v. *Lee*, 1 At. 147.

(*p*) *George* v. *Howard*, 7 Pr. 651.

(*q*) *Custance* v. *Cunninghame*, 13 B. 363.

(*r*) *King* v. *Dennison*, 1 V. &

B. 279: *Watson* v. *Hayes, sup.*

(*s*) *Rogers* v. *Rogers*, 3 P. W. 193.

(*t*) *King* v. *Dennison, sup.;* *Wood* v. *Cox, sup.*

(*u*) *Tregonwell* v. *Sydenham*, 3 Dow, 210.

will be no resulting trust, but the whole property will go to the devisee beneficially, subject only to the charge.

Art. 19.—*Resulting Trusts where Trusts declared are Illegal.*

When a person has intentionally vested property in another for an illegal purpose, then if the trustee expressly relies (*a*) upon the maxim "*In pari delicto potior est conditio possidentis*," the settlor cannot recover it back (*b*), except in the following cases, namely,—

α. Where the illegal purpose is not carried into execution and nothing is done under it, there is a locus pœnitentiæ, and the mere intention to effect an illegal object will not deprive the settlor of the right to the beneficial ownership, to which the trustee has no honest claim; and there will consequently be a resulting trust in favour of the settlor (*c*).

β. Where the effect of allowing the trustee to retain the property might be to effectuate an unlawful object, or to defeat a legal prohibition, or to protect a fraud, equity will, on the ground of public policy, enforce a resulting trust in favour of the settlor, so as to prevent the illegal trust being carried into effect (*d*).

(*a*) *Haigh* v. *Kaye*, L. R., 7 Ch. 469.

(*b*) *Duke of Bedford* v. *Coke*, 2 V. sen. 116; *Curtis* v. *Perry*, 6 V. 739; *Cottington* v. *Fletcher*, 2 At. 156; *Brackenbury* v. *Brackenbury*, 2 J. & W. 391; *Taylor* v. *Chester*, L. R., 4 Q. B. 309; *Ayerst* v. *Jenkins*, L. R., 16 Eq. 275.

(*c*) *Symes* v. *Hughes*, L. R., 9 Eq. 475; *Childers* v. *Childers*, 1 D. & J. 482; *Davies* v. *Otty*, 35 B. 208; *Birch* v. *Blagrave*, Amb. 264; *Platamone* v. *Staple*, G. Coop. 250.

(*d*) See per Lord Selborne in *Ayerst* v. *Jenkins*. L. R., 16 Eq. 283: and see per Knight Bruce, L. J., in *Reynell* v. *Spry*, where he said, "Where the parties are not in pari delicto, and where public policy is considered as advanced by allowing either party, or at least the more excusable of the two, to sue for relief, relief is given to him." And see also to same effect, *Law* v. *Law*, 3 P. W. 393, and *St. John* v. *St. John*, 11 V. 535.

ILLUST.—1. Thus in *Symes* v. *Hughes* (*e*), the plaintiff, being in pecuniary difficulties, assigned certain leasehold property to a trustee with the **view of defeating his creditors**, and two and a half years afterwards was adjudicated bankrupt, but obtained the sanction of his creditors, under sect. 110 of the Bankruptcy Act, 1861, to an arrangement, by which his estate and effects were re-vested in him, he covenanting to prosecute a suit for the recovery of the assigned property, and to pay a composition of two and sixpence in the pound to his creditors, in case his suit should prove successful. Lord Romilly, M. R., in delivering judgment, said: "The assignment was made for an illegal purpose, and it is said that, such being the case, the court will not interfere. I think the correct answer to this was given by Mr. Southgate, namely, that where the purpose for which the assignment was given is not carried into execution, and nothing is done under it, the mere intention to effect an illegal object when the assignment was executed, does not deprive the assignor of his right to recover the property from the assignee who has given no consideration for it."

2. So, again, the plaintiff, being **apprehensive of an indictment** for bigamy (conviction for which involved forfeiture of property), conveyed his real estate to the defendant, on a parol agreement to retransfer when the difficulty should have passed over. It subsequently transpired that the plaintiff was not liable to be indicted, and thereupon he filed a bill praying for a retransfer of his property; and it was held, that although there was no express trust, inasmuch as there was no written proof of it, yet there was a resulting trust to which the statute did not apply, and as there was no illegality in fact, but only in intention, the court ordered the transfer prayed for (*f*).

3. And where a father conveyed the legal estate in pro-

(*e*) *Supra.*   (*f*) *Davies* v. *Otty, sup.*

perty to his daughter, with the intention of thus **escaping from serving as sheriff**, but afterwards repented, and paid the fine, Lord Hardwicke said, " I am of opinion that the conveyance ought not to take effect against his intention *unless he had actually taken the oath*" that he had not the requisite qualification (*g*).

4. Where a settlor attempts to settle property so as to **contravene the policy of the law** with regard to perpetuities, such trusts will not only not be carried into effect, but the person nominated to carry them out is held to be a mere trustee for the settlor or his representatives. For the attempt was made either through ignorance or carelessness, or else with a direct intention to contravene the law. In the former case, as there would be no delictum, the usual maxim would not apply. In the latter, equity would not allow the trustee to retain the property and so put it in his power to carry out the illegal intentions of the testator, and to defeat the policy of the law (*h*).

5. And so again, where land or the proceeds of land is devised to charitable uses, or is devised to one who is under a secret agreement with the testator pledged to apply it to **charitable purposes**, then, notwithstanding the improper intentions of the testator, yet, as the object of allowing the gift to stand would probably be to effect an object prohibited by law, there will be a resulting trust in favour of the testator's heir-at-law or residuary devisee, as the case may be (*i*).

6. But where a father granted land to his son, in order to give him a **colourable qualification** to shoot game under the old game laws, and without any intention of conferring any beneficial interest upon him, the court would not enforce any resulting trust in favour of the father, on the

(*g*) *Birch* v. *Blagrave, sup.*
(*h*) *Carrick* v. *Errington,* 2 P. W. 361; *Tregonwell* v. *Sydenham,* 3 Dow, 194; *Gibbs* v. *Rumsey,* 2 V. & B. 294.

(*i*) *Arnold* v. *Chapman,* 1 V. sen. 108; *Addlington* v. *Cann,* Barn. 130; *Springett* v. *Jennings,* L. R., 10 Eq. 488 : but see *Rowbotham* v. *Dunnett,* L. R., 8 Ch. Div. 430.

ground probably, that he and the son were in pari delicto, and that there would be no detriment to the public in allowing the son to retain the estate (k). Of course, if there had been no illegality (if, for instance, a bare legal estate had been a sufficient qualification), there would have been a resulting trust (l).

7. So in *Ayerst* v. *Jenkins* (m), a widower, two days before going through the ceremony of **marriage with his deceased wife's sister** (which ceremony was known to both parties to be invalid), executed a deed, by which it was recited that he was desirous of making a settlement and provision for the lady, and had transferred certain shares into the names of trustees, upon the trusts thereinafter declared, being for the separate and inalienable use of the lady during her life, and after her death as she should by deed or will appoint. They afterwards lived together as man and wife until the widower's death. Some time afterwards, his personal representative instituted a suit to set aside the settlement, on the ground that it was founded on an immoral consideration; but Lord Selborne said, "Relief is sought by the representative, not merely of a particeps criminis, but of a voluntary and sole donor, on the naked ground of the illegality of his own intention and purpose, and that, not against a bond or covenant or other obligation resting in fieri, but against a completed transfer of specific chattels, by which the legal estate in those chattels was absolutely vested in trustees for the sole benefit of the defendant. I know of no doctrine of public policy which requires or authorizes a court of equity to give assistance to such a plaintiff under such circumstances. When the immediate and direct effect of an estoppel in equity against relief to a particular plaintiff might be *to effectuate an unlawful object, or to defeat a legal prohibition, or to protect a*

(k) *Brackenbury* v. *Brackenbury*,   (l) *Childers* v. *Childers*, 1 D. &
2 J. & W. 391.   J. 482.
                                        (m) L. R., 16 Eq. 283.

fraud, such an estoppel may well be regarded as against public policy. But the voluntary gift of part of his own property by one particeps criminis to another, is in itself neither fraudulent nor prohibited by law; and the present is not the case of a man repenting of an immoral purpose before it is too late, and seeking to recall, while the object is yet unaccomplished (*n*), a gift intended as a bribe to iniquity. If public policy is opposed, as it is, to vice and immorality, it is no less true, as was said by Lord Truro in *Benyon* v. *Nettlefold* (*o*), that the law in sanctioning the defence of particeps criminis does so on the grounds of public policy,—namely, that those who violate the law must not apply to the law for protection."

ART. 20.—*Resulting Trusts upon Purchases in Another's Name.*

When real (*a*) or personal (*b*) property is taken in the names of the purchaser and others generally, or in the names of others without that of the purchaser, or in one name, or in several, and whether jointly or successively, there is a primâ facie presumption of a resulting trust in favour of the man or men who, by parol (*c*) or other evidence, is or are proved to have advanced the purchase-money (*d*) in the character of purchaser (*e*). But this presumption may be rebutted—

α. By parol (*f*) or other evidence;

β. By the fact that the person or persons in whose name or names the purchase was made was or were the wife, child or children of the pur-

---

(*n*) As in *Symes* v. *Hughes, sup.*
(*o*) 3 M. & G. 102.
(*a*) *Dyer* v. *Dyer*, 2 Cox, 93.
(*b*) *Ebrand* v. *Dancer*, 2 Ch. Ca. 26; *Wheeler* v. *Smith*, 1 Gif. 300.
(*c*) 29 Car. II. c. 3, s. 8; *Bartlett* v. *Pickersgill*, 1 Ed. 515;

Ryall v. *Ryall*, 1 Atk. 59; *Leach* v. *Leach*, 10 Ves. 517.
(*d*) *Dyer* v. *Dyer, sup.; Wray* v. *Steele*, 2 V. & B. 388.
(*e*) *Bartlett* v. *Pickersgill, sup.*
(*f*) *Rider* v. *Kidder*, 10 V. 360.

chaser (g), or was or were some person or persons
towards whom he stood in close relationship, and
in loco parentis (h) ; in any of which cases a primâ
facie presumption will arise that the purchaser intended the ostensible grantee or grantees to take
beneficially. But this last presumption is also
capable of being rebutted by evidence, or by surrounding circumstances (i).

Illust.—1. If one discharge the purchase-money by
way of loan to the person in whose name the property is
taken, there will be no resulting trust, because the lender
did not advance the purchase-money as purchaser (k).

2. Where the purchase-money is **advanced partly by
the person** in whose name the property is taken, and
partly by another, then, if they advance it in equal shares,
they will (in the absence of evidence or circumstances
showing a contrary intention (l)) take as joint tenants,
because the advance being equal the interest is equal;
but if in unequal shares, then a trust results to each of
them, in proportion to his advance (m).

3. In *Crabbe* v. *Crabbe* (n), a father transferred a sum of
stock from his own name into the **name of his son**, and of
a broker, and told the latter to carry the dividends to the
son's account. The father, by a codicil to his will executed
subsequently, bequeathed the stock to another; but it was
held that the son took absolutely, the Master of the Rolls
saying, "If the transfer is not ambiguous, but a clear and

(g) *Soar* v. *Foster*, 4 K. & J.
152 ; *Beckford* v. *Beckford*, Loft,
490.

(h) *Beckford* v. *Beckford, sup. ;
Currant* v. *Jago*, 1 Coll. 261;
Tucker v. *Burron*, 2 H. & M. 515;
Forrest v. *Forrest*, 13 W. R. 380.

(i) *Tunbridge* v. *Cane*, 19 W. R.
1047; *Williams* v. *Williams*, 32
B. 370.

(k) *Bartlett* v. *Pickersgill, sup.*,
and see also *Areling* v. *Knipe*, 19

Ves. 441.

(l) See *Robinson* v. *Preston*, 4
K. & J. 505; *Edwards* v. *Fashion*,
Pr. Ch. 332; *Lake* v. *Gibson*, Eq.
Ca. Ab. 290; *Bone* v. *Polland*, 24
Bea. 288.

(m) *Lake* v. *Gibson*, 1 Eq. C.
A. 291; *Rigden* v. *Vallier*, 3 Atk.
735.

(n) 1 M. & K. 511; and see also
Birch v. *Blagrave*, Amb. 264.

unequivocal act, as I must take it on the authorities, for
explanation there is no place; if then it cannot be permitted to explain, still less can it be allowed to qualify
the operation of the previous act. The transfer being held
an advancement, nothing contained in the codicil, nor any
other matter ex post facto, can ever be allowed to alter
what had been already done." In short, a resulting trust
will not be allowed to arise, merely because a donor
subsequently changes his mind and repents him of his
generosity.

4. But a declaration made by the father *at or before* the
date of the purchase is admissible **to rebut the presumption,** although it might not be good as a declaration of
trust on account of its not being reduced into writing; for
" as the trust would result to the father were it not rebutted by the sonship as a circumstance of evidence, the
father may counteract that circumstance by the evidence
arising from his parol declaration"(*o*).

5. **Surrounding circumstances** may also tend to rebut
the presumption. Thus, where a father, upon his son's
marriage, gave him a considerable advancement, and
having several younger children who had no provision, he
sold an estate; but 500*l*. only of the purchase-money being
paid, he took a security for the residue in the joint names
of himself and his said son, and he himself received the
interest and a great part of the principal without any
opposition from the son, as did his executrix after his
death, the son writing receipts for the interest; it was held
that the son took nothing; the Lord Chancellor saying,
" Where a father takes an estate in the name of his son it
is to be considered as an advancement; but that is liable
to be rebutted by subsequent acts; so if the estate be
taken jointly, so as the son may be entitled by survivorship, that is weaker than the former case, and still

(*o*) *Williams* v. *Williams*, 32 B. 370.

depends on circumstances. The son knew here that his name was used in the mortgage, and must have known whether it was for his own interest or only as a trustee for the father, and instead of making any claim, his acts are very strong evidence of the latter; nor is there any colour why the father should make him any further advancement when he had so many children unprovided for" (*l*). The dictum of the learned chancellor, that the presumption may be rebutted by subsequent acts, cannot be taken to mean subsequent acts of the father, which are only admissible against, and not for him (*m*); but must, it is apprehended, refer only to **subsequent acts of the son** (and only to them when there is nothing to show that the father did actually intend to advance the son (*n*)), or to subsequent acts of the father so acquiesced in by the son as to raise the presumption that the son always knew that no benefit was intended him. It is also to be remarked, that the fact of the father having previously made provision for the son, would not of *itself* have been sufficient to rebut the usual presumption, although, taken together with other circumstances, it is a strong link in the chain (*o*).

6. So the relationship of **solicitor and client** between the son and the parent has been considered a circumstance that will, of itself, rebut the presumption of advancement (*p*).

7. In *Re De Visme* (*q*) it was laid down, that where a **married woman** had, out of her separate estate, made a purchase in the name of her children, no presumption of advancement arose, inasmuch as a married woman was under no obligation to maintain her children. But, with

(*l*) *Pole* v. *Pole*, 1 V. sen. 76; *Stock* v. *McAvoy*, L. R., 15 Eq. 55.
(*m*) *Reddington* v. *Reddington*, 3 Ridge, 197.
(*n*) *Sidmouth* v. *Sidmouth*, 2 B. 455; *Hepworth* v. *Hepworth*, L. R.,

11 Eq. 10.
(*o*) See per Lord Loughborough, 3 Ridge, 190.
(*p*) *Garrett* v. *Wilkinson*, 2 D. & S. 244.
(*q*) 2 De G., J. & S. 17.

great respect, it is submitted that the true ground for presuming that a parent intends to advance his child, is not duty, but natural love and affection. On this point, the judgment of Vice-Chancellor Stuart in *Sayre* v. *Hughes* (r) is worthy of study. In that case, a widowed mother, after making her will in favour of her two daughters, transferred East India Stock which had stood in her own name into the names of herself and the unmarried daughter, and died: and the Vice-Chancellor said, "If stock be found standing in the names of two persons, the presumption of law is that it is their property. But if there be evidence that one of them purchased the stock, and that the name of the other was used without any consideration proceeding from that person, the want of consideration induces the court to presume a resulting trust. The more simple case, and that generally referred to in the reported decisions, is the case of a purchase by one person in the name of another. As soon as you have the fact of the purchase in evidence, and show that the purchase-money was paid by a person other than the person to whom the conveyance was made, the fact of want of consideration almost necessarily creates the presumption of a resulting trust. In the case, however, of a father purchasing property in the name of a son, and having the conveyance made to the son—the father paying the purchase-money—the circumstance of a relationship raises a presumption of benefit intended for the son, which rebuts the notion of a resulting trust. In the case of *Grey* v. *Grey* (s), before Lord Nottingham, there was, beyond the simple facts of the purchase and the conveyance, the fact of the receipt of the profits by the father. Where the conveyance is to one person and the purchase-money paid by another, the receipt of the profits by the person who paid the purchase-money, in an ordinary case strengthens the presumption that he is the beneficial

(r) L. R., 5 Eq. 376.   (s) 2 Sw. 594.

owner, but in the case of a father and a son this circumstance was not enough to rebut the presumption of benefit
to the son. The same doctrine extends to a purchase by a
person in loco parentis. Lord Cottenham in *Powys* v.
Mansfield (*t*), commenting upon the meaning of that expression, said, 'It means a person in such a relation towards
the individual in question as raises a presumption of an
intention to benefit him.' It has been argued, that a
mother is not a person bound to make an advancement to
her child, and that a widowed mother is not a person
standing in such a relation to her child as to raise a
presumption that in a transaction of this kind a benefit
was intended for the child. In the case of *Re De Visme*
it was said, that a mother does not stand in such a
relationship to a child as to raise a presumption of benefit
for the child. The question in that case arose on a petition in lunacy, and it seems to have been taken for
granted that no presumption of benefit arises in the case
of a mother. But *maternal affection as a motive* of bounty
is perhaps the strongest of all, although the duty is not so
strong as in the case of a father, inasmuch as it is the duty
of a father to advance his child. That, however, is a
moral obligation, and not a legal one." His honor then
reviewed the circumstances of the case, in order to see
whether they rebutted the presumption of advancement,
and, finding that they did not, decided in favour of the
daughter.

8. With regard to the presumption of advancement in
favour of persons to whom the purchaser stands **in loco
parentis**, it has been held that the presumption arose in
the case of an illegitimate child (*u*), a grandchild *when the
father was dead* (*r*), and the nephew of a wife who had
been practically adopted by the husband as his child (*w*).

(*t*) 3 M. & C. 359.
(*u*) *Beckford* v. *Beckford*, Loft,
290.

(*r*) *Ebrand* v. *Dancer*, Ch. Ca. 26.
(*w*) *Currant* v. *Jago*, 1 Coll. Ch.
261.

But it would seem that the person alleged to have been in loco parentis must have intended to put himself in the situation of the person described as the natural father of the child with reference to those parental offices and duties which consist in making provision for a child; and the mere fact that a grandfather took care of his daughter's illegitimate child and sent it to school, has been held to be insufficient to raise the presumption; Vice-Chancellor Page Wood saying, "I cannot put the doctrine so high as to hold that if a person educate a child to whom he is under no obligation either morally or legally, the child is therefore to be provided for at his expense" (x).

ART. 21.—*Profits made by Persons in Fiduciary Positions.*

Where a person holds, or has the management of property, either as an express trustee, or as one of a succession of persons partially interested under a settlement, or as a guardian, agent, or other person clothed with a fiduciary character, he must not gain any personal profit by availing himself of his position; and if he does so, he will be a mere trustee of such profit for the benefit of the persons equitably entitled to the property, in respect of which such profit was gained.

ILLUST.—1. Thus, in the leading case of *Sandford* v. *Keech* (a), a lessee of the profits of a market had devised the lease to a trustee for an infant. On the expiration of the lease, the trustee applied for a renewal, but the lessor would not renew, on the ground that the infant could not enter into the usual covenants. Upon this, the **trustee took a lease to himself** for his own benefit; but it was decreed by Lord King, that he must hold it in trust for the infant, his lordship saying, "If a trustee, on the refusal

(x) *Tucker* v. *Burron*, 2 H. &   (a) Sel. Ch. Ca. 61.
M. 515; 11 Jur., N. S. 525.

to renew, might have a lease to himself, few trust estates
would be renewed to cestuis que trust."

2. And so also a **tenant for life** of leaseholds (even though
they be held under a mere yearly tenancy (*b*)), who claims
under a settlement, cannot renew them for his own sole
benefit; for he cannot avail himself of his position, as the
person in possession under the settlement, to get a more
durable term, and so to defeat the probable intentions of
the settlor, that the lease should be renewed for the benefit
of *all* persons claiming under the settlement (*c*). And upon
similar grounds, if a tenant for life accepts money in consideration of his allowing something to be done which is
prejudicial to the trust property (as for instance the
unopposed passage of an act of parliament sanctioning a
railway), he will be a trustee of such money for all the
persons interested under the settlement (*d*).

3. The same principle applies to **mortgagees** (*e*), **joint
tenants** (*f*), **partners** (*g*), and owners of land subject to a
charge (*h*).

4. So **directors** of a company, cannot avail themselves
of their position to enter into beneficial contracts with the
company (*i*); nor can they buy property, and then sell it
to the company at an advanced price. So promoters of a
company hold a fiduciary relation towards the company (*k*).
Directors cannot receive commissions from other parties,

(*b*) *James* v. *Deane*, 15 V. 236
(*c*) *Eyre* v. *Dolphin*, 2 B. & B.
290; *Mill* v. *Hill*, 3 H. L. C.
828; *Yew* v. *Edwards*, 1 D. & J.
598; *James* v. *Deane*, *sup.*
(*d*) *Pole* v. *Pole*, 2 Dr. & S.
420.
(*e*) *Rushworth's* case, Free. 13.
(*f*) *Palmer* v. *Young*, 1 Ver.
276.
(*g*) *Featherstonhaugh* v. *Fenwick*,
17 V. 311; *Clegg* v. *Fishwick*, 1
M. & G. 294; *Bell* v. *Barnett*, 21
W. R. 119; but as to partners,
see *Dean* v. *MacDowell*, L. R., 8

Ch. Div. 345.
(*h*) *Jackson* v. *Welsh*, L. & G.
t. Plunket, 346; *Winslow* v. *Tighe*,
2 B. & B. 195; *Webb* v. *Lugar*, 2
Y. & C. 247.
(*i*) *Great Luxembourg Rail. Co.*
v. *Magnay*, 25 B. 586; *Aberdeen
Rail. Co.* v. *Blackie*, 1 Macq. 461;
Flanagan v. *G. W. Rail. Co.*, 19
L. T., N. S. 345.
(*k*) *Hitchens* v. *Congreve*, 1 R.
& M. 150; *Fawcett* v. *Whitehouse*,
ibid. 132; *Beck* v. *Kantorowicz*, 3
K. & J. 230; *Bagnall* v. *Carlton*,
L. R., 6 Ch. Div. 371.

on the sale of any of the property of the company (*l*), and generally they cannot deal for their own advantage with any part of the property or shares of the company (*m*).

5. Agents come under the same principle (*n*). Thus, where A., being aware that B. wished to obtain shares in a certain company, represented to B. that he, A., could procure a certain number of shares at 3*l*. a share, and B. agreed to purchase at that price, and the agreement was carried out; but B. afterwards discovered that A. was in fact the owner of the shares, having just previously bought them for 2*l*. a share; it was held that A. was an agent for B., and must be ordered to repay to B. the difference between the price given by B., and that given by A. for the shares (*o*).

6. So a **solicitor** who purchases property from a client, must, if the sale be impeached, not only show that he gave full value for it, but also that the client was actually benefited by the transaction. And persons who subsequently purchase from the solicitor with notice of the transaction are under a similar liability (*p*).

ART. 22.—*General Equitable Claims.*

In every case (not coming within the scope of any of the preceding articles) where the person in whom real or personal property is vested, has not the whole equitable interest therein, he is pro tanto a trustee for the persons having such other equitable interest (*a*).

(*l*) *Gaskell* v. *Chambers*, 26 B. 360.

(*m*) *York, &c. Co.* v. *Hudson*, 16 B. 485.

(*n*) *Morrett* v. *Paske*, 2 At. 54; *Kimber* v. *Barber*, L. R., 8 Ch. 56.

(*o*) *Kimber* v. *Barber, sup.*

(*p*) *Topham* v. *Spencer*, 2 Jur., N. S. 865.

(*a*) This article, doubtless, includes all those relating to constructive trusts which have preceded it, but as it would be a quite endless task to enumerate every kind of constructive trust, for they are, as has been truly said, conterminous with equity jurisprudence, I have thought it better to call special attention

ILLUST.—1. Thus, where a binding contract is entered into between two persons for the sale of property by one to the other, then, in the words of Lord Cairns, in *Shaw* v. *Foster* (b), "There cannot be the slightest doubt of the relation subsisting in the eye of a court of equity between the **vendor and the purchaser.** The vendor is a trustee of the property for the purchaser; the purchaser is the real beneficial owner in the eye of a court of equity of the property, subject only to this observation, that the vendor (whom I have called a trustee) is not a mere dormant trustee; he is a trustee having a personal and substantial interest in the property, a right to protect that interest, and an active right to assert that interest if anything should be done in derogation of it. The relation therefore of trustee and cestui que trust subsists, but subsists subject to the paramount right of the vendor and trustee to protect his own interest as vendor of the property." He is, however, only trustee pro tanto, and his duties are strictly matter of contract (c).

2. In the converse case, where the vendor has actually conveyed the property, but the purchaser has not paid the purchase-money, or has only paid part of it, the vendor has a **lien** upon the property for the unpaid portion (d); and the purchaser will hold the estate as a trustee pro tanto, unless by his acts or declarations the vendor has plainly manifested his intention to rely, not upon the estate, but upon some other security, or upon the personal credit of the individual (e). A mere collateral security will not, however, suffice (f); but where it appears that a bond, covenant, mortgage or annuity was itself the actual con-

to these classes which are most important, and to bring all others within one sweeping general clause.

(b) L. R., 5 H. L. 338; *Earl of Egmont* v. *Smith*, L. R., 6 Ch. Div. 475.

(c) See per Lord Westbury in *Knox* v. *Gye*, L. R., 5 H. L. 656; but see *Smith* v. *Earl Egmont*, L. R., 6 Ch. Div. 469.

(d) *Mackreth* v. *Symmons*, 1 Lead. Ca. 295.

(e) Ibid.

(f) *Collins* v. *Collins*, 31 B. 346; *Hughes* v. *Kearney*, 1 Sch. & L. 134.

sideration—the thing bargained for—and not a mere collateral security for the purchase-money (g), there will be no lien, and consequently no trust.

3. It need scarcely be pointed out that a mortgagor, in the case of an **equitable mortgage**, is pro tanto a trustee for the mortgagee; for even where there is no written memorandum, a deposit of title deeds is of itself evidence of an agreement for the mortgage of the property (h); and in accordance with the maxim, that equity regards that as done which ought to be done, the mortgagor holds the legal estate in trust to execute a legal mortgage to the mortgagee.

4. Upon the death of a mortgagee, the **mortgaged property** (if assured to him in fee) descended at law, previous to the Vendor and Purchaser Act 1874, to his heir; but being in reality only a security for money, it **equitably belonged** to his personal representatives, and the heir was, therefore, held to be a trustee only for the administrators or executors of the mortgagee (i).

5. So a **mortgagee in possession** is constructively a trustee of the rents and profits, and bound to apply them in a due course of administration (k). But there has been considerable conflict of opinion as to the extent of his responsibility. For instance, it has been held that he is liable, even after transferring the mortgage without the mortgagor's consent (l); but this decision has been ques-

(g) 1 Lead. Ca. 317; *Buckland* v. *Pocknell*, 13 Sim. 499; *Parrott* v. *Sweetland*, 3 M. & K. 655; *Dixon* v. *Gayfere*, 21 B. 118; *Dyke* v. *Rendall*, 2 D. M. & G. 209; and see *Re Brentwood Brick and Coal Co.*, L. R., 4 Ch. Div. 562.

(h) *Russell* v. *Russell*, 1 Lead. Ca. 674; *Ex parte Wright*, 19 V. 258; *Pryce* v. *Bury*, 2 Dr. 42; *Ferris* v. *Mullins*, 2 Sm. & Gif. 378;

Ex parte Moss, 3 D. & S. 599.
(i) *Thornborough* v. *Baker*, 2 Lead. Ca. 1030. But see 37 & 38 Vict. c. 78, ss. 4, 5.
(k) Lew. 169; *Coppring* v. *Cooke*, 1 Ver. 270; *Bentham* v. *Haincourt*, Pr. Ch. 30; *Parker* v. *Calcraft*, 6 Mad. 11; *Hughes* v. *Williams*, 12 V. 493; *Maddocks* v. *Wren*, 2 Ch. Rep. 109.
(l) *Venables* v. *Foyle*, 1 Ch. Ca. 3.

tioned, and, it is respectfully apprehended, rightly so (m). In another case, it was said that a mortgagee in possession who, after the mortgagor's death, bought up the widow's right to dower, was obliged to hold it in trust for the heir, upon his paying the purchase-money (n); and although this case has called forth much comment (o), it is difficult to distinguish it in principle from the class of cases treated of in the last article.

6. Upon similar principles, a court of equity converts a party who has obtained property by **fraud** "into a trustee for the party who is injured by that fraud; but that, being a jurisdiction founded on personal fraud, it is incumbent on the court to see that a fraud, or malus animus, is proved by the clearest and most indisputable evidence; it is impossible to supply presumption in the place of proof" (p).

(m) Lew. 169; and consider *Ringham* v. *Lee*, 15 Sim. 400.

(n) *Baldwin* v. *Bannister*, cited in *Robinson* v. *Pett*, 3 P. W. 251.

(o) *Dobson* v. *Land*, 8 Ha. 330;

Arnold v. *Garner*, 2 Ph. 231; *Mathison* v. *Clarke*, 3 Dr. 3.

(p) Per Lord Westbury in *McCormick* v. *Grogan*, L. R., 4 H. L. 88.

Division III.

THE ADMINISTRATION OF A TRUST.

SUB-DIV. I.—PRELIMINARY.

SUB-DIV. II.—THE ESTATE OF THE TRUSTEE.

SUB-DIV. III.—THE TRUSTEE'S DUTIES.

SUB-DIV. IV.—THE TRUSTEE'S POWERS.

SUB-DIV. V.—THE AUTHORITY OF THE CESTUIS QUE TRUST.

SUB-DIV. VI.—THE DEATH, RETIREMENT, OR REMOVAL OF A TRUSTEE.

SUB-DIVISION I.—PRELIMINARY.

ART. 23.—*Who are Fit Persons to be appointed Trustees.*

EVERY person who can hold property, may have property vested in him as trustee ; but where the trust
is a special trust, he can only execute it, where he is,
in the eye of the law, competent to exercise discretion (*a*).

ILLUST.—1. An **infant** may be appointed a trustee, for he
is capable of holding property, but he cannot properly
carry out a special trust during his minority. In *King* v.
Bellord (*b*), V.-C. Page Wood said : " The contest arises
thus : a testator having chosen to devise estates upon
trusts requiring discretion as to the expediency, as to the
time, and as to the manner of a sale, to three persons, one
of whom is an infant, the question is, whether a contract for
sale entered into by those three trustees is a valid contract
which the court can specifically perform. There can be no
doubt that if a man by his will gives an infant a simple
power of sale without an interest, the infant may exercise
it. . . . . It is to be observed that all the cases relied on
with reference to powers, have gone upon the principle,

(*a*) *King* v. *Bellord*, 1 H. & M.   (*b*) *Sup.;* but consider *Re Card-*
343.   *ross*, L. R., 7 Ch. Div. 728.

that the infant in executing the power is a mere conduit
pipe; so that when the estate is created, the infant is
merely the instrument by whose hand the donor acts (c).
This principle fails altogether to reach the case of a devise
in trust to an infant. It is not in the power of a testator
to confer upon an infant that discretion which the law does
not give him, although he may make the infant his hand—
his agent—to execute his purpose. He cannot give an
estate to an infant, and say that he may sell it, when the
law says that he cannot do so." An additional objection
to making an infant a trustee consists in the fact that he
cannot be made liable for a breach of trust arising from
negligence (d), although he would seem to be liable for
actual fraud if it can be shown that he had sufficient ability
to contrive a fraud (e).

2. An **alien** may, since the passing of the statute 33 &
34 Vict. c. 14, hold real estate, and may therefore (it is apprehended) be either a settlor or a trustee. Prior to that
act he could purchase lands for an estate of freehold, but
could not take them by operation of law, as, for instance,
by descent or jure mariti (f); and even if he took them by
purchase he was liable to be ousted by the crown on inqui-
sition found, and could not make a good title. Thus, in
Fish v. *Klein* (g), a testator devised and bequeathed the
residue of his real and personal estate to his wife and one
Klein (an alien) upon trust to sell the same. The estate
was sold for 60,000l., but doubts having arisen as to
Klein's capacity to convey the estate to a purchaser, the
matter came before the court; and the then Master of the
Rolls said: "The estate being out of Klein, it is impossible
to consider his alienee in any better situation as to title
than Klein himself." No doubt, however, the crown could

(c) *Grange* v. *Tiving*, Bridg. 107.
(d) *Hindmarsh* v. *Southgate*, 2
Russ. 324.
(e) *Evroy* v. *Nicholas*, 2 Eq.
Ca. Ab. 489; *Stikeman* v. *Daw-*
son, 1 D. & S. 503; *Wright* v.
Snowe, 2 ib. 321; *Davies* v. *Hodg-*
son, 25 B. 177.
(f) Lew. 25.
(g) 2 Mer. 431.

have made a good title, and could have executed the trust (*h*), but there would seem to be no means of forcing the crown to execute a trust (*i*); although, it is apprehended, that *practically*, by means of a petition of right, the crown would be as amenable to the court in this matter as an individual.

3. **A married woman** may undoubtedly be a trustee (*k*), but she is not a desirable person for the office. No doubt she can exercise powers collateral, or in gross, or appendant (*l*); but she can only execute a trust to sell, unaccompanied by a power of appointment, with her husband's consent and joinder; for not only is he the party liable (*m*), but as she takes a mere legal estate, she takes it subject to her legal disabilities and incidents (*n*); and it is apprehended, that even where there is a *power* vested in her to sell, she would not be capable of entering into a binding contract to execute the power, as it is no question affecting her separate estate (*o*).

Art. 24.—*Disclaimer of a Trust.*

No one is bound to accept the office of trustee (*a*). Both the office and the estate may be disclaimed before acceptance, either by deed (*b*) or (save in the case of a married woman, who *must* disclaim by deed (*c*)) by doing an act which is tantamount to a disclaimer (*d*). The disclaimer should be made

---

(*h*) Lew. 29.
(*i*) *Paulett* v. *Att.-Gen.* Hard. 467; *Hodge* v. *Att.-Gen.* 3 Y. & C. 342.
(*k*) *Smith* v. *Smith*, 21 B. 385.
(*l*) *Godolphin* v. *Godolphin*, 1 V. sen. 21.
(*m*) *Smith* v. *Smith*, 21 B. 385.
(*n*) Lew. 33.
(*o*) *Avery* v. *Griffin*, L. R., 6 Eq. 607.

(*a*) *Robinson* v. *Pett*, 2 Lead. Ca. 238.
(*b*) *Stacey* v. *Elph*, 1 M. & K. 199.
(*c*) 8 & 9 Vict. c. 106, s. 7.
(*d*) *Stacey* v. *Elph*, sup.; *Townson* v. *Tickell*, 3 B. & A. 31; *Begbie* v. *Crook*, 2 B. N. C. 70; *Bingham* v. *Clanmorris*, 2 Moll. 253; but see *Re Ellison*, 2 Jur., N. S. 262.

within a reasonable period, having regard to the
circumstances of the particular case (*e*).

ILLUST.—1. Thus, even though a person may have **agreed**
in the lifetime of a testator to be his executor, he is still
at liberty to recede from his promise at any time before
proving the will (*f*).

2. A prudent man will of course always disclaim by deed,
in order that there may be no question of the fact; but a
disclaimer by counsel at the bar is sufficient (*g*); and in
Stacey v. *Elph* (*h*), where a person, named as executor and
trustee under a will, did not formally renounce probate
until after the death of the acting executor, nor formally
disclaim the trusts of the will, but purchased a part of the
real estate, and took a conveyance from the tenant for life
and the heir-at-law *to whom the estate must have descended
on disclaimer of the trust*, it was held that he had by his
conduct disclaimed the office and estate of trustee under the
will; and Sir J. Leach, M.R., said: "In this case there is
no ambiguity in the conduct of the defendant; he never
interfered with the property, except as the friend or agent
of the widow; and it is plain from the confidence which the
testator appears to have placed in him by his will that he
was a particular friend of the family. . . . . It is true he
never executed a deed disclaiming the trust, but **his conduct disclaimed the trust**; in the purchase of the small
real estate made by him, he took by feoffment from the
widow and eldest son of the testator, in whom the estates
could only vest by the disclaimer of the trustee." In *Re
Ellison's Trusts* (*h*), however, Sir W. Page Wood, V.-C.,
expressed some doubt whether a freehold *estate* could be
disclaimed by parol, or otherwise than by deed; but his

(*e*) See *Doe* v. *Harris*, 16 M. &
W. 522; *Paddon* v. *Richardson*, 7
D. M. & G. 563; *James* v. *Frear-
son*, 1 Y. & C. C. C. 370.

(*f*) *Doyle* v. *Blake*, 2 Sch. & L.
239.

(*g*) *Foster* v. *Dawber*, 8 W. R.
646.

(*h*) *Supra*.

honour's attention does not appear to have been called to *Stacey* v. *Elph*, and as the case was only an unopposed petition for the appointment of new trustees, it can hardly be taken as an authority against the rules above laid down.

ART. 25.—*Acceptance of the Trust.*

A person may accept the office of trustee expressly, or he may do so constructively, by doing such acts as are only referable to the character of trustee or executor (*a*), or by long acquiescence.

ILLUST.—1. A trustee **expressly** accepts the office, by executing the settlement (*b*), or by making an express declaration of his assent (*c*).

2. Permitting an action concerning the trust property to be brought in his name (*d*), or otherwise allowing the trust property to be dealt with in his name (*e*), is such an **acquiescence** as will be construed to be an acceptance of the office.

3. So, where the office of executor is clothed with certain trusts, or where the executor is also nominated the trustee of real estate under a will, he is construed to have accepted the office of trustee if he **takes out probate** to the will (*f*); and acceptance of the trusts of a will is constructive acceptance of the office of trustee of estates, devised thereby, of which the testator was trustee (*g*).

4. In *Conyngham* v. *Conyngham* (*h*), one Coleman was appointed trustee of a will, but he never expressly accepted the appointment. One of the trusts was in respect

(*a*) Spence, 918.
(*b*) *Buckeridge* v. *Glasse*, 1 Cr. & Ph. 134.
(*c*) *Doe* v. *Harris*, 16 M. & W. 517.
(*d*) *Montford* v. *Cadogan*, 17 V. 485.

(*e*) *James* v. *Frearson*, 1 Y. & C. C. C. 370.
(*f*) *Mucklow* v. *Fuller*, Jac. 198; *Ward* v. *Butler*, 2 Moll. 533.
(*g*) *Re Perry*, 2 Curt.655; *Brooke* v. *Haynes*, L. R., 6 Eq. 25.
(*h*) 1 V. sen. 522.

of the rents of a plantation then in lease to the testator's
son. Coleman acted as the agent of the son, who was
also heir-at-law, and received the rents of the estate from
him. It was held, that by so **interfering with the trust
property,** he could not repudiate the trust, and say that he
merely acted as the son's agent. He received the property
from the person who was nominally to have remitted the
rents, and it was incumbent on him, if he would not have
acted as trustee, to have refused, and not to leave himself
at liberty to say he acted as trustee or not. It is, however,
not every interference with trust property which will be
construed as an acceptance of the office of trustee : for if
such interference be *plainly* (not *ambiguously*) referrible to
some other ground, it will not operate as an acceptance (*i*) ;
nor will merely taking charge of a trust until a new trustee
can be found, be, of itself, a constructive acceptance (*k*).

5. Where a trustee, with notice of the trust, has indulged
in a passive acquiescence for some years, he will be presumed to have accepted it, in the absence of any satisfactory
explanation (*l*).

(*i*) *Stacey* v. *Elph*, 1 M. & K.
195; *Dove* v. *Everard*, 1 R. & M.
281; *Lowry* v. *Fulton*, 9 Sim. 115.
(*k*) *Evans* v. *John*, 4 B. 35.

(*l*) *Wise* v. *Wise*, 2 J. & Lat.
412; *Re Uniacke*, 1 J. & Lat. 1;
Re Needham, *ib.* 34.

SUB-DIVISION II.

The Estate of the Trustee and its Incidents.

Art. 26.—*Cases in which the Trustee takes any Estate.*

α. Where the trust is a simple trust, and the trust property is of freehold tenure, then, in consequence of the Statute of Uses, the trustee takes no estate unless the property be limited *to his use*, or unless there be a clear intention to vest an estate in him. But where the trust is a special trust the statute does not apply, and the trustee will take an estate.

β. Where the trust property is of copyhold or leasehold tenure, or is pure personalty, the Statute of Uses is inapplicable, and the trustee takes the legal estate, whether the trust be simple or special.

Illust.—1. Thus, where a freehold estate is limited to trustees, and the words used are "in trust **to pay to** " a specified person the rents and profits, there the trustees take the legal estate, because they must receive before they can make the required payments. But where the words are "in trust **to permit** and suffer A. B. to take the rents and profits," there the use is divested out of them and executed in the party, the purposes not requiring that the legal estate should remain in them (*a*).

2. Where, however, the trustees are to **permit** and suffer the cestui que trust to receive the *net* or **clear rents** and profits, the trustees take the legal estate, it being presumed that the trustees are to take the *gross* rents, and after payment of outgoings, to hand over the *net* rents to the cestui que trust (*b*).

(*a*) Per Parke, J., *Barker* v. *Greenwood*, 4 M. & W. 429; *Doe d. Leicester* v. *Biggs*, 2 Taunt. 109; *Doe* v. *Bolton*, 11 A. & E. 188.

(*b*) *Barker* v. *Greenwood, sup.;* *White* v. *Parker*, 1 Bing. N. C. 573; *Shapland* v. *Smith*, 1 Bro. C. C. 75.

3. So, again, where the trustees are to **exercise any control** or discretion they take an estate; as, for instance, where the cestui que trust is empowered to give receipts for the rents with the *approbation* of the trustees (c), or the trust is for the separate use of a married woman, who consequently requires protection, the trustees take the legal estate (d); at all events, where the trust is created by will. But where it is created by deed, it would seem that the common law courts, not recognizing the separate estate of a feme convert, would (at all events before the Judicature Act, 1873) have held that such a trust was a simple trust, and therefore came within the Statute of Uses (e).

4. Where property is devised to trustees **charged with payment of debts**, and subject thereto in trust for A., there, as the trustees are not directed *to pay* the debts, they have no duties, and consequently, take no estate (f).

5. Where the **language is ambiguous**, and may be read either as implying a simple or a special trust, the question must be determined according to the general rules of construction. Thus, the words "to pay or permit him to receive" would, if contained in a deed, create a special trust, inasmuch as of two inconsistent expressions in a deed the first prevails; whereas the same words occurring in a will would create a simple trust, as the testator's last words are preferred (g).

6. In *Houston* v. *Hughes* (h), it was held that, notwithstanding the Statute of Uses, under a devise of freeholds and copyholds to A. and his heirs, in trust for B. and his heirs, the circumstance that A. took an estate in the copyholds was an argument in favour of an **intention** that he should take the legal estate in the freeholds. It is, how-

(c) *Gregory* v. *Henderson*, 4 Taunt. 772.
(d) *Harton* v. *Harton*, 7 T. R. 652.
(e) *Williams* v. *Waters*, 14 M. & W. 166; see *Nash* v. *Allen*, 1

H. & C. 167.
(f) *Kenrick* v. *Lord Beauclerk*, 3 B. & P. 175.
(g) *Doe* v. *Biggs*, 2 Taunt. 109.
(h) 6 B. & C. 403.

ever, apprehended that a similar limitation in a deed would
be construed far more strictly.

ART. 27.—*The Quantity of Estate taken by the Trustees.*

Whenever a trust is created a legal estate sufficient
for the execution of the trust is, if possible, implied;
but the legal estate limited to the trustee is not
carried further than the complete execution of the
trust necessarily requires (*a*). In applying this rule,
the following principles are of importance :—

α. Deeds are construed strictly, and take effect
according to their strict legal meaning, unless the
very object and intention of the instrument would
be defeated by such a construction (*b*).

β. Wills are construed loosely, and although no
estate or an insufficient estate be expressly given to
trustees, the legal estate is impliedly vested in them
as long as the execution of the trust requires it,
and (unless there are recurring trusts (*c*)), no
longer (*d*).

γ. A devise to trustees and their heirs, primâ facie
passes the fee simple (*e*) (and if the trusts by their
nature extend over an indefinite period that presumption is irrebutable (*f*)); but if a less estate
would certainly enable the trustees to fulfil all the
trusts, and it can be pointed out on the face of the
settlement what other estate the trustees can take,
but not otherwise, the primâ facie absolute nature
of the gift is destroyed, and the trustees take such

(*a*) Lew. 189.
(*b*) *Venables* v. *Morris*, 7 T. R.
342; *Wykham* v. *Wykham*, 18 V.
395; *Colemore* v. *Tyndall*, 2 Y. & J.
605; and see *Re Bird*, L. R.,
3 Ch. Div. 214, where the word
"heirs" was omitted, but it being
necessary that the trustees should
take the fee, the settlement was
ordered to be rectified by adding
the word.

(*c*) See *Harton* v. *Harton*, 7
T. R. 652.
(*d*) *Doe* v. *Nicholls*, 1 B. & C.
336; *Watson* v. *Pearson*, 2 Ex.
581; *Bush* v. *Allen*, 5 Mod. 63;
Doe v. *Homfray*, 6 A. & E. 206.
(*e*) Per Williams, J., *Doe* v.
Davies, 1 Q. B. 430; and see
Blagrave v. *Blagrave*, 4 Ex. 550.
(*f*) *Ib.*, per Patteson, J.

an estate only as is sufficient for the execution of the trust (*g*). Provided, that where the settlement is a will made since the passing of the Wills Act, and the trust property is real estate, no indefinite chattel interest, and no freehold with an indefinite chattel interest superadded, can be implied or expressly given ; and where such estates would have been previously implied, *or* where there is no cestui que trust for life, *or* where there is one, but the trusts may continue beyond his life, in every such case the trustee takes the fee simple, or other the whole estate or interest which the testator could dispose of (*h*).

Illust.—1. In *Colemore* v. *Tyndall* (*i*), under a settlement, lands were limited to the use of A. for life, and after his death to the use of B. and his heirs during the life of A. to support contingent remainders, remainder to the use of C. for life, remainder to the same B. and his heirs

(*g*) *Ib.*; and see per Erle, J., *Poad* v. *Watson*, 6 E. & B. 606; and generally as to the rule, see per Jessel, M. R., *Collier* v. *Walters*, L. R., 17 Eq. 262.

(*h*) This proviso is intended and believed to give the effect of the 30th and 31st sections of the Wills Act, 1 Vict. c. 26. By the first of these sections it is enacted that where any real estate (other than or not being a presentation to a church) shall be devised to any trustee or executor, such devise shall be construed to pass the fee simple, or other the whole estate or interest which the testator had power to dispose of by will, in such real estate, unless a definite term of years absolute or determinable, or an estate of freehold, shall be given to him expressly or by implication. The 31st section enacts, that where any real estate shall be devised to a trustee without any express limitation of the es-

tate to be taken by such trustee, and the beneficial interest in such real estate, or in the surplus rents and profits thereof, shall not be given to any person for life, or shall be given for life, but the purposes of the trust may continue beyond the life of such person, such devise shall be construed to vest in such trustee the fee simple or other the whole legal estate which the testator had power to dispose of by will, and not an estate determinable when the purposes of the trust shall be satisfied. Both these sections have been subjected to much criticism, and even now their meaning is by no means clear (see Low. 195: Sug. R. P. Stats. 380; 2 Jar. Wills, 296; Hawkins's Wills, 30); but it is apprehended that the effect of the 30th section is as above stated.

(*i*) 2 Y. & J. 605; and see also *Cooper* v. *Kynock*, L. R., 7 Ch. 398.

during the life of C. to support contingent remainders, remainder to the first and other sons of C. in tail male,
remainder to divers other uses, remainder to the said B.
and his heirs (without saying during the life of the tenant
for life) to support and preserve contingent remainders,
with divers remainders over.   The question arose whether,
under the last limitation to B. and his heirs, he took the
fee simple, or whether he only took that which was necessary for the purpose of the trust, namely, an estate *pur autre
vie;* but the court held that it was not a sufficient ground
for restricting an estate limited **in a deed** to a trustee and
his heirs to an estate for life, that the estate given to the
trustee seemed to be longer than was essential to its purpose; and the Lord Chief Baron, quoting from the judgment of Lord Chief Justice Willes in *Parkhurst* v. *Smith,*
said: "Though the intent of the parties be never so clear,
it cannot take place contrary to the rules of law, nor can
we put words in a deed which are not there, nor put a
construction on the words of a deed directly contrary to the
plain sense of them; but where the *intent* is *plain and
manifest,* and the *words doubtful and obscure,* it is the duty
of the judges to endeavour to find out such a meaning in
the words as will best answer the intent of the parties."
And the Lord Chief Baron also said: "As to the notion
that whenever an estate is limited to a person professedly
as a trustee, he shall, whatever terms may be used, take
only the estate requisite to enable him to perform his trust,
and this though of a freehold, and in a deed, I do not find
it supported by any authority, nor even by any dictum."

2. On the other hand, where by **will** the rents of certain
lands are directed to be paid to a married woman by the
testator's executors, there is an implied devise to the
executors of such an estate in the land as will enable them
to execute the trust (*k*).

3. So if land be devised to trustees without any words

(*k*) *Bush* v. *Allen,* 5 Mod. 63.

of limitation, and they are expressly **directed to sell** (*l*), or impliedly authorized to do so (*m*), certainly or contingently (*n*), or are authorized to **lease indefinitely** or to **mortgage** (*o*), or to do any other act which requires the complete control over the property (*p*), the trustees will take (and even before the Wills Act would have taken) an estate in fee simple, or other the whole estate which the testator could dispose of.

4. But where there are **recurring trusts** which require the legal estate to be in the trustees, with intervening limitations, which taken alone would vest the legal estate in the persons beneficially entitled, and there is no repetition before each of the recurring trusts of the gift of the legal estate to the trustees, the legal estate is held to be in the trustees throughout, and the intermediate estates are equitable and not legal (*q*). To show the importance of this principle, it is well to refer to the leading case of *Harton* v. *Harton* (*r*), where the limitations were to trustees in trust for A. for life for her separate use, remainder to the heirs of her body, remainder to B. for life for her separate use, with remainder to the heirs of *her* body. Here the separate use gave the trustees an estate during A.'s life and also during B.'s life; but had it not been for this last trust, they would not have taken the legal estate during the intermediate trust in favour of the heirs of A.'s body. As, however, there was a recurring trust they did so; and, therefore, as the estate of A., and the estate given to the heirs of her body, were both equitable estates, the rule in Shelley's case applied and A. took an estate tail.

(*l*) *Shaw* v. *Weigh*, 2 Str. 798; *Bagshaw* v. *Spencer*, 1 V. 144; *Watson* v. *Pearson*, 2 Ex. 581.

(*m*) *Gibson* v. *Lord Montfort*, 1 V. 485.

(*n*) *Ib.*

(*o*) *Doe* d. *Cadogan* v. *Ewart*, 7 A. & E. 636; *Watson* v. *Pearson*, *sup.*; *Doe* v. *Willan*, 2 B. & Al.

84; but see *Heardson* v. *Williamson*, 1 Ke. 33; *Ackland* v. *Lutley*, 9 A. & E. 879.

(*p*) *Villiers* v. *Villiers*, 2 Atk. 72.

(*q*) *Harton* v. *Harton*, *sup.*; *Hawkins* v. *Luscombe*, 2 Sw. 391; *Brown* v. *Whiteway*, 8 Ha. 145; *Toller* v. *Atwood*, 15 Q. B. 929.

(*r*) *Supra.*

5. In *Collier* v. *Walters* (s) a testator by will, dated in
1827, had devised his estate to trustees and their heirs
upon trust that they and their heirs should stand seised of
the same during the life of W. C., and also until the whole
of the testator's debts and the legacies thereinafter mentioned were paid, upon trust to let the same and apply the
rents in discharge of his debts, after payment of which,
they were to apply the rents in payment of legacies, and
finally hold the property upon trust to pay the rents to
W. C. and his assigns during his life; and after the decease of W. C. and payment of the debts and legacies and
all expenses, the testator devised the property to the heirs
of the body of W. C., with remainders over. In 1830, the
debts and legacies being paid, the trustees conveyed the
estate to W. C. for life, who shortly afterwards, relying on
the rule in Shelley's case, suffered a common recovery and
barred the entail. Upon his right to do this coming in
question Sir Geo. Jessel, M. R., said: "The first observation to make upon this will is this, that there is a gift to
trustees and their heirs, and that the trustees and their
heirs are to stand seised (they get legal seisin of something,
and it was not denied that they must get an estate of freehold of some kind or other) 'for and during the term of
the natural life of my brother William, and also until the
whole of my just debts and all interest due thereon have
been paid.' Now the rule is this, that trustees under a devise to them and their heirs **prima facie take a fee.** . . . . .
Now this kind of case was again considered in *Poad* v.
Watson (t), and there Mr. Justice Coleridge puts the rule
in this way, 'The paramount rule is to look to the intention as appearing on the whole will. But there are
secondary rules, one of which is that the words of devise
to trustees and their heirs are to have their natural effect
to give a fee simple, unless something shows that it is cut
down to an estate terminating at some time ascertained at

(s) *Supra.*   (t) *Supra.*

the time of the testator's death. If no precise period for
the termination can be shown, it remains an estate in fee.'
Then Mr. Justice Erle says: 'These are words clearly
meaning that the testator gave the trustees a fee simple ;
but if a less estate would certainly enable the trustees to
fulfil all the trust, the fee simple would be cut down to that
estate.' . . . . That rule is therefore a rule which I think
is clearly and fairly settled by authority, and should govern
me in construing this will. Now there is another rule
which may be collected from all the authorities, that you
cannot cut down the estate in fee simple unless you can
point out on the face of the will what less estate the trustees
take. Upon that there is immense difficulty here." Commenting upon the various suggestions of counsel, his lordship continued : " The first, that they took an estate for life
with a chattel interest superadded, clearly will not do. . . .
If you are to imply a chattel interest from a gift to the
trustees upon trust to pay debts and legacies, the chattel
interest will be implied from the moment of the testator's
death ; and it is impossible, therefore, to hold that they
took during the life of W. C., and then took a superadded
estate by implication upon trust to pay debts and legacies.
Then, as regards the concurrent chattel interest and life
estate, did anyone ever hear of such a thing as taking a
chattel interest and a freehold estate together ? . . . . .
These two being rejected, Mr. Badnall to-day suggested a
third, that they took a freehold interest for the life of the
tenant for life, and, if necessary, a further chattel interest
until the debts were paid." His lordship here gave reasons why, on the special wording of the will, this proposi-
tion was untenable, and continued : " These suggestions
being out of the way, I think I am at liberty to say that
human ingenuity cannot suggest a fifth. Therefore we are
reduced to this. The first rule being that those who say
they do not take a fee shall point out what estate they
take, they cannot suggest any estate which in my opinion

can be fairly and properly implied from the words used in this will." His lordship therefore held, that the trustees took the legal fee, and that W. C. consequently, under the rule in Shelley's case, took an equitable estate tail.

OBS.—The rule restricting the estate taken by trustees to the quantity necessary for the performance of the trust gave rise to the doctrine of **indefinite terms, and determinable fees.** Thus, where property was devised to trustees upon trust out of the rents and profits to pay debts, &c., it was held that they took an indefinite term necessary to enable them to pay the debts (*u*). And where the devise was to trustees and their heirs, in trust to raise and pay money, it was held that they took the fee, only until the money was raised (*r*). The 30th and 31st sections of the Wills Act put an end to both these doctrines with regard to wills executed since that act; but, apart from its provisions, it is considered improbable that either doctrine would now be adopted (*w*), and indeed the doctrine of determinable fees has been expressly overruled (*x*).

ART. 28.—*Devolution of the Legal Estate.*

α. Where there are two or more trustees, they take as joint tenants; and upon the death of one of them, the estate survives to his co-trustees or trustee.

β. Upon the death of a sole or last surviving executive trustee intestate, the trust property descends to his real or personal representatives, according to its nature.

γ. Upon the death of a sole or last surviving bare trustee intestate, since the passing of the Vendors and Purchasers Act, 1874, the trust property de-

---

(*u*) *Doe* v. *Simpson*, 5 East, 162: *Ackland* v. *Lutley*, 9 A. & E. 879; *Heardson* v. *Williamson*, 1 Kee. 33.
(*r*) *Glover* v. *Monckton*, 3 Bing. 13.

(*w*) Hawkins on Wills, 149.
(*x*) *Doe* d. *Davies* v. *Davies*, 1 Q. B. 430; *Blagrave* v. *Blagrave*, 4 Ex. 550.

scends to his personal representatives, whether it be
real or personal property.

ILLUST.—1. On the decease of a sole or last surviving
trustee of leaseholds, intestate as to trust estates, the legal
estate devolves on his executor; and if the executor dies
similarly intestate as to trust estates, the legal estate vests
in his executor; for an executor of an executor represents
the original testator; but if the executor of the trustee had
died wholly intestate, or without naming an executor, then
an administrator de bonis non of the trustee would have to
be appointed to convey the legal estate, as an administrator
of an executor does *not* represent the original testator.

ART. 29.—*Devise of the Trustee's Estate.*

A trustee can devise or bequeath the legal estate in
the trust property (*a*), and it will pass under a
general devise or bequest of his property, unless
the will contain expressions authorizing a narrower
construction, or the disposition of the estate so
devised or bequeathed is such as a testator would
be unlikely to make of property not his own (*b*).

ILLUST.—1. Thus, where a testator subjects the property,
passing under a general devise, to the payment of debts or
legacies (*c*), or directs them to be sold (*d*), or devises them
to persons as tenants in common (*e*), or to a numerous and
unascertained class (*f*), or limits them in strict settle-

(*a*) Whether the *devisee* can
execute the trust is a totally different question, as to which see
Art. 52, *infra.* Constructive trust
estates (as land agreed to be sold)
pass under a devise of trust estates.
Lysaght v. *Edwards*, L. R., 2 Ch.
Div. 499.

(*b*) (*Braybrooke* v. *Inskip*, 8 V.
436; *Ex parte Morgan*, 10 V. 101;
Langford v. *Angel*, 4 Ha. 313.

(*c*) *Re Morley*, 10 Ha. 293; *Re
Packman & Moss*, L. R., 1 Ch.
Div. 214; but see *Re Brown &
Sibley*, 24 W. R. 783.

(*d*) *Re Morley*, *sup.*

(*e*) *Martin* v. *Laverton*, L. R.,
9 Eq. 568.

(*f*) *Re Finney*, 3 Gif. 465; see
also *Re Packman & Moss*, *sup.*; and
compare with *Re Brown & Sibley*,
sup.

ment (*y*), or in any other way which makes it impossible to say the intention could be to give a dry trust estate (*z*), trust estates will not pass.

ART. 30.—*Bankruptcy of the Trustee.*

The property of a bankrupt divisible among his creditors, does not comprise property which can be identified (*a*) as property held by him as trustee for any other person (*b*), even though he may have converted it into property of a different character (*c*), and although it is property in his order and disposition at the commencement of the bankruptcy (*d*).

ILLUST.—1. If goods consigned to a factor be sold by him and reduced into money, yet if **the money can be identified**—as, for instance, where it has been kept separate and apart from the factor's own monies, or kept in bags, or the like (*e*), or has been changed into bills or notes (*f*), or any other form (*g*),—the employer, and not the creditors of the factor, will, upon his bankruptcy, be entitled to the property into which it has been converted; for the creditors of a defaulting trustee can have no better right to the trust property than the trustee himself (*h*), and it makes no difference in this respect that the trustee committed a breach of trust in converting the property, for an abuse of

---

(*y*) *Braybrooke* v. *Inskip, sup.*

(*z*) *Ib.;* and see *Att.-Gen.* v. *Vigor,* 8 V. 276.

(*a*) *Tooke* v. *Hollingworth,* 5 T. R. 277; *Ex parte Dumas,* 1 At. 234.

(*b*) 32 & 33 Vict. c. 71, s. 15; *Houghton* v. *Kœnig,* 18 C. B. 235; *Winch* v. *Keeley,* 1 T. R. 619.

(*c*) *Taylor* v. *Plumer,* 3 M. & S. 575; *Scott* v. *Surman,* Willes, 404.

(*d*) *Ex parte Barry,* L. R., 17 Eq. 113; *Ex parte Marsh,* 1 Atk. 158. As to constructive trustees, *Ex parte Pease,* 19 V. 46; *Whitefield* v. *Brand,* 16 M. & W. 282.

(*e*) *Tooke* v. *Hollingworth, sup.*

(*f*) *Ex parte Dumas,* 2 V. sen. 582.

(*g*) *Frith* v. *Cartland,* 2 H. & M. 417.

(*h*) *Ib.*

trust can confer no right on the person abusing it, or those claiming through him (*i*).

2. But where the trust property has become so **mixed up** with the bankrupt's private property as to lose its identity (or earmark, as it is usually called), for instance, where it has been converted into money, which has been put in circulation (*k*), or has otherwise become indistinguishable, then, as the right of the cestui que trust is only to have the actual trust property, or that which stands in its place, and as the actual property is gone, and that which stands in its place cannot be identified, the cestui que trust can only prove against the bankrupt's estate as one of his general creditors (*l*).

ART. 31.—*The Incidents of the Trustee's Estate at Law.*

At law, the estate of the trustee is subject to the same incidents as if he were the beneficial owner, except where such incidents are modified by act of parliament.

ILLUST.—1. Thus he is the proper person **to bring actions** arising out of wrongs formerly cognizable by common law courts, and which necessitated the possession of the legal estate in those bringing them (*a*); and it is apprehended that the Judicature Acts have made no distinction as to this.

2. So at law, the estate of the trustee in real property is **liable to curtesy** (*b*), **dower** (*c*), and, if of copyhold tenure, to freebench (*d*); but of course the persons so taking could only take as trustees for those beneficially entitled (*e*).

(*i*) *Taylor* v. *Plumer, sup.*
(*k*) *Miller* v. *Race,* 1 Bur. 457; see per Lord Kenyon.
(*l*) *Ex parte Dumas,* 1 Atk. 234; *Ryall* v. *Rolle, ib.* 172; *Scott* v. *Surman, sup.*
(*a*) *May* v. *Taylor,* 6 M. & G. 261.

(*b*) *Bennett* v. *Davis,* 2 P. W. 319.
(*c*) *Noel* v. *Jevon,* Fre. 43; *Nash* v. *Preston,* Cro. Car. 190.
(*d*) *Hinton* v. *Hinton,* 2 V. sen. 638.
(*e*) *Noel* v. *Jevon, sup.;* *Lloyd* v. *Lloyd,* 4 Dr. & War. 354.

Formerly it was also liable to forfeiture and escheat, but there can no longer be forfeiture or escheat of a trust estate (*f*).

3. So, again, **trustees of copyholds** who take an *estate* must be admitted by the lord of the manor on the customary terms (*g*).

4. Where a debtor to the trust estate becomes bankrupt, the trustee is the **proper person to prove** without the concurrence of the cestui que trust (*h*), unless in the case of a simple trust. Where it is as likely as not that the debtor has paid the cestui que trust direct, then it lies in the discretion of the judge to require the concurrence of the cestui que trust (*i*).

5. The trustee of a private trust is, as legal owner, **liable to be rated** in respect of the trust property (*k*).

6. If the trustee, in pursuance of the trust, carry on a business for the benefit of the cestui que trust, he will yet be **personally liable to the creditors** of the business (*l*), and may be made a bankrupt (*m*).

7. On the other hand, the ordinary legal incident of **voting** for members of parliament does not belong to the trustee in respect of the trust estate, as the act 6 & 7 Vict. c. 18, s. 74, confers that right on the cestui que trust. It would, however, seem that the trustee still retains the right of voting for coroners (*n*).

(*f*) 13 & 14 Vict. c. 60, s. 46.

(*g*) *Wilson* v. *Hoare*, 2 B. & Ad. 350.

(*h*) *Ex parte Green*, 2 Dea. & Ch. 116.

(*i*) *Ex parte Dubois*, 1 Cox, 310; *Ex parte Gray*, 4 Dea. & Ch. 778.

(*k*) *Reg.* v. *Sterry*, 12 A. & E. 84; *Reg.* v. *Stapleton*, 4 B. & S. 629.

(*l*) *Farhall* v. *Farhall*, L. R., 7 Ch. 123; *Owen* v. *Delamere*, L. R., 15 Eq. 134.

(*m*) *Wightman* v. *Townroe*, 1 M. & S. 412; *Ex parte Garland*, 10 V. 119; *Farhall* v. *Farhall, sup.*

(*n*) *Burgess* v. *Wheate*, 1 Ed. 251; 58 Geo. 3, c. 95, s. 2, repealed by 7 & 8 Vict. c. 92; *Reg.* v. *Day*, 3 E. & B. 859.

ART. 32.—*Trustee's Estate on total Failure of Cestuis que trust.*

Where a trust does not exhaust the whole of the trust property, and there is no one in whose favour the trust can result, then, if the trust property be real estate, the trustee takes absolutely (*a*), and if personal estate, it goes to the crown as bona vacantia (*b*).

ILLUST.—1. In the leading case of *Burgess* v. *Wheate* (*c*), the settlor conveyed **real estate** unto and to the use of trustees, in trust for herself, her heirs and assigns, to the intent that she should appoint, and for no other use whatever. She subsequently died without having appointed, and without heirs; and it was held that (there being holders of the legal estate—namely, the trustees) the crown could not claim by escheat, and that the trustees (no person remaining who could sue them in equity) retained, as the legal proprietors, the beneficial interest also.

2. But if the settlor in the last case had appointed or devised her equitable interest to C., in **trust for purposes which could not take effect,** then, as between the original trustees and C., the latter would be entitled to the property as the nominee under the will. The court will, as between those parties, only carry out the testator's directions, and will not inquire how far the directions can be executed in their integrity (*d*).

3. The rule also applies to a **constructive trustee.** Thus a mortgagee in fee, whose mortgagor dies intestate and without heirs, takes the property absolutely, subject to the mortgagor's debts (*e*). Whether this would be the case if the mortgagee was a mere equitable mortgagee, seems to be more doubtful; but it is submitted that, on the principle of *Onslow* v. *Wallis*, the result would be the same as if he were the legal mortgagee.

(*a*) *Burgess* v. *Wheate*, 1 Ed. 177.

(*b*) *Taylor* v. *Haygarth*, 14 Sim. 8; *Middleton* v. *Spicer*, 1 B. C. C. 201.

(*c*) *Supra.*

(*d*) *Onslow* v. *Wallis*, 1 M. & G. 506; and see *Jones* v. *Goodchild*, 3 P. W. 33.

(*e*) *Beale* v. *Symonds*, 16 B. 406.

SUB-DIVISION III.

The Duties of a Trustee.

Art. 33.—*A Trustee must exercise reasonable care.*

Except where courts of equity have imposed distinct and stringent duties upon trustees (which duties are mentioned in the succeeding articles of this sub-division), they are only bound to exercise a reasonable discretion, and to use such due diligence and care as men of ordinary prudence and vigilance would use in the management of their own affairs (*a*). But, nevertheless, the mere fact that a trustee who has done an act which is, in fact, a breach of trust, did so under the advice of a professional man, will not excuse him (*b*). Yet it is apprehended that it would be strong evidence of diligence where the alleged breach is alleged to have arisen from mere negligence, and not from the breach of some distinct duty.

Illust.—1. Thus, it is their duty to **realize debts** owing to the trust estate with all convenient speed (*c*), but they are not bound to commence legal proceedings when, in the exercise of a reasonable discretion, they consider it inexpedient to do so. For instance, in a case where one cestui que trust would have been ruined by the immediate realization of a debt due from him to the trust estate, and the other cestuis que trust (his children) would have been seriously prejudiced, the House of Lords held, that the

(*a*) *Brice* v. *Stokes*, 2 Lead. Cas. 865; *Massey* v. *Banner*, 1 J. & W. 247.
(*b*) *Doyle* v. *Blake*, 2 Sch. & L. 243; *Re Knight*, 27 B. 49.

(*c*) *Buxton* v. *Buxton*, 1 M. & C. 93. As to its effect as evidence of diligence, see and consider judgment of Jessel, M.R., in *Re Cooper, infra*, Illust. 6, and also Illust. 9.

trustee exercised a reasonable discretion in refraining from suing the debtor and in allowing him time, and that the trustee was consequently discharged from liability for any consequent losses (*d*).

2. So trustees may **release or compound debts** due to the trust estate, where they bonâ fide and reasonably believe that that course is for the benefit of their cestuis que trust (*e*). Yet they must not be negligent, nor must they fail to exert themselves to realize a debt (*f*).

3. Thus where trustees allowed rents to get in arrears which they might have recovered by proper diligence, it was held that they were liable to make good the arrears, though without interest, the judge saying: "If there be **crassa negligentia** and a loss sustained by the estate, it falls upon the trustee " (*g*).

4. Where a trustee indebted to the trust becomes bankrupt it is his duty **to prove the debt,** and if he neglect to do so he will be liable for the loss, notwithstanding that he may have obtained his certificate ; for, as was observed by Sir J. Romilly, M.R. : " Suppose a person owing money to a trust estate becomes bankrupt, and the trustee is a distinct and separate person, knowing of the bankruptcy, he is bound to prove the debt ; if he does not, he commits a breach of trust, and would be held liable for all that he might have received under the commission if he had proved the debt as he ought to have done. Is the case altered because the trustee is himself the debtor ? I think not ; the original debt, no doubt, is barred, but the amount of the dividends which the trustee might have received under the commission is a liability subsequently attaching to the

(*d*) *Ward* v. *Ward*, 2 H. L. C. 784.

(*e*) *Blue* v. *Marshall*, 3 P. W. 381 ; *Forshaw* v. *Higginson*, 8 D., M. & G. 827.

(*f*) *Wiles* v. *Gresham*, 5 D., M. & G. 770 ; *Lawson* v. *Copeland*, 2 B. C. C. 156 ; *Bailey* v. *Gould*, 4 Y. & C. 221 ; *Ticker* v. *Smith*, 2 S. & G. 46 ; *Caffrey* v. *Daley*, 6 V. 488.

(*g*) *Tebbs* v. *Carpenter*, 1 Mad. 291 ; and see as to interest, *Lawson* v. *Copeland, sup.; Wiles* v. *Gresham*, 2 Dr. 258; *Rowley* v. *Adams*, 2 H. L. C. 725.

trustee in that character, and is not affected by the bankruptcy or the certificate " (*h*).

5. So, again, where a settlor has, for valuable consideration, covenanted to settle property, a trustee who neglects to **enforce the covenant** is liable for any loss occasioned thereby (*i*).

6. Or, again, **if** a trustee **neglect to register** the trust instrument (where it requires to be registered), and the settlor is thereby enabled to effect a mortgage on the property, the trustee will be liable (*k*).

7. In the exercise of due diligence, **trustees for sale** will, of course, use their best endeavours to sell to the best advantage. They should, therefore (in general), abstain from **joining with the owners of contiguous property** in a sale of the whole together, unless, indeed, such a course would be clearly beneficial to their cestuis que trust, for by doing so they expose the trust property to deterioration on account of the flaws or possible flaws in the title to the other property; but "suppose there were a house belonging to trustees, and a garden and forecourt belonging to somebody else, it must be obvious that those two properties would fetch more if sold together than if sold separately; you might have a divided portion of a house belonging to trustees, and another divided portion belonging to somebody else. It would be equally obvious if these two portions were sold together, that a more beneficial result would thereby take place. . . . . But in those cases where it is not *manifest on a mere inspection* of the properties that it is more beneficial to sell them together, then you ought to have reasonable evidence that it is a prudent and right thing to do, and that evidence, as we know by experience, is obtained from surveyors and other persons who are competent judges " (*l*).

(*h*) *Orrett* v. *Corser*, 21 B. 52.
(*i*) *Woodhouse* v. *Woodhouse*, L.
R., 8 Eq. 514.
(*k*) *Macnamara* v. *Carey*, 1 Ir.
R., Eq. 9; *Kingdon* v. *Castleman*,

W. N. (1877) 15.
(*l*) Per Jessel, M. R., *Re Cooper
& Allen's Contract*, L. R., 4 Ch. D.
517.

8. "Where trustees for sale are **joint owners** with a third party, or are reversioners, it is obvious that they may in general join in a sale; for everybody knows that as a general rule (of course there are exceptions to every rule) the entirety of a freehold estate fetches more than the sum total of the undivided parts, or the separate values of the particular estate and the reversion" (*m*).

9. Again, trustees for sale ought not to do any act which will depreciate the property, and so they ought not *unnecessarily* to **limit the title** (*n*), for no reasonable man would unnecessarily depreciate his own property by such means.

10. Again, if trustees for sale, or those who act under their authority, fail in reasonable diligence in **inviting competition**, or if they contract to sell under circumstances of great **improvidence** or waste, they will be personally responsible (*o*). It is therefore the duty of trustees for sale to inform themselves of the **real value** of the property, and for that purpose to employ, if necessary, some experienced person to value the same (*p*).

11. The same principle holds good in the case of **trustees for purchase**, or for investing trust moneys on mortgage, who ought to clearly satisfy themselves of the value of the property, and for that purpose to employ a valuer of their own, and not trust to the valuer of the vendor or mortgagor; for a man may bonâ fide form his opinion, but he looks at the case in a totally different way when he knows on whose behalf he is acting; and if the trustees rely upon the vendor's valuer, and he, however bonâ fide, values the property at more than its true value, they will be liable (*q*).

12. Trustees for purchase, or for investment on mort-

(*m*) *Ib.*
(*n*) See *Hobson* v. *Bell*, 2 B. 17; *Rede* v. *Oakes*, 10 Jur., N. S. 1246.
(*o*) *Ord* v. *Noel*, 5 Mad. 440; and *Anon.*, 6 Mad. 11; *Peehel* v. *Fowler*, 2 Anst. 550.

(*p*) *Oliver* v. *Court*, 8 Pr. 165; *Campbell* v. *Walker*, 5 V. 680; and see per Jessel, M. R., *Re Cooper & Allen*, L. R., 4 Ch. D. 816.
(*q*) *Ingle* v. *Partridge*, 34 B. 412.

gage, should also take reasonable care that they get a
good **marketable title**, and that they do not, by conditions
of sale, bind themselves not to require one (*r*); and, except
in very exceptional cases, they should never purchase without getting the legal estate; for although a man may be
himself willing to take the risk of leaving an outstanding
legal estate, he is not justified in incurring that risk for
other people (*s*).

13. Upon similar grounds, a trustee who is empowered
to invest trust funds *at his discretion*, is not entitled to lend
them on mere **personal security;** for that would not be a
reasonable exercise of his discretion (*t*); and it would seem
that it would not be proper for him to invest in foreign
securities (*u*), or foreign railways (*w*), or in trade (*x*); but
the reason of this is, that (as will be seen hereafter) there
is a special duty of care cast upon trustees for investment.
Where a trustee is directed to invest on *security* at his discretion, he cannot properly **invest in shares,** for they are
not a security at all, but only a right to participate in
profits (*y*).

14. **Trustees for investment** on mortgage, cannot, without
risk, advance more than two-thirds of the actual value of
freehold estate (*z*); and if it be house property, not more
than one-half (*a*); and if it be trade property, the value of
which depends upon the continued prosperity of the trade,
it would be hazardous to advance even so much as that (*b*).

(*r*) *E. C. R. Co.* v. *Hawkes*, 5
H. L. C. 363.

(*s*) Lew. 440. And as to ad-
vancing trust money on a covenant to surrender copyholds, see
Wyatt v. *Sharratt*, 3 B. 498; and
as to equitable mortgages generally, *Norris* v. *Wright*, 14 B. 308;
Lockhart v. *Reilly*, 1 D. & J. 476.

(*t*) See *Pocock* v. *Beddington*,
5 V. 794; *Potts* v. *Britton*, L. R.,
11 Eq. 433; *Bethell* v. *Abraham*,
L. R., 17 Eq. 24; and see *Ryder*
v. *Bickerston*, 3 Sw. 81, n. (*a*).

(*u*) *Bethell* v. *Abraham*, L. R.,
17 Eq. 24.

(*w*) *Ib.*

(*x*) *Cock* v. *Goodfellow*, 10 Mod.
489.

(*y*) *Harris* v. *Harris*, 29 B. 107.

(*z*) *Stickney* v. *Sewell*, 1 M. &
C. 8; *Drosier* v. *Brereton*, 15 B.
221.

(*a*) *Budge* v. *Gummow*, L. R.,
7 Ch. 719; *Stretton* v. *Ashmall*, 3
Dr. 12.

(*b*) *Ib.*; and *Royds* v. *Royds*, 14
B. 54.

But, nevertheless, if they exceeded these limits, yet if they acted bonâ fide and used reasonable care, they would not be liable (c).

15. A trustee is not responsible for a **mere error** of judgment, if he has exercised a reasonable discretion, and has acted with diligence and good faith. Thus, where an executor omitted to sell some foreign bonds for a year after the testator's death, although pressed to do so by his co-executor, and although there was a direction in the will to convert with all reasonable speed, he was held irresponsible for a loss caused by the bonds falling in price; for although the conclusion he came to was unfortunate, yet having exercised a bonâ fide discretion, the mere fact of the loss was not sufficient to charge him (d). As to what constitutes a reasonable delay, that depends on the particular circumstances affecting each case, but, primâ facie, a trustee ought not to delay realization beyond a year, even where he has apparently unlimited discretion (e); and if he procrastinates beyond that period, the onus will be cast upon him of proving that the delay was reasonable and proper (f).

16. A trustee will not be liable if the trust **property be stolen,** provided he has taken reasonable care of it (g).

17. A trustee is not bound to **insure** leasehold premises against loss by fire. In *Bailey* v. *Gould* (h), it was sought to charge an executor who had neglected to continue an insurance; but Baron Alderson said: "It was a contingent claim, which the testator might by possibility himself have realized, but which he did not. . . . . It was no claim

(c) Lew. 287.

(d) *Buxton* v. *Buxton, sup.;* and see *Paddon* v. *Richardson,* 7 D., M. & G. 563.

(e) *Sculthorpe* v. *Tipper,* L. R., 13 Eq. 232; and as to the propriety of an executor allowing the testator's money invested on mortgage to remain so until wanted, see *Orr* v. *Newton,* 2 Cox,

276; *Robinson* v. *Robinson,* 1 D., M. & G. 252.

(f) See per Wood, L. J., in *Graybourne* v. *Clarkson,* L. R., 3 Ch. 606, and *Hughes* v. *Empson,* 22 B. 181.

(g) *Morley* v. *Morley,* 2 Ch. C. 2; *Jones* v. *Lewis,* 2 V. 240.

(h) 4 Y. & C., Ex. 221; and *Dobson* v. *Land,* 8 Ha. 216.

existing at the time of the testator's decease. What *then*
existed the executors did possess, that is, the leasehold
premises. Being in their possession, a fire, for which they
were not to blame, occurred. It was a mere misfortune
which took place. Can the loss be said to have happened
by their default in not keeping up a contingent claim?
Was this property which, but for their default, they might
have got? It is very difficult to say that it was."

18. Trustees being liable for gross negligence, they are,
à fortiori, liable where they combine reckless disregard
of the interests of their cestuis que trust with mala fides.
Thus, where one trustee retires from the trust *for the purpose* of enabling his co-trustee to commit a breach of trust,
or in order, as he thinks, to relieve himself from the
responsibility of the wrongful act meditated by his co-trustee, he will be held as fully responsible as if he had been
particeps criminis (*i*).

19. Even a quasi trustee, such as a vendor before completion of the sale, is obliged to take due care of the property, and to see that it does not become unnecessarily
depreciated by want of care (*k*).

ART. 34.—*Trustee must see that he hands the Trust
Property to the right Person.*

The whole responsibility of handing the trust property
to the persons entitled falls upon the trustee; and
if he hands it to the wrong person, either through
mistake on his part or in consequence of some fraud
practised upon him, he will have to make the loss
good, however careful he may have been. In cases
of doubt, therefore, the trustee should apply to the
court for its direction (*a*).

ILLUST.—1. Thus where a trustee makes a payment to
one who produces a **forged authority** from the cestui que

(*i*) *Norton* v. *Pritchard*, Reg.
Lib. B. 1844, 771; *Le Hunt* v.
Webster, 9 W. R. 918; *Palairet*
v. *Carew*, 32 B. 567.

(*k*) See *E. Egmont* v. *Smith*,
L. R., 6 Ch. Div. 475.
(*a*) *Talbot* v. *E. Radnor*, 3 M. &
K. 252; *Mulin* v. *Blagrave*, 25 B.

trust, the trustee, and not the cestui que trust, will have to bear the loss; for, as was said by Lord Northington (b), " a trustee, whether he be a private person or a body corporate, must see to the reality of the authority empowering him to dispose of the trust money; for if the transfer is made without the authority of the owner, the act is a nullity, and in consideration of law and equity the right remains as before."

2. So, again, trustees who paid over the trust fund to wrong persons upon the faith of a marriage certificate which turned out to be a forgery, were made responsible for so much of the trust fund as could not be recovered from those who had wrongfully received it (c).

3. A trustee who, by mistake, pays the capital to the tenant for life instead of investing it and paying him the income only, will have to make good the loss to the estate, although he will, as will be seen hereafter (d), be entitled to be recouped out of the life estate (e).

OBS.—It is difficult to see how the law, as above stated, could have come into being, except upon the false analogy of a trustee, to a banker or creditor. As has been shown in the last article, a trustee is in the position of a gratuitous bailee; he must take reasonable care of the trust property, and if it is lost or stolen he is discharged from responsibility, provided that he was guiltless of negligence. If, then, a careful trustee is not responsible for property stolen from his custody, upon what conceivable ground should he be held responsible for property obtained from him by false pretences or forgery, which are crimes far more subtle, and against which it is much more difficult to safeguard oneself. It is humbly suggested, therefore, that

137; *Ashby* v. *Blackwell*, 2 Ed. 302; *Eaves* v. *Hickson*, 30 B. 136; *Sporle* v. *Burnaby*, 10 Jur., N. S. 1142.

(b) *Ashby* v. *Blackwell*, *sup.*

(c) *Eaves* v. *Hickson*, *sup.*; and see also *Bostock* v. *Floyer*, L. R.,

1 Ch. 26; and *Sutton* v. *Wilder*, L. R., 12 Eq. 373.

(d) *Infra*, Art. 61.

(e) *Barratt* v. *Wyatt*, 30 B. 442; *Davies* v. *Hodgson*, 25 B. 177; *Griffiths* v. *Porter*, ib. 236.

in these instances the law might be reconsidered with advantage.

***

ART. 35.—*Trustees must not in general depute their Duties.*

A trustee may not depute his duties or authority (*a*), either to a stranger (*b*) or to his co-trustees or co-trustee (*c*), save only—

   α. Where he is obliged to do so from necessity (*d*);

   β. Where by doing so he is acting conformably to the common usage of mankind, and as prudently as if acting for himself, and according to the usage of business (*e*); or

   γ. Where the settlement has authorized his doing so (*f*).

But even where he *may* safely permit another to receive trust property, he will not be justified in allowing it to remain in such other person's custody for a longer period than the circumstances of the case require (*g*).

ILLUST.—1. Thus a **trustee for sale,** who leaves the whole conduct of the sale to his co-trustee, cannot shield himself from responsibility for the latter's negligence by saying that he left the matter entirely in his hands (*h*). But, on the other hand, there is no objection to his employing an agent where such a course is conformable to the common usage of mankind, and the trustee acts as pru-

(*a*) See per Lord Langdale, *Turner* v. *Corney,* 5 B. 517.

(*b*) *Adams* v. *Clifton,* 1 Russ. 297; *Turner* v. *Corney, sup.; Chambers* v. *Minchin,* 7 V. 196; *Wood* v. *Weightman,* L. R., 13 Eq. 434.

(*c*) *Langford* v. *Gascoigne,* 11 V. 333; *Clough* v. *Bond,* 3 M. & C. 497; *Cowel* v. *Gatcombe,* 27 B. 568; *Eaves* v. *Hickson,* 30 B. 136.

(*d*) *Bennett* v. *Wyndham,* 4 De G. & J. 259; *Jay* v. *Campbell,* 1

Sch. & L. 341; *Re Bird,* L. R., 16 Eq. 203.

(*e*) St. § 1269; *Ex parte Belchier,* Amb. 219; *Clough* v. *Bond, sup.*

(*f*) *Kilbee* v. *Sneyd,* 2 Moll. 199; *Doyle* v. *Blake,* 2 Sch. & L. 245.

(*g*) *Brice* v. *Stokes,* 2 Lead. Cas. 865; *Gregory* v. *Gregory,* 2 Y. & C. 313; *Re Fryer,* 3 K. & J. 317.

(*h*) *Oliver* v. *Court,* 8 Pr. 166; *Re Chertsey Market,* 6 Pr. 285; *Hardwicke* v. *Mynd,* 1 Anst. 109.

---

dently as he would have done for himself (*i*). But he must not allow such agent to receive the purchaser's money, or he will be responsible for its loss (*k*); and, therefore, if "trustees for sale join with any other person in a joint sale of the trust property, and any other property, whether that person be a trustee himself or be a beneficial owner, they must take care that their share of the purchase-money is paid to them, and the purchaser must take care of that likewise, because he can only pay trust money to the trustees. Therefore, when they do join with other people the purchase-money must be apportioned before the completion of the purchase, and must be paid by the purchaser, the apportioned part coming to the trustees to be paid to them" (*l*).

2. And so where a trustee **handed money to a solicitor** for the purpose of reinvestment, and the solicitor professed to have, but in reality had not, invested it, but had used it for his own purposes, and himself paid interest on it for some years until his death, it was held that the trustee was liable (*m*), for he ought not to have entrusted the money to a solicitor when there was no necessity; and it is not in the eye of the law (although it is probably in point of fact) the usage of mankind to do so, as may be seen in the frequent case of a purchaser of property, who makes himself liable to the vendor if he pays the purchase-money to the vendor's solicitor without express authority (*n*).

3. In *Hopgood* v. *Parkin* (*o*), the late Lord Romilly carried the liability of trustees for the acts and defaults of their agents to a height which, it is with humility suggested, was by no means justified, either on principle or authority. In that case, trustees, having trust funds to lend on mortgage, employed a solicitor to investigate the

(*i*) *Ex parte Belchier, sup.*
(*k*) Lew. 383.
(*l*) Per Jessel, M. R., *Re Cooper & Allen's Contract*, L. R., 4 Ch. D. 815.

(*m*) *Bostock* v. *Floyer*, L. R., 1 Eq. 29; but see *Re Bird*, L. R., 16 Eq. 203; and *infra*, Illust. 4.
(*n*) Dart, 656.
(*o*) L. R., 11 Eq. 70.

mortgagor's title. Owing to the **solicitor's negligence,**
in failing to make proper inquiries as to previous incum-
brances, the trust moneys advanced on the mortgage were
to a large extent lost, and his lordship held that the
trustees must replace them. But it is difficult to understand upon what grounds the learned judge based his
opinion. The trustees were right in investing on mortgage; they were right in employing a skilled person to
investigate the real value of the security; indeed, it is
apprehended, from the remarks of Sir George Jessel, M. R.,
in *Re Cooper* (*p*), which have been quoted in the 7th illustration to Article 33, that it was the *duty* of the trustees to
employ a skilled person. In addition to which, there was
a moral necessity for them to employ a skilled agent to
investigate the title, and they were but acting conformably
to the general " usage of mankind, and as prudently for
the trust as for themselves, and according to the usage of
business" (*q*). If, then, they were right in employing
the solicitor to investigate the title for them, upon what
possible ground could they be holden responsible for their
agent's default. As Lord Hardwicke said, in *Ex parte Belchier* (*r*), if the defendant " is chargeable in this case, no
man in his senses would act. . . . . This court has laid
down a rule with regard to the transactions of assignees,
and more so of trustees, so as not to strike a terror into
mankind acting for the benefit of others, and not for their
own;" and his lordship then proceeded to lay down the
rule as above stated. It is with great respect submitted,
that Lord Romilly confused the case with those in which
it has been held that a trustee is responsible for a *breach
of trust* which he has committed bonâ fide and under skilled
advice. The distinction is, however, clear. The trustees
had not *done* anything wrong. They had not committed
any breach of trust at the instance of another. They had
merely lent money through the medium of an agency,

(*p*) *Supra.*   (*r*) *Supra.*
(*q*) Per Lord Hardwicke, *Ex parte Belchier*, Amb. 219.

which they were entitled, and indeed bound, to employ, on the ground of moral necessity, and they ought therefore to have been discharged from the loss. Had there been a distinct breach of some duty which the settlor had cast upon the trustees, then, although they might have taken and followed the best advice procurable, they would no doubt have been properly held responsible; but here, the only possible breach of duty was the *negligence* of an agent, and, as has been said above, a trustee is only responsible for his agent where he has improperly employed one.

4. In *Re Bird* (s), on the other hand, Vice-Chancellor Bacon seems (if I may say so, with great submission,) to have gone to the opposite extreme. There, one of three executors employed the solicitor of the testatrix for the purpose of obtaining a settlement with a creditor of the testatrix. The solicitor subsequently informed the executor that the compromise had been effected, and requested a cheque for the amount, which the executor sent. No compromise had ever been made, and the **solicitor appropriated the money** to his own use. Here it might have been anticipated that the executor would have been held liable, as, in accordance with *Bostock* v. *Floyer* (t), he ought to have paid the money to the creditor personally and not to the solicitor; but the Vice-Chancellor decided that he was not liable, saying, " It seems to me that the executor has done just what any prudent man would think himself safe in doing. He finds that the testatrix had in her lifetime employed Mr. Hunt as her solicitor. He had been employed as her solicitor on various matters; his credit was not called in question, his ability was not doubted. He had arranged for her some other claims, and when, after her death, a claim is made by these two companies, naturally enough Mr. Hunt is employed to conduct the business, namely, the compromise of these claims. Having employed this attorney to negotiate for a compromise, and being told by him ' I have got

(s) L. R., 16 Eq. 203.   (t) L. R., 1 Eq. 29.

I 2

these terms for you, and 310*l.* is payable,' the executor puts into his hands the 310*l.* What negligence is there in that? What incautious trusting to some other person's representation? It is all in the ordinary course of the business then being transacted, and I cannot think that the executor has neglected any caution which it was incumbent on him to exercise." Whether or not the present state of the law will permit of a trustee entrusting a solicitor with money, it is suggested that his honor's decision is in accordance with that summa ratio which the simpleminded believe to be equivalent to the summum jus.

5. A trustee will be liable where he has *unnecessarily* left trust moneys in the hands of a **banker or broker who fails,** when he ought to have invested them, or where he has paid money to a banker or broker for investment and has neglected for some time to make inquiries as to such investment(*u*); and the *usual* clause indemnifying him against the acts or defaults of others will not protect him(*v*).

6. On the other hand, where money has been deposited in a bank **pending investment,** and not for an unnecessary length of time, the trustee will not be liable for the failure of the bank (*w*), for it is according to the common usage of mankind to make use of banks for the safe custody of their money.

7. So a trustee may appoint stewards, bailiffs, workmen, and other agents of the like kind, for there is a **moral necessity** for him to do so (*x*).

8. So where one executor lives at a distance from the testator's place of abode, he may remit money to his coexecutor who lives in the immediate vicinity, for the purpose of paying the testator's debts, for "he is considered to do this of **necessity.** He could not transact business without trusting some person, and it would be impossible

(*u*) *Challen* v. *Shippam*, 4 Ha. 555; *Rehden* v. *Wesley*, 29 B. 213; *Matthews* v. *Brise*, 6 B. 239.

(*v*) *Rehden* v. *Wesley*, *sup.*

(*w*) *Johnson* v. *Newton*, 11 Ha. 160; *Fenwick* v. *Clarke*, 31 L. J., Ch. 728; and per Lord Hardwicke, *Ex parte Belchier*, *sup.*

(*x*) *Ibid.*

for him to discharge his duty if he is made responsible where he remitted money to a person to whom he would himself have given credit, and would in his own business have remitted money in the same way" (y).

9. Again, trustees may **remit money** through the medium of a respectable bank, as being the most convenient and the safest mode (z); but they should pay the money into the bank *as* trustee eo nomine (a).

10. A trustee may safely permit his co-trustee to *receive* or *collect* trust moneys (b); and even though he **join in the receipt** for such moneys, and thereby acknowledge that he has received them, he will not be liable *if he can prove* (c) that he did not in fact receive them, and only joined in the **receipt for the sake of conformity** (d). For one of several trustees cannot alone give a good receipt, unless expressly empowered to do so, and all must, therefore, join (e); so that, although at law the signature of a trustee is (or rather was (f)) conclusive evidence that the money came to his hands, "equity, which pursues truth, will decree according to the justice and verity of the fact" (g), and will hold that, under the circumstances, seeing that it is an act which the very nature of his office will not permit him to decline (h), it does not amount to an admission that he actually received the money. It was formerly thought that executors could not claim this privilege, on the ground that one alone could give a good discharge; but this notion has been greatly modified by the case of *Wesley* v. *Clarke* (i), and it may now be con-

---

(y) Per Ld. Redesdale, *Joy* v. *Campbell*, 1 Sch. & L. 341; *Ex parte Griffin*, 2 Gl. & J. 114. See, however, *Chambers* v. *Minchin*, 7 V. 193; *Langford* v. *Gascoigne*, *sup.*

(z) *Knight* v. *Earl of Plymouth*, 1 Dick. 120.

(a) *Wren* v. *Kirton*, 11 V. 380.

(b) *Townley* v. *Sherborne*, 2 Lead. Ca. 858; *Re Fryer*, 3 K. & J. 317.

(c) *Brice* v. *Stokes*, 2 Lead. Ca. 865.

(d) *Fellows* v. *Mitchell*, 1 P. W. 81: *Re Fryer, sup.*

(e) Lew. 233. See *Re Belchier*, *sup.*; *Walker* v. *Symonds*, 3 Sw. 63; *Lee* v. *Sankey*, L. R., 15 Eq. 204.

(f) Not so since the régime of the Judicature Acts.

(g) See per Lord Henley, *Harden* v. *Parsons*, 1 Ed. 147.

(h) Lew. 233.

(i) 1 Ed. 357.

sidered as settled that, "if the receipt be given for the purpose of mere form, the signing will not charge the person not receiving; but if it be given under circumstances purporting that the money, though not actually received by both executors, was *under the control of both*, such a receipt shall charge; and the true question in these cases seems to have been whether the money was under the control of both executors" (*k*). An executor is, however, more strictly responsible than an ordinary trustee for any act by which he reduces any part of the testator's property into the sole possession of his co-executor (*l*).

11. Although a trustee may safely permit his co-trustee to receive trust moneys, he will, nevertheless, be liable if he **permit him to retain them** for a longer period than the circumstances of the case necessitate (*m*). Thus in *Walker* v. *Symonds* (*n*), D., one of three trustees, received part of the trust money, and, with the assent of the other trustees, invested it in East India Co.'s bills, payable *to him*. These were paid off, and thereupon S., another of the trustees, wrote to D., requesting him to invest the money. D., however, begged that it might remain in his hands on mortgage. The other trustees assented to this. The mortgage was, however, never prepared, although S. made frequent applications to D., who finally died insolvent five years after first receiving the money. Upon this state of facts Lord Eldon said: "The money was laid out with the consent of the trustees on India bills, payable to D., a palpable breach of trust, by placing the fund under his control, secured by little more than a promissory note payable to himself. It was probable that in 1793 the money due on the bills would be paid, and it would be

(*k*) Per Lord Redesdale, *Joy* v. *Campbell*, 1 Sch. & L. 341.

(*l*) *Townsend* v. *Barber*, 1 Dick. 356; *Candler* v. *Tillett*, 22 B. 263; *Hovey* v. *Blakeman*, 4 V. 608; *Clough* v. *Dixon*, 3 M. & C. 497; *Lees* v. *Sanderson*, 4 Sim. 28.

(*m*) *Brice* v. *Stokes, sup.*; *Thompson* v. *Finch*, 8 D., M. & G. 560; *Walker* v. *Symonds*, 3 Sw. 1; *Hanbury* v. *Kirkland*, 3 Sim. 265; *Styles* v. *Guy*, 1 M. & G. 422; *Egbert* v. *Butler*, 21 B. 560; *Rodbard* v. *Cooke*, 25 W. R. 555.

(*n*) *Supra*.

lodged in his hands; and although the court will proceed
as favourably as it can to trustees who have laid out the
money on a security from which they cannot with activity
recover it, yet no judge can say that they are not guilty of
a breach of trust if they suffer it to lie out on such a security *for so long a time.* The trustees were guilty of a
breach of trust in permitting the money to remain on bills
payable to D. alone, and in leaving the state of the funds
unascertained for five years."

ART. 36.—*Trustees should obey the Terms of the
Settlement.*

Trustees are bound to carry out the *duties* prescribed
by the settlement.

ILLUST.—1. Thus, if trustees are **directed to call in**
trust-moneys, and to lay them out on a purchase, and they
fail to do so, and the fund is lost, they are liable for the
loss so sustained (*a*).

2. So if a trustee for sale **omits to sell** property when it
ought to be sold, and it is afterwards lost, although without any default on his part, he is liable for the loss which
would not have happened had he not failed in performing
an obvious duty (*b*).

3. So where the settlement orders trust funds to be
invested on **particular securities**, the trustees are bound
so to invest them.

4. So where there are any **conditions** attached to the
exercise of any of their functions, they must strictly perform those conditions. As for instance, where they are
authorized to lend to a husband with the consent of his
wife, they cannot make the advance without getting the
required consent, even though he subsequently get it (*c*).

5. On the same principle, where an estate is given in
trust for A. for life, and **after his death** upon trust **to sell**

(*a*) *Craven* v. *Craddock*, W. N.   (*b*) St. § 1269, n.
1868, p. 229.   (*c*) *Bateman* v. *Davis*, 3 Mad. 98.

and pay the proceeds to another, the trustees cannot sell during the life of A., even with his consent, unless all the persons who are to receive the proceeds are sui juris and join in the sale; for the settlor, having prescribed the date of the sale, the trustees must follow out his direction (*d*).

ART. 37.—*Trustees must not favour particular Cestuis que trust.*

Trustees must honestly exercise their functions for the benefit of all parties claiming under the settlement, and must not favour individual cestuis que trust at the expense of the others (*a*).

ILLUST.—1. Thus where trustees are **empowered to sell** real estate and to lay out the proceeds in the purchase of another estate, they would not be justified in selling to promote the exclusive interests of the tenant for life; but they must look to the intention of the settlement, and whether another and better purchase is practicable, and not merely probable; or at all events there must be some strong reasons of family prudence (*b*).

2. Conversely, if lands be devised to trustees upon trust to sell for payment of debts, and subject thereto upon trusts for divers persons successively, the trustees must not raise the money by **sale of the timber,** for that would be a hardship on the tenant for life (*c*).

3. Where money is directed to be laid out in the purchase of land to be settled on a person for life with or without impeachment of waste, with remainders over, the trustees should not purchase an estate with an **overwhelming proportion of trees** on it, for if the tenant for life be impeachable for waste he would lose the fruit of so much as was the value of the timber; and if he be not impeach-

---

(*d*) *Leedham* v. *Chawner*, 4 K. & J. 458; *Want* v. *Stallibrass*, L. R., 8 Ex. 175.

(*a*) See Lew. 379; *Cargill* v. *Oxmantown*, 3 Y. & C. 369; *Watts* v. *Girdlestone*, 6 B. 188; *Marshall* v. *Sladden*, 4 D. & S. 468.

(*b*) *Mortlock* v. *Buller*, 10 V. 309; *Mahon* v. *Stanhope*, cit. 2 Sug. Pow. 412.

(*c*) *Davies* v. *Westcombe*, 2 Sim. 425.

able he could, by felling the timber, possess himself of a great part of the corpus of the trust property (*d*).

4. Upon a similar trust to the foregoing, trustees should not purchase **mining property**, nor an advowson, both of which might give an undue preference to one cestui que trust (*e*).

5. Again, where trustees have a **choice of investments**, they must not exercise that choice for the *sole* benefit of the tenant for life by investing upon a more productive but less secure property (*f*); and where any change of investment is to be made with the consent of the tenant for life, and he *improperly* withholds his consent, the court will compel him to give it (*g*).

6. Upon the same equitable principles, it is a general rule that where a testator subjects the residue of his personal estate to a series of limitations, directly or by way of trust, without any particular directions as to investment or mode of enjoyment, there, in the absence of indications of a contrary intention, such part of the residue as may consist of **goods of a perishable nature** (such as leaseholds), or as may be invested in securities which yield a high rate of interest, but are not authorized by the court, **must be converted** and put into such investments as to be securely available for all persons interested. And if the residue comprises property of a **reversionary nature**, that also must be converted. The one rule protects the remainderman,— the other the tenant for life (*h*).

ART. 38.—*Trustee must not set up Jus tertii.*

A trustee, who has acknowledged himself as such, must not set up or aid the adverse title of a third party against his cestui que trust (*a*). But (quære)

(*d*) *Bingers* v. *Lamb*, 16 V. 174.
(*e*) Lew. 439.
(*f*) *Raby* v. *Ridehalgh*, 7 D., M. & G. 104; and *Stuart* v. *Stuart*, 3 B. 430.
(*g*) *Costello* v. *O'Rourke*, 3 Ir.

Rep. 172.
(*h*) *Howe* v. *Earl of Dartmouth*, 2 Lead. Ca. 262; *Brown* v. *Gellatly*, L. R., 2 Ch. 751.
(*a*) *Newsome* v. *Flowers*, 30 B. 461.

he may decline to execute the trust, if he receives
information making it doubtful whether he ought
to execute it; and he has a right to have the direction of the court on the subject (c).

ILLUST.—1. In *Newsome* v. *Flowers* (*sup.*), a chapel was
vested in trustees, in trust for Particular Baptists. Subsequently a schism took place, and part of the congregation
seceded, and went to another chapel. Still later, the surviving trustees were induced (not knowing the real object)
to appoint new trustees, and vest the property in them.
Immediately afterwards, the new trustees, who were in
fact attached to the seceding congregation, brought an
action to obtain possession of the chapel. Their appointment was however set aside, and it was held that they
could not raise the adverse claims of the seceders as a
defence against the congregation of the chapel who were
their cestuis que trust; Lord Romilly saying, "It is a
common principle of law, that a tenant who has paid rent
to his landlord cannot say, 'You are not the owner of the
property.' The fact of his having paid rent prevents his
doing it. The same thing occurs where persons are made
trustees for the owner of property; if they acknowledge
the trust for a considerable time, they cannot say that any
other persons are their cestuis que trust."

2. Nor, however honestly trustees may believe that the
trust property belongs of right to a third party, are they
justified in refusing to perform the trust they have once
undertaken or in communicating with such other person
on the subject; but they must assume the validity of the
title of their cestuis que trust until it be impeached (d).

3. If however they believe that there is a bonâ fide
claimant adverse to their cestuis que trust, and that they
may make themselves **personally liable** in case they carry
out the trust in favour of their cestuis que trust, they may,
it would seem, come to the court for its direction, and in

(c) *Neale* v. *Davis*, 5 D., M. &   (d) *Beddoes* v. *Pugh*, 26 B. 407;
G. 258.   Lew. 253.

the meanwhile refuse to carry out the trust. The late
Lord Justice Knight Bruce, however, energetically dissented
from this view, saying: "Even if by paying the fund to
their cestuis que trust they would make themselves personally liable to the adverse claimant in the event of his
being successful, they were and are bound to perform the
trust which they undertook" (e). The doctrine as enun-
ciated in the rule has however been since assented to, and
is at all events primâ facie correct (f).

ART. 39.—Investment of Trust Funds (a).

In the absence of express directions in the settlement,
trustees can safely invest trust funds on the
following securities only:—

α. On real securities, or in any of the government or bank annuities (b) ;

(e) *Neale* v. *Davis, sup.*
(f) *Neligan* v. *Roche*, Ir. R., 7
Eq. 332.
(a) It is apprehended that
this article is a correct digest of
the law of the court as modified
by statute. The 22 & 23 Vict.
c. 35, s. 32, gave trustees power
to invest in the securities mentioned in sub-clause β, and that
act has not been impliedly repealed, as appears from its confirmation by 23 & 24 Vict. c. 38,
s. 12, and 30 & 31 Vict. c. 132,
ss. 1 and 2. By 23 & 24 Vict.
c. 145, s. 25, trustees of settlements executed after that date
are empowered to invest in any
of the parliamentary or public
funds or government securities.
This would, at first sight, seem
to be restrictive of the powers of
the 22 & 23 Vict. c. 35, but it is
evidently not so, as that act is
impliedly confirmed and extended
by 30 & 31 Vict. c. 132, which
enacts, that, except where expressly forbidden by the instrument creating the trust, it shall
be lawful for every trustee, executor or administrator to invest
any trust fund in his possession,
or under his control, in any securities the interest of which is
guaranteed by parliament, to the
same extent and in the same
manner as they may invest in
East India Stock under sect. 1
of that act. This act, however,
would seem to be subject, in the
case of settlements executed since
the 28th August, 1860, to the
proviso in the article. At all
events it would not be safe to
assume that it was not. The act
23 & 24 Vict. c. 38, s. 11, authorizing investment in any securities in which funds under the
control of the court may be invested, has at present had no
application, as such funds can
only be invested in Bank Stock,
East India Stock, Exchequer Bills,
Two and a Half per Cent. Annuities, and mortgage of freeholds
or copyholds.
(b) *Baud* v. *Farrell*, 7 D., M. &
G. 628.

β. Where under the circumstances it is reasonable and proper, in stock of the banks of England or Ireland, or in any (c) East India Stock (d), or in any security the interest of which may be guaranteed by parliament (e): Provided, that where the settlement is dated subsequently to the 28th August, 1860, *and* there is a person under no disability entitled in possession to receive the income of the trust fund for life, or for a term of years determinable with life, or for any greater estate, no investment can be made, except in consols, without his written consent (f).

ILLUST. 1.—Thus a trustee cannot (unless expressly authorized to do so) lend money on **personal security,** however apparently good (g), or however apparently trustworthy (h); and as Lord Kenyon said, in *Holmes* v. *Dring* (i), this "ought to be rung into the ears of every one who acts in the character of trustee."

2. So, again, a trustee must not invest on **trade security**; as for instance in the shares of a public company, which are in reality no security at all, but merely documents conferring a right to speculative profits (k). It was on this ground, that before the passing of the acts of parliament before referred to, trustees were not entitled to invest even in stock of the Bank of England, or in East India Stock (l).

3. Where there is a tenant for life, and those in remainder object to funds being invested in East India Stock, it would not in general be considered **"reasonable and proper"** for trustees to invest in it; because the market price of that stock is usually higher than the rate at which it is

(c) 30 & 31 Vict. c. 132, s. 1.
(d) 22 & 23 Vict. c. 35, s. 32, made retrospective by 23 & 24 Vict. c. 38, s. 12.
(e) 30 & 31 Vict. c. 132, s. 2.
(f) 23 & 24 Vict. c. 145, s. 25.
(g) *Holmes* v. *Dring*, 2 Cox, 1.

(h) *Styles* v. *Guy*, 1 M. & G. 423.
(i) *Supra*.
(k) Lindley, 682.
(l) *Howe* v. *Earl of Dartmouth*, Lead. Ca. 262.

redeemable; and therefore, although it pays a higher rate
of interest than consols, the consequence of investing in it
might be to benefit the tenant for life at the expense of
those in remainder (*m*). If, however, there were special
circumstances which might make such an investment beneficial to the remainderman in præsenti, although not in
futuro, the trustee would be justified in making the investment; as for instance, where property is settled on a
parent for life with remainder to his children, and it is
very important that the parent should have an increased
income *for the better support and education of the children* (*n*).
And it would seem that where a trustee acts bonâ fide and
to the best of his discretion, he is entitled to the protection
of the court, notwithstanding that the court would not
have sanctioned such an investment had the fund been
under its control (*o*).

ART. 40.—*Trustee should be ready with his Accounts.*

It is the duty of a trustee to give accurate information to his cestuis que trust as to the state of the
trust property; and for that purpose he should
keep clear accounts thereof (*a*).

ILLUST.—1. Thus, where owners of a privateer, acting
for themselves and the crew in the sale of the prizes,
neglected to render accounts, and delayed the distribution
of the proceeds, they were charged with interest on the
balances and were condemned in costs (*b*). Where, however, the trustees are executors, it would seem that they
would not be mulcted in costs, unless they pertinaciously

(*m*) *Cockburn* v. *Peel*, 3 D., F.
& J. 170; *Ungless* v. *Tuff*, 9 W.
R. 729; *Waite* v. *Littlewood*, 41
L. J., Ch. 636.

(*n*) *Cockburn* v. *Peel*, *sup.*, per
Turner, L. J.: and see *Montefiore*
v. *Guedalla*, W. N. 1868, 87; *Re
Ingram*, 11 W. R. 980.

(*o*) *Cockburn* v. *Peel*, *sup.*; *Hume*
v. *Richardson*, 4 D., F. & J. 29.

(*a*) *Springett* v. *Dashwood*, 2
Giff. 521; *Burrows* v. *Walls*, 5
D., M. & G. 253; *Pearse* v. *Green*,
1 J. & W. 140.

(*b*) *Ibid.*

refused to render their accounts; for an executor is said to have a right to have his accounts taken in court.

ART. 41.—*Trustee must not make private Advantage out of Trust Property.*

It is the duty of a trustee to act wholly and entirely for the benefit of his cestuis que trust, and without reference to his own interests; he must not make any use of the trust property for his own private purposes, even though he would thereby do no actual injury to it, or to the cestuis que trust (*a*); nor must an executive trustee purchase it (*b*) from himself, or his colleagues (*c*), however fair and honourable his intentions may be (*d*), unless by leave of the court acting for cestuis que trust who are not sui juris (*e*). He is also incapable of making a valid purchase even from his cestuis que trust so long as he remains a trustee, unless he can affirmatively prove that the cestuis que trust were fully and distinctly informed of, and understood the nature of, the transaction, and waived all objections, and that he disclosed to them all facts tending to enhance the value of the transaction (*f*). A trustee cannot, by retiring just before a sale takes place (with all his knowledge of the property fresh in his mind), thereby qualify himself to be a purchaser (*g*).

ILLUST.—1. Lord Eldon once directed an inquiry whether

(*a*) *Webb* v. *Earl Shaftesbury*, 7 V. 488; *Ex parte Lacey*, 6 V. 625; and see *Re Imperial Land Co. of Marseilles*, L. R., 4 Ch. Div. 566; *Aberdeen Town* v. *Aberdeen University*, L. R., 2 Ap. Ca. 544.
(*b*) *Fox* v. *Mackreth*, 1 Lead. Ca. 115.
(*c*) *Whichcote* v. *Lawrence*, 3 V. 740; *Morse* v. *Royal*, 12 V. 374.
(*d*) *Ex parte Lacey*, sup.
(*e*) *Campbell* v. *Walker*, 5 V. 682; *Farmer* v. *Deane*, 32 B. 327; and see *Tennant* v. *Trenchard*, L.

R., 4 Ch. 517.
(*f*) *Randall* v. *Errington*, 10 V. 427; *Coles* v. *Trecothick*, 9 V. 247; *Spring* v. *Pride*, 4 D., J. & S. 395; and see *Morse* v. *Royal*, sup.; *Clark* v. *Swaile*, 2 Ed. 134. This provision does not extend to a purchase by the trustees of the trustees' marriage settlement, *Hickley* v. *Hickley*, L. R., 2 Ch. Div. 190.
(*g*) *Ex parte James*, 8 V. 352; *Spring* v. *Pride*, sup.

the right of **sporting over the trust property** could be let for the benefit of the cestuis que trust, and, if not, he thought that the game should belong to the heir of the settlor; the trustee might appoint a gamekeeper, if necessary, for the preservation of the game, but must not keep an establishment of mere pleasure for his own enjoyment (h).

2. So, again, it need hardly be pointed out that he must not actively import **trust moneys into his trade** or business, or use them in speculations of his own, and if he does so (as has been said before) he will be a constructive trustee of the profits, and if there be no profits he will be liable for the breach of trust, and will have to pay compound interest at five per cent., as will be seen hereafter (i). Where, however, there has been no *active* breach of trust, but only an omission on the part of a trustee, in whose business the settlor had money invested, to settle up the accounts, and properly invest the balance, such an omission will not make him liable to account for the profits (j).

3. The case of *Sandford* v. *Keech* which has been cited as the first illustration of Article 21, is another instance of the application of the rule now under consideration.

4. An **agent** employed for the sale of an estate cannot purchase it for himself, for he is a constructive trustee (k).

5. Trustees cannot lease or mortgage the trust estate to one of themselves, and if they do so the lessee will have to account for the profits (l).

6. The rule as to selling to himself, only applies where the express or constructive trustee is in the nature of an executive trustee, for where he is the mere depository of the legal estate without any duties, he may be a purchaser. For instance, **trustees to preserve contingent remainders** (m),

---

(h) *Webb* v. *Earl Shaftesbury*, sup.

(i) Art. 67.

(j) *Vyse* v. *Foster*, L. R., 8 Ch. 335.

(k) *Re Boyle*, 1 M. & G. 495.

(l) *Ex parte Hughes*, 6 V. 617; *Stickney* v. *Sewell*, 1 M. & C. 8; *Francis* v. *Francis*, 5 D., M. & G. 108.

(m) *Sutton* v. *Jones*, 15 V. 587; *Pooley* v. *Quilter*, 4 Dr. 189.

or persons nominated trustees who have disclaimed (n).
But one who was originally an executive trustee, and has
become a mere bare trustee by performance of the trusts,
would, it is apprehended, be disqualified; for he would
have had an opportunity of becoming acquainted with the
property and its value, and if he chose to conceal that
value it might be impossible to establish it against him (o).

7. In reference to **sales by the cestuis que trust**, the
transaction was upheld where a cestui que trust took
the whole management of a sale upon himself, and then
agreed to sell a lot, which he had bought in, to one of the
trustees for sale (p).

8. So where a client was very desirous of selling property, and after vainly endeavouring to do so, finally **sold
it to his solicitor** (who was of course a constructive trustee),
and it was proved that the transaction was fair and the
price adequate, and indeed more than could have been
obtained elsewhere at the time, and the client quite understood his position, it was held that such a sale was good
and binding, although it lay upon the solicitor to prove
that it was unimpeachable (q).

9. The rule as to the extreme fairness to be observed in
purchasing from cestuis que trust does not apply to persons
who are only **constructive trustees** by virtue of some business contract entered into with the so-called cestuis que
trust. Thus, mortgagees can freely purchase from their
mortgagors (r), partners from the representatives of a
deceased partner (s), and other persons bearing similar
relations enjoy a similar freedom; for though contracting
parties may by a metaphor be said to be trustees for each
other, the trust is strictly limited by the contract. They

(n) *Stacey* v. *Elph*, 1 M. & K.
195.
(o) *Ex parte Bennett*, 10 V. 381.
(p) *Coles* v. *Trecothick*, 9 V.
234; and *Clark* v. *Swaile*, 2 Ed.
134.
(q) *Spencer* v. *Topham*, 22 B.

573; 2 Jur., N. S. 865; *Gibson*
v. *Jeyes*, 6 V. 278; *Johnson* v.
Fesenmayer, 3 D. & J. 13; *Edwards* v. *Merrick*, 2 Ha. 60.
(r) *Knight* v. *Majoribanks*, 3 M.
& G. 10.
(s) *Chambers* v. *Howell*, 11 B. 6.

are trustees only to the extent of their obligation to perform that contract, and the trust is limited to the discharge of that obligation (*t*).

10. Where there are **infant cestuis que trust**, the court will, on the application of the trustee, allow him to purchase, if it can see that, *under the circumstances*, it is clearly for the benefit of the cestuis que trust, but not otherwise (*u*).

ART. 42.—*Trustee must in general act gratuitously.*

A trustee has no right to charge for his time and trouble (*a*) except in the following cases:—

α. Where the settlement provides for it (*b*).

β. Where he has, at the time of accepting the trust, expressly stipulated for a remuneration (*c*), and the cestuis que trust have freely and without unfair pressure assented to such stipulation (*d*).

γ. Where the trust is before the court, and the trustee has, before accepting the trust, expressly stipulated for such remuneration (*e*).

δ. Where one who is not an express trustee has properly traded with another's money under circumstances which make him a constructive trustee of the profits (*f*).

ε. Where the trust property is in the West Indies, and it is the custom of the local courts to allow remuneration (*g*).

ILLUST.—1. Thus a trustee who is a **solicitor** will not be allowed to charge for his time and trouble or for his professional attendance; for, as was somewhat drily said by Lord Lyndhurst in *New* v. *Jones* (*h*), "a trustee placed in

(*t*) See per Westbury, L. C., in *Knox* v. *Gye*, L. R., 5 H. L. 675; but see per Jessel, M. R., *Egmont* v. *Smith*, L. R., 6 Ch. Div. 469.

(*u*) *Farmer* v. *Deane*, 32 B. 327; *Campbell* v. *Walker*, 5 V. 681.

(*a*) *Robinson* v. *Pett*, 2 Lea. Ca 215.

(*b*) *Ib.*; *Webb* v. *Earl of Shaftesbury*, 7 V. 480; *Willis* v. *Kibble*,

1 B. 559.

(*c*) *Re Sherwood*, 3 B. 338; *Douglas* v. *Archbut*, 2 D. & J. 148.

(*d*) *Ayliffe* v. *Murray*, 2 At. 58.

(*e*) *Barrett* v. *Hartley*, 12 Jur., N. S. 426; *Moore* v. *Froud*, 3 M. & C. 48.

(*f*) *Brown* v. *Litton*, 1 P.W. 140.

(*g*) *Chambers* v. *Goldwin*, 9 V. 267.

(*h*) 9 Jar. Prec. 338.

the position of a solicitor might, if allowed to perform the duties of a solicitor and to be paid for them, find it very often proper to institute and carry on legal proceedings which he would not do if he were to derive no emolument from them himself, and if he were to employ another person."

2. Nor in general will a trustee, whether express or constructive, be permitted to claim a salary or any remuneration for **managing a trade** or business (*i*).

3. But this does not apply to one who *rightfully* becomes possessed of another's money and rightfully trades with it; for he will be entitled to a **reasonable remuneration,** although he is of course a constructive trustee of the profits of the trade (*k*). For instance, in *Brown* v. *Litton* (*l*) the plaintiff's testator was the captain of a ship, who being on a voyage, had 800 dollars which he intended to invest in trade. The captain died, and the defendant, who was the mate of the ship, becoming captain in his place, took possession of these 800 dollars, and by judiciously trading with them made considerable profits. Upon a bill being filed against him for an account, the Lord Keeper Harcourt said: "He ought clearly to account for the profits made of the money; the primary intention in carrying abroad this money, was to invest it in trade, and not to return with it home again, and therefore the defendant having observed the intent of the testator in trading therewith, and having taken such a prudent care in the management of it as (it may be presumed) he would have taken of his own money, the defendant would not have been liable for any loss that might have happened, and to recompense him for his care in trading with it, the master shall settle a proper salary for the pains and trouble he has been at in the management thereof."

(*i*) *Stocken* v. *Dawes*, 6 B. 371;   284; *Wedderburn* v. *Wedderburn*,
Burdon v. *Burdon*, 1 V. & B. 170.   22 B. 84.
     (*k*) *Brown* v. *De Tastet*, Jac.   (*l*) 1 P. W. 140.

SUB-DIVISION IV.

THE POWERS AND AUTHORITY OF A TRUSTEE.

ART. 43.—*General Authority of a Trustee.*

IN addition to the power and authority expressly given to him by the settlement, and subject to any restrictions contained therein, a trustee may, without application to the court, do such acts as the court would sanction if applied to (*a*). No rule can be laid down as to what acts the court will sanction, as that must depend upon the particular circumstances of each case; but in general the court will sanction—

α. Acts which are reasonable and proper for the realization, protection, or benefit of the trust property (*b*); and

β. Acts which are reasonable and proper for the protection, safety, support, or reputation of a cestui que trust who is incapable of taking care of himself or herself (*c*):

Provided, that such acts do not benefit one cestui que trust at the expense of another or others (*d*), and do not interfere with any *legal* beneficial interest.

ILLUST.—1. Thus, in *Ward* v. *Ward* (*e*), where, by the immediate realization of the trust property, the trustee would have ruined one cestui que trust from whom a large debt

(*a*) *Lee* v. *Brown*, 4 V. 369; *Inwood* v. *Twyne*, 2 Ed. 153; *Seagram* v. *Knight*, L. R., 2 Ch. 630.
(*b*) *Ward* v. *Ward*, 2 H. L. C. 784; *Waldo* v. *Waldo*, 7 Sim. 261; *Bright* v. *North*, 2 Ph. 220; *Bowes* v. *E. L. Water Co.*, Jac. 324.
(*c*) *Sisson* v. *Shaw*, 9 V. 288; *Maberly* v. *Turton*, 14 V. 499;

Cotham v. *West*, 1 B. 381; *Ex parte Green*, 1 J. & W. 253; *Re Haworth*, L. R., 8 Ch. 415; *De Witte* v. *Palin*, L. R., 14 Eq. 251; *Swinnock* v. *De Crispe*, Free. 78.
(*d*) *Seagram* v. *Knight*, *sup.*; *Lee* v. *Brown*, *sup.*; *Wood* v. *Patteson*, 10 B. 544.
(*e*) *Supra.*

K 2

was due to the trust estate, and would have very seriously prejudiced others, and instead of doing so, the trustee made an **arrangement with the debtor** for payment of the money by instalments, it was held, that he was justified in having taken that course, because he had exercised a sound discretion, and such as the court would have approved of.

2. So, again, as was said by Lord Cottenham in *Bright* v. *North* (*f*), every trustee is entitled to be allowed the reasonable and proper expenses incurred in **protecting property** committed to his care. But if they have a right to protect property from immediate and direct injury, they must have the same right where the injury threatened is indirect but probable; and, therefore, his lordship allowed the trustees (who were, in that instance, trustees of public works) the expenses of opposing a bill in parliament which would have been prejudicial to those works if passed.

3. So, again, in cases where the court would, if applied to, authorize the **cutting down of timber** which has arrived at maturity, and which would only degenerate if allowed to stand; or where it is necessary to cut it for the purpose of thinning it, the trustee may fell it on his own authority (*g*).

4. On the same principle, a trustee who has the management of property, may grant a **reasonable agricultural lease** (*h*), unless expressly or impliedly (*i*) restrained from doing so by the settlement; but he may not grant a mining lease, for that would benefit the tenant for life at the expense of the reversioner (*k*).

5. On the other hand, trustees must not do acts, however beneficial they may possibly be to the property, if they are in their nature **unreasonable** and problematical. For instance, they ought not to make merely ornamental improve-

(*f*) 2 Ph. 220.
(*g*) *Waldo* v. *Waldo*, 7 Sim. 261. See *Seagram* v. *Knight, sup*.
(*h*) *Naylor* v. *Arnitt*, 1 R. & M. 501; *Bowes* v. *E. L. Water Co.*, Jac. 324; *Att.-Gen.* v. *Owen*, 10

V. 560.
(*i*) *Evans* v. *Jackson*, 8 Sim. 217; and see *Michells* v. *Corbett*, 34 B. 376.
(*k*) *Wood* v. *Patteson*, 10 B. 544.

ments (*l*), nor take down a mansion-house for the purpose of rebuilding a better one (*m*), nor build a villa for the mere improvement of the estate (*n*). If, however, they are, by the settlement, expressly given a power " generally to superintend the management of the estate," it would seem that their powers of management are almost unlimited, so long as they are exercised bonâ fide (*o*).

6. With regard to acts for the **benefit of the cestuis que trust**, a familiar instance occurs in the case of trusts of personalty for married women, where, if the trustee paid over the fund to the husband, the wife would probably get no benefit from it. In such cases, the trustee is justified, if he thinks fit, in refusing to pay the money to the husband, and in paying it into court instead, so that the wife may have every facility for enforcing her equity to a settlement (*p*).

7. So trustees might always allow, by way of **maintenance**, a competent part of the income of property to the father of an infant cestui que trust (*q*), where the father could not support it *according to its position* (*r*) ; and, if an orphan, to the mother (*s*), or stepfather (*t*), whether they could do so or not. And a trustee *may* under special circumstances, as for instance, where the capital is considerably under a thousand pounds (*u*), allow maintenance out

(*l*) *Bridge* v. *Brown*, 2 Y. & C. 181.

(*m*) *Bleazard* v. *Whalley*, 2 Eq. Rep. 1093.

(*n*) *Vyse* v. *Foster*, L. R., 8 Ch. 309.

(*o*) *Bowes* v. *E. Strathmore*, 8 Jur. 92; and see also as to powers of building, &c., *Re Leslie*, L. R., 2 Ch. Div. 185; and consider principle in *Gisborne* v. *Gisborne*, L. R., 2 Ap. Ca. 300.

(*p*) Wat. 360; *Re Swan*, 2 H. & M. 34; *Re Bendyshe*, 3 Jur., N. S. 727.

(*q*) *Sisson* v. *Shaw*, 9 V. 288; *Maberly* v. *Turton*, 14 V. 499;

Cotham v. *West*, 1 B. 381.

(*r*) Maintenance has been allowed to a father with an income of 6,000*l*. a year, *Jervoise* v. *Silk*, 1 G. Coop. 52.

(*s*) *Douglas* v. *Andrews*, 12 B. 310.

(*t*) Lew. 492, commenting on *Billingsley* v. *Critchett*, 1 B. C. C. 268, as affected by 4 & 5 Will. 4, c. 76, s. 57.

(*u*) *Barlow* v. *Grant*, 1 Ver. 255; *Ex parte Green*, 1 J. & W. 253; *Re Howarth*, L. R., 8 Ch. 415; *De Witte* v. *Palin*, L. R., 14 Eq. 251.

of the capital; but a trustee would not be wise to take upon himself the responsibility of breaking into the capital (*r*).

8. Upon the same principle, a trustee may apply part of an infant's capital for its **advancement** in the world (*w*).

9. But where, by making an advancement, the trustee would injure the **contingent rights** of another cestui que trust, he will do it at his peril as against such other (*x*). For instance, where 100*l.* was bequeathed, upon trust to apply the income towards the maintenance and education of A. during his minority, and upon trust to pay the corpus to him on attaining twenty-one, but in case of his dying before that age, upon trust for X., it was held that, as against X., the trustees had no authority to advance part of the capital to A., who died before attaining his majority (*y*).

10. On the principle that the court in general **cannot interfere with legal interests**, it is apprehended that a trustee for another for life only (the trustee merely taking an estate *per autre vie*) would not be justified, without the consent of the *legal* remainderman, in cutting timber which had arrived at maturity (as in Illustration 3), inasmuch as, not being the trustee for the remainderman, he could not do acts for the benefit of the estate generally which would be in derogation of the latter's legal rights (*z*); nor could he invest the proceeds so as to equitably arrange the benefit between the tenant for life and the remainderman.

(*r*) See *Walker* v. *Wetherell*, 6 V. 255.

(*w*) *Swinnock* v. *Crispe*, Free. 78; *Boyd* v. *Boyd*, L. R., 4 Eq., 305 ; *Roper-Curzon* v. *Roper-Curzon*, L. R., 11 Eq. 452.

(*x*) *Worthington* v. *McCrear*, 23 B. 81; *Re Breed*, L. R., 1 Ch. Div. 226; but under power conferred by Trustees and Mortgagees Act, 1860, trustees of settlements dated since then may allow maintenance to infants contingently entitled, *Re Cotton*, L. R., 1 Ch. Div. 232, in cases where upon their shares becoming vested they would be entitled to past income, *Re George*, L. R., 5 Ch. Div. 837.

(*y*) *Lee* v. *Brown*, 4 V. 362.

(*z*) See and consider *Seagram* v. *Knight*, L. R., 2 Ch. 630, and compare with *Waldo* v. *Waldo*, 7 Sim. 261, and *Gent* v. *Harrison*, John. 517.

ART. 44.—*Implied Powers of Trustees under recent Settlements.*

The trustees of every settlement executed since the 28th August, 1860, can exercise the powers set out in Lord Cranworth's Act in relation to the conduct of sales and exchanges of real estate, the conveyance thereof to the purchaser, and the investment of the purchase-money, and also in relation to the renewal of renewable leaseholds, the raising of money for the purposes of the settlement, the maintenance of infant cestuis que trust, and the accumulation of the income: Provided, that the settlement does not expressly negative the exercise of such powers (*a*).

OBS.—The reader must not assume that trustees of settlements prior to August, 1860, had *not* any of these powers, for, in point of fact, as we have seen, trustees possessed most of them. But the act has defined, and put into a concrete form, powers which were formerly exercisable by trustees with more or less risk, inasmuch as their exercise was not so much a matter of absolute discretion, as a question of what was, *under the circumstances*, such an act as would meet with the approval of the court. Some of the powers are however quite new, such as the power to give valid receipts for purchase-money.

———

ART. 45.—*Delegation of the Powers of a Trustee.*

A power involving the exercise of special *personal* discretion or confidence, can only be validly executed by the persons nominated for that purpose, except in cases of absolute necessity (*b*); but a

(*a*) Trustees and Mortgagees' Act, 1860 (Lord Cranworth's Act),   23 & 24 Vict. c. 145.
(*b*) *Stuart* v. *Norton*, 9 W.R. 320.

power to do a merely ministerial act, and involving
no personal discretion, may be delegated (*b*).

ILLUST.—1. Thus, a **power of leasing** cannot be delegated, for in its exercise much judgment is required. The
fitness and responsibility of the lessee, the adequacy of the
rent, the length of the term to be granted, and the nature
of the covenants, stipulations and conditions which the
lease should contain, are matters requiring knowledge and
prudence (*c*).

2. But a trustee may appoint an attorney merely **to pass the
legal estate**, as such an act involves no discretion (*d*). And
where trustees had power to elect a clergyman, it was held
that they could not appoint proxies *to vote;* but when the
choice was once made, they could appoint proxies for the
purpose of signing the formal presentation (*e*).

3. A power to give **valid receipts** and discharges is a
power involving confidence, and a receipt given by an
agent or proxy (even though he be a co-trustee) will be
invalid (*f*).

4. The rule as to the impossibility of delegating discretionary or confidential powers is so stringent, that where a
settlement contains no power to appoint new trustees *with
similar* powers to those conferred on the trustees appointed
by the settlor, it is **not even competent for the court** to
confer such powers upon new trustees, save only where the
power is *so interwoven with the trust itself, that there can
be no execution of the trust without the exercise of the power,*
in which case the power must of *necessity* be exercised by
the new trustees (*g*).

5. Thus, where there are trustees for sale, with a power
to give valid discharges for the purchase-money, and it

(*b*) Sug. Pow. 179; Farwell,
Pow. 358, 360.
(*c*) *Robson* v. *Flight*, 4 D., J. &
S. 614.
(*d*) Farwell, Pow. 361.

(*e*) *Att.-Gen.* v. *Scott*, 1 V. sen.
413.
(*f*) *Crewe* v. *Dicken*, 4 V. 97.
(*g*) Lew. 412.

becomes necessary to appoint new trustees, the power is
properly exercisable by them; for without the power they
could not sell the property, and the settlor's intentions
would be frustrated. They therefore take the power of
necessity (*i*).

6. On the other hand, a power of distribution of the trust
property among a class, in such proportions as the trustee
should deem proper, could not, in the absence of express
directions to that effect, be executed by a new trustee.

Art. 46.—*Suspension of Trustees' Powers by Suit.*

Where a suit has been commenced for the execution
of the trust, and a decree has been made, the
trustees have no authority to exercise their powers,
except with the sanction of the court (*a*) ; but such
a suit does not take away the *legal powers* of an
executor, so as to invalidate the title of persons
claiming under a disposition made by him in exercise of those powers, where no injunction has been
granted, and no receiver appointed, and the alienee
has no notice of any actual breach of trust (*b*) ; nor
does a decree absolve a trustee from the performance of his *duties* (*c*). *v. Swin 477, 515.*

ILLUST.—1. Thus a trustee cannot prosecute or defend
legal proceedings (*d*), nor execute a power of sale (*e*), nor
make repairs (*f*), nor invest (*g*), nor exercise any other
power, after a decree in an administration suit, without
applying to the court to sanction his doing so.

2. In *Berry* v. *Gibbons* (*h*), on the other hand, a decree

(*i*) *Ib.*; *Drayson* v. *Pocock*, 4
Sim. 283; *Byam* v. *Byam*, 19 B.
58; *Bartley* v. *Bartley*, 3 Dr. 385;
Lord v. *Bunn*, 2 Y. & C. 98.

(*a*) *Mitchelson* v. *Piper*, 8 Sim.
64; *Shewen* v. *Vanderhorst*, 2 R.
& M. 75; *Minors* v. *Battison*, L.
R., 1 Ap. Cas. 428.

(*b*) *Berry* v. *Gibbons*, L. R., 8

Ch. 747.
(*c*) *Garner* v. *Moore*, 3 Dr. 277.
(*d*) *Jones* v. *Powell*, 4 B. 96.
(*e*) *Walker* v. *Smallwood*, Amb.
676.
(*f*) *Mitchelson* v. *Piper*, *sup.*
(*g*) *Bethell* v. *Abraham*, L. R.,
17 Eq. 24.
(*h*) *Supra.*

had been made in a creditors' suit, for the administration of the *personal* estate of a testator, but no receiver had been appointed, nor any injunction granted to restrain the executrix from dealing with the assets. More than two years after the decree, the executrix, who was also the sole legatee, opened an account with a bank *as* such executrix. The account becoming overdrawn, she deposited with the bank a picture, belonging to the testator's estate, by way of security. It was contended, that although the bank had no notice of the suit, yet that it being a lis pendens, they ought to have searched the register. But Lord Justice James said: "In my opinion, the executrix had the legal right to make such a deposit. In order to deprive them (the bank) of the benefit of it, there must be evidence to show that they had notice of there being some breach of trust in the transaction. Now it appears to me that the bankers did nothing but what was in the usual course of business, and that there is nothing to fix them with any notice of a breach of trust. The doctrine of lis pendens has no bearing on the case; for a mere administration decree, no receiver having been appointed, nor any injunction granted to prevent the executrix from dealing with the assets, would not take away her legal powers so as to invalidate the title of persons claiming under a disposition made by her in exercise of those powers."

SUB-DIVISION V.

THE AUTHORITY OF THE CESTUIS QUE TRUST.

ART. 47.—*The Authority of the Cestui que trust in a Simple Trust.*

THE cestui que trust in a simple trust is entitled to have the legal estate vested in him or his as-signee (*a*).

ART. 48.—*The Authority of One of several Cestuis que trust partially interested in a Special Trust.*

The authority of one of several cestuis que trust in a special trust, who is only partially and not abso-lutely entitled to the trust property, in general depends upon the terms of the trust as construed by the court; but if sui juris, the cestui que trust cannot be restrained from assigning his or her interest, save only in the case of a married woman, who may by apt words in the settlement be re-strained from doing so during her coverture, but not afterwards (*b*).

ILLUST.—1. In *Tidd* v. *Lister* (*c*), real and personal pro-perty was devised and bequeathed to trustees, upon trust to pay debts and funeral expenses, to keep the buildings on the real estate insured, to satisfy the premiums upon certain policies effected on the lives of the testator's sons, to allow each of his sons an annuity, and, subject thereto, in trust for his daughter for life, with divers remainders over. The personal estate sufficed to pay all but the insurance premiums, and the daughter, who was a feme covert, filed

(*a*) *Smith* v. *Wheeler*, 1 Mod. 17; *Brown* v. *How*, Barn. 354; *Att.-Gen.* v. *Gore*, *ib.* 150; *Kaye* v. *Powell*, 1 V. 408.

(*b*) *Tybus* v. *Smith*, 3 B. C. C. 340, n.; *Re Ellis*, L. R., 17 Eq.,

409; *Horlock* v. *Horlock*, 2 D., M. & G. 644; *Tullet* v. *Armstrong*, 4 M. & C. 392; *Re Gaffee*, 1 M. & G. 547; *Buttanshaw* v. *Marten*, Johns. 89.

(*c*) 5 Mad. 429.

a bill praying to be let into possession, upon securing the amount of the premiums of the policies. But Sir John Leach refused her request, on the ground that the testator had placed the direction of the property in the hands of the trustees, which was for the advantage of those who were to take in succession, and that a court of equity ought not to disappoint the testator's intention by delivering over the possession to the tenant for life, unprotected against her natural tendency to favour herself at the expense of those in remainder. "There may be cases in which it is plain, from the expressions in the will, that the testator did not intend the property should remain under the personal management of the trustees: there may be cases in which it is plain from the nature of the property that the testator could not mean to exclude the cestui que trust for life from the personal possession of the property; as in the case of a family residence. There may be very special cases in which the court would deliver the possession of the property to the cestui que trust for life, although the testator's intention appeared to be that it should remain with the trustees; as where the personal occupation of the trust property is beneficial to the cestui que trust, in which case the court, by taking means to secure the due protection of those in remainder, would, in substance, be performing the trust according to the intention of the testator."

2. The interest of a cestui que trust (save only in the case of a married woman during her coverture) **cannot be made inalienable** (*d*), except by means of a shifting clause giving it over, or practically giving it over, to some other person upon alienation (*e*); in which case, the real interest of the cestui que trust is merely contingent. The contingency upon which it ceases being an attempt at

(*d*) *Snowdon* v. *Dales*, 6 Sim. 524; *Green* v. *Spicer*, 1 R. & M. 395; *Brandon* v. *Robinson*, 18 V. 429; *Hood* v. *Oglander*, 34 B. 513.

(*e*) See *Oldham* v. *Oldham*, L. R., 3 Eq. 404; *Billson* v. *Crofts*, L. R., 15 Eq. 314; *Re Aylwin*, L. R., 16 Eq. 585; *Ex parte Eyston*, L. R., 7 Ch. Div. 145.

alienation, it follows that he has nothing to alien. But
where he has an interest, and there is a mere restraint
on alienation, without any new trust being raised by an
attempt at alienation, the restraint is wholly nugatory.
For instance, a trust to apply income for another's maintenance entitles him to have the income paid to him or to
his alienee; for no one in remainder is injured by it (*f*).

3. Even where a **married woman who is tenant in tail**
for her separate use is restrained from anticipation, she can
bar the entail and turn her estate into a fee simple; for
she does not thereby anticipate her interest, but only
enlarges it. As was said by Sir G. Jessel, M. R., in *Cooper*
v. *Macdonald* (*g*), "What is the meaning of the fetter?
The meaning is exactly that which was expressed by the
old common form of conveyancers, 'so as in nowise to
deprive herself of the benefit thereof by way of anticipation.' The meaning was to give the actual enjoyment to
the married woman for her own benefit, not for the benefit
of anybody else; and it is absurd, it appears to me, to
extend such an equitable provision as this, so as to prevent
a married woman enlarging the estate tail into an estate
in fee simple for her own benefit. That is not an alienation so as to deprive herself of anything. . . . Why should
I construe that clause against anticipation—which was in-
vented by a Lord Chancellor for the benefit of a married
woman—to her damage and injury?"

ART. 49.—*The Authority of the Cestuis que trust collec-
tively in a special Trust.*

If there is only one cestui que trust, or several
cestuis que trust all of one mind, and he or they
are sui juris, the specific performance of the trust
may be arrested, and the trust modified, or turned

(*f*) *Younghusband* v. *Gisborne*, (*g*) L. R., 7 Ch. Div. 292.
1 Coll. 400.

into a simple trust; for the cestuis que trust are in equity the absolute owners (*a*), save only in the case of a married woman restrained from anticipation, who is during her coverture incapable of dealing with her interest (*b*).

ILLUST.—1. Thus where a testator gave his residuary personal estate to J. J., an infant, and directed his executors to place it out at interest to accumulate, and to pay the principal to the infant on his **attaining twenty-four**, and in the meantime to allow 60*l.* a year for his maintenance, and the testator gave the residue over on the infant's dying under twenty-one; the court held that the residue was absolutely given to the infant on his attaining twenty-one, and that, therefore, he was entitled to have the residue and accumulations at once transferred to him (*c*).

2. And so in *Magrath* v. *Morehead* (*d*), the settlor by his will directed his property to be divided into nine shares, and gave one and a half share to each of his two daughters, "**to be settled** on themselves at their marriage." The two daughters having attained twenty-one, and being unmarried, it was held that they were entitled to their shares absolutely.

3. In *Gosling* v. *Gosling* (*e*), a testator by codicil, after devising an estate in Surrey to his trustees, upon trust for certain persons, concluded as follows : " It is my particular desire, that no one shall be put in possession of my estate, or shall enjoy the rent, dividends and profits of any part thereof, or of any property left by my will or codicil, until he shall **attain the age of twenty-five** years; and in the meantime the rents, dividends, and profits to accumulate." A devisee claimed to have the estate transferred to him before attaining twenty-five, and Vice-Chancellor Page Wood said : " The principle of this court has always been

(*a*) Lew. 569, and see cases quoted as examples.
(*b*) *Stanley* v. *Stanley*, L. R., 7 Ch. Div. 589; and cases cited *sup.*

Art. 48, n. (*b*).
(*c*) *Josselyn* v. *Josselyn*, 9 Sim. 63.
(*d*) L. R., 12 Eq. 491.
(*e*) Johns. 265.

to recognize the right of all persons who attain the age of
twenty-one to enter upon the absolute use and enjoyment
of the property given to them by a will, notwithstanding
any directions by the testator to the effect that they are
not to enjoy it until a later age, unless, during the interval,
the property is given for the benefit of another. If the
property is once theirs, it is useless for the testator to
attempt to impose any fetter upon their enjoyment of it
in full, so soon as they attain twenty-one. And upon that
principle, unless there is in the will, or in some codicil to
it, a clear indication of an intention on the part of the
testator, not only that his devisees are not to have the enjoyment of the property he has devised to them, until they
attain twenty-five, but that some other person is to have
that enjoyment, or unless the property is so clearly taken
away from the devisees up to the time of their attaining
twenty-five, as to induce the court to hold that, as to the
previous rents and profits, there has been an intestacy, the
court does not hesitate to strike out of the will any direction
that the devisees shall not enjoy it in full until they attain
the age of twenty-five years." The learned Vice-Chancellor
therefore allowed the plaintiff's claim.

4. Again, in *Re Brown* (*f*) there was a bequest of consols
in trust to **purchase a life annuity** for a lady, to be held
for her separate use without power of anticipation ; and in
case of her illness or incapacity, the testator gave the
trustees a discretionary power as to the application of the
annuity for her maintenance. The legatee *being unmarried*,
and the restraint on anticipation being therefore nugatory,
it was held that she was entitled to a transfer of the
consols (*g*).

5. A similar result follows where the legatee, restrained

(*f*) 27 B. 324.
(*g*) See also *Tullett* v. *Armstrong*, 4 M. & C. 377; *Buttanshaw* v. *Martin*, Johns. 89; *Wright*
v. *Wright*, 2 J. & H. 655; *Cooke*
v. *Fuller*, 26 B. 99 ; *Barton* v.
Briseoe, Jac. 603 ; *Re Gaffee*, 1
M. & G. 547 ; *Re Linyee*, 23 B.
241.

from anticipating, becomes discovert afterwards (h), or is divorced, or about to be divorced (i), or has a protection order under 20 & 21 Vict. c. 85 (k), and à fortiori where she is judicially separated by a magistrate's order under 41 Vict. c. 19, s. 4.

6. So where a testatrix gave a sum of 20,000l. stock, to be laid out by the trustees of her will in the purchase of a government annuity, in the name and for the benefit of her godson for the term of his natural life, and directed that the annuitant should not be entitled to have the value of his annuity in lieu thereof, and that if he should sell it, it should cease, and form part of her residuary estate, it was held that the annuitant was absolutely entitled to the annuity, and that he could make a good title to it to a purchaser (l).

7. On similar principles, where an estate is directed to be sold and the proceeds to be divided amongst several persons, no one singly can elect that his own share shall not be disposed of, but shall remain realty (m); for the other undivided shares would not sell so beneficially; but if all of them agree to take the land unconverted, they can insist upon their right to do so (n).

(h) Buttanshaw v. Martin, sup.
(i) Re Linyee, sup.
(k) Cooke v. Fuller, sup.
(l) Hunt v. Foulston, L. R., 3 Ch. Div. 285.

(m) Lew. 784; Holloway v. Radcliffe, 23 B. 163.
(n) Harcourt v. Seymour, 2 Sim., N. S. 45; Cookson v. Reay, 5 B. 22; Dixon v. Gayfere, 17 B. 433.

SUB-DIVISION VI.

THE DEATH, RETIREMENT, OR REMOVAL OF A TRUSTEE,
AND THE EFFECT THEREOF IN RELATION TO THE
OFFICE OF TRUSTEE.

ART. 50.—*Survivorship of the Authority and Powers of
the Trustees.*

UPON the death of a trustee, the office, as well as the
estate, survives to the remaining trustees (*a*); and
notwithstanding that there is a power for the
appointment of new trustees (*b*), the survivors can
carry out the trust and exercise all such powers as
are necessary for the carrying out of the trust (*c*),
unless there be something in the settlement which
specially manifests an intention to the contrary (*d*).

ILLUST.—Thus where there was a devise and bequest of
freehold and other property, and all other the testator's
real and personal estate to two persons, their executors and
administrators, upon trust, by sale or otherwise at their
discretion, to raise and invest a certain sum of money and
apply the interest as therein directed, and one of the
trustees died, and the other proceeded to sell the estate;
it was held, on an objection to the title, that the surviving
trustee might exercise the option of selling and the power
of sale; and the Vice-Chancellor said: "The argument proceeds, as it appears to me, on an entire disregard of the
distinction between powers and trusts. No doubt where it

(*a*) *Warburton* v. *Sandys*, 14
Sim. 622; *Eyre* v. *Countess of
Shaftesbury*, 2 P. W. 121—124.
(*b*) *Warburton* v. *Sandys, sup.*
(*c*) *Lane* v. *Debenham*, 11 Ha.
188; *Eyre* v. *Countess of Shaftes-*

bury, sup.; Re Cooke's Contract,
L. R., 4 Ch. Div. 454.
(*d*) *Foley* v. *Wortner*, 2 J. & W.
245; and see *Jacob* v. *Lucas*, 1 B.
436.

is a naked power given to two persons, that will not survive to one of them unless there be express words or a necessary implication. . . . When, on the other hand, a testator gives his property, not to one party subject to a power in others, but to trustees upon special trusts, with a direction to carry his purposes into effect, it is the duty of the trustee to execute the trust. If an estate be devised to A. and B. upon trust to sell, and thereby raise such a sum, it is, I think, a novel argument, that after A.'s death B. cannot sell the estate and execute the trust" (e).

ART. 51.—*Devolution of the Office of Executive Trustee on Death of the last Survivor.*

Upon the death of a last surviving trustee, intestate as to the trust estate, it depends upon the language of the settlement whether his heir or personal representative, as the case may be, can execute a special trust. If it is to be collected from the settlement that the office was intended to be a personal one, it does not devolve on the heir or personal representative. If, on the other hand, the trust is directed to be performed by the trustee, *his heirs, executors, &c.*, it will devolve on those persons.

ILLUST.—1. Thus where the settlor gives personal property to A. B. upon certain trusts, then upon the death of A. B., although the *estate* vests in his executor, the latter will be unable to execute the trusts; for, as was said by Lord Cottenham in *Mortimer* v. *Ireland* (a), "whether the property is real or personal is no matter; for suppose a man appoints a trustee of real and personal estate simpliciter, adding nothing more, this cannot make his representative a trustee. . . . The property may vest in the

(e) *Lane* v. *Debenham, sup.;* and (a) 11 Jur. 721.
Re Cooke's Contract, sup.

representative, but that is quite another question from his
being trustee."

2. But where leaseholds were assigned to two trustees,
their executors and administrators, then upon the death of
the survivor, his executors or administrators can carry out
the trust, unless (it is said) he has himself expressly or
impliedly forbidden the doing so, as by bequeathing the
leaseholds to another, and so going out of his way to
prevent them devolving upon the executors or administrators (z).

ART. 52.—*Devise of the Office of Trustee.*

When a last surviving executive trustee devises the
trust property, the devisee can only execute the
trust if it was by the settlement confided to the
trustees *and their assigns* (a). In the absence of
these words, new trustees must be appointed (b).

ILLUST.—1. Thus if the settlor vest the trust property in
A. and his heirs, upon trust that A. and his heirs shall sell,
and A. dies and devises the trust property to B., new trustees must be appointed to carry out the sale; for B. cannot
sell, inasmuch as there was no power given by the settlement to A.'s assigns to carry out the trust; and A.'s heir
cannot sell, because by devising the estate to B., A. deprived him of the character of heir (c).

2. And so again, where (d) personalty was assigned to
trustees, their executors and administrators, in trust, and
the surviving trustee bequeathed it to A. and B., and
appointed A., B. and C. his executors, it was held that A.
and B. could not execute the trust, for the trustee had no
power to bequeath it; nor could A., B. and C. as executors

(z) See per Kindersley, V.-C., *Re Burtt*, 1 Dr. 319.
(a) *Hall* v. *May*, 3 K. & J.
585; *Titley* v. *Wolstenholme*, 7 B.
425; *Saloway* v. *Strawbridge*, 1 K.
& J. 371.
(b) See *Re Burtt*, 1 Dr. 319.
(c) *Cook* v. *Crawford*, 13 Sim. 91.
(d) *Re Burtt*, *sup.*

execute it, for by bequeathing the property to A. and B. alone, the trustee had deprived his executors of the trust. It is suggested that where *real* property is vested in one and his heirs, upon trust that he and *his executors* carry out certain directions, and the trustee devises it to another, such devise, although nugatory, would not deprive the executors of the trust; for it would not deprive them of the estate, which would, in the absence of the devise, have descended to the heir and not devolved upon them.

3. Where the trust property was confided to a trustee, his heirs *and assigns*, it was held, that although the settlement contained a power to appoint new trustees, the word *assigns* might reasonably be construed to give the trustee a discretionary power of preventing the inconvenience which might attend the devolution of the trust upon his heir (*z*).

Art. 53.—*Retirement and Removal of a Trustee.*

Where the settlement contains no power to appoint new trustees, *and* it is dated before the 28th day of August, 1860 (*a*), a trustee can only be discharged from his office—

α. With the consent of himself and all his cestuis que trust, who must, in order to give a valid consent, be sui juris (*b*); or

β. By the court, which will act at the instance of the trustee, or at the instance of any of the cestuis que trust where the trustee has behaved improperly (*c*), or is incapable of acting properly (*d*), or is a felon (*e*), or a bankrupt (*f*), or is residing

(*z*) *Hall* v. *May, sup.*; see Mr. Lewin's observations on this case, Trusts, 204.

(*a*) Lord Cranworth's Act, 23 & 24 Vict. c. 145, s. 37, which implies a power to appoint new trustees in settlements executed after the 28th August, 1860.

(*b*) *Wilkinson* v. *Parry*, 4 Russ. 276.

(*c*) *Millard* v. *Eyre*, 2 V. 94; *Paliaret* v. *Carew*, 32 B. 567.

(*d*) *Buchanan* v. *Hamilton*, 5 V. 722.

(*e*) 15 & 16 Vict. c. 55, s. 32.

(*f*) 32 & 33 Vict. c. 71, s. 32; *Re Barker*, L. R., 1 Ch. Div. 43.

abroad (*g*), or cannot be heard of (*h*). And the court can discharge an old trustee without necessarily appointing a new one in his place, if it be difficult or impossible to do so (*i*). The costs of the application will come out of the estate if the trustee is justified in retiring (*k*), or where the removal is not caused by impropriety on his part.

ILLUST.—The only points in this article which need illustration are the circumstances which will **justify a trustee in retiring**. In *Forshaw* v. *Higginson* (*l*), the late Master of the Rolls said : " It is quite settled that a trustee cannot from mere caprice retire from the performance of his trust without paying the costs occasioned by that act ; it is also quite clear, that any circumstances arising in the administration of the trust which have altered the nature of his duties justify him in leaving it, and entitle him to receive his costs ; but I think that to justify him in that course the circumstances must be such *as arise out of the administration of the trust, and not those relating to himself individually.* Here the circumstances which in my opinion justify his saying, ' I cannot proceed with the administration of the trust with my co-trustee,' arose out of his private circumstances, not out of the administration of the trust. If, therefore, on the application of the trustee to be discharged, the cestuis que trust had said, ' You must pay the cost of the appointment of new trustees,' which would have been the mere cost of an indorsement on a deed, and he had refused to do this, I should not have supported him in instituting a suit by giving him the costs thereby occasioned. But that is not the present case. . . . . *No person can be compelled to remain a trustee* and act in the

(*g*) *Buchanan* v. *Hamilton, sup.;* *Re Bignold,* L. R., 7 Ch. 223.

(*h*) *Re Harrison,* 22 L. J., Ch. 69.

(*i*) *Re Stokes,* L. R., 13 Eq. 333.

(*k*) *Coventry* v. *Coventry,* 1 Kee. 758 ; *Greenwood* v. *Wakeford,* 1 B. 581; *Forshaw* v. *Higginson,* 20 B. 485 ; *Re Stokes, sup.;* and see *Barker* v. *Peile,* 2 Dr. & S. 340.

(*l*) *Supra.*

execution of the trust. As already stated, if the circumstances preventing his continuing to perform his duties arose from any act of his own, or anything relating to himself, I think he ought to pay the costs of the appointment of a new trustee; but if the persons upon whom the appointment of a new trustee depends absolutely refuse to take steps for that purpose, what is he to do? In my opinion, the only course he could take was to say what every trustee may say, 'I will apply to, and have the trust executed by the court, and I will ask to be discharged from the trusts as incidental to that relief.'"

ART. 54.—*Appointment of new Trustees by the Court.*

Whenever it is expedient to appoint a trustee or trustees, whether of a settlement of which no trustees were originally appointed (*a*), or the original trustees of which have died, retired, or been removed, and it is found inexpedient, difficult, or impracticable to do so without the assistance of the court, the court may appoint such a trustee or trustees (*b*), and may, by order, vest in such new trustees or trustee any lands (*c*) subject to the trust (*d*), and the right to call for the transfer of any stock, or to receive the dividends thereof, and the right to sue for and recover any chose in action, or any interest in respect thereof (*e*).

ART. 55.—*Express Power to appoint new Trustees.*

Where there is an express power to appoint new trustees contained in the settlement (and such a

(*a*) *Dodkin* v. *Brunt*, L. R., 6 Eq. 580; *D'Adhemar* v. *Bertrand*, 35 B. 19; and see 15 & 16 Vict. c. 55, s. 9.

(*b*) 13 & 14 Vict. c. 60, ss. 32, 33.

(*c*) Quære, leaseholds; see *Re Mundel*, 6 Jur., N. S. 880, and *Re Robinson*, 9 Jur., N. S. 885.

(*d*) 13 & 14 Vict. c. 60, s. 34.

(*e*) *Ib.*, s. 35.

power is implied in every settlement executed since the 28th August, 1860 (*a*), such a power must be executed strictly (*b*). But unless there clearly appears to be an intention to the contrary (*c*), the original number of trustees may be increased or diminished (*d*).

ILLUST.—1. Thus, where the power was vested in "the surviving or continuing trustees or trustee, or the heirs, executors, or administrators of the last surviving and continuing trustee," and the two trustees were desirous of retiring, it was held that they could not do so by appointing two new trustees in their place by one deed, but that one must appoint a new trustee in the place of the first retiring trustee, and then the new trustee must appoint one in the place of the second retiring trustee (*e*). This case is a singular instance of that verbal subtlety which makes men of the world so distrustful of legal interpretation. It all turned upon the idea, that trustees who were *about to retire could not be said to be continuing*, but that if one retired first, the other would be a continuing trustee, although he might intend to retire the next day. If, in addition to the words "surviving and continuing," the words "or other trustee or trustees" had been added, the two retiring trustees might have appointed two new ones by the same deed (*f*).

2. So again, the words "unfit and incapable" are very strictly construed. Thus, where a new trustee was to be appointed if a trustee became incapable of acting, it was held that the bankruptcy of one of the trustees did not fulfil the condition, as it only rendered him *unfit* but not

(*a*) 23 & 24 Vict. c. 145, s. 27.
(*b*) See *Stones* v. *Rowton*, 17 B. 30.
(*c*) See *Emmett* v. *Clarke*, 3 Gif. 32; *Lord Lonsdale* v. *Beckett*, 4 D. & J. 255.
(*d*) *Meinertzhagen* v. *Davis*, 1 Coll. 335; *Millar* v. *Priddon*, 1 D., M. & G. 335; *Re Bathurst*, 2 S. & G. 169.
(*e*) *Stones* v. *Rowton*, *sup.;* but comp. *Cafe* v. *Bent*, 5 Ha. 24.
(*f*) *Lord Camoys* v. *Best*, 19 B. 414.

incapable (*g*). And so where the words were "unable to act," it was held that absence in China or Australia did not *disable* (*h*), although it clearly unfitted (*i*) a trustee for the office.

(*g*) *Turner* v. *Maule*, 15 Jur. 761; see *Re Watts*, 9 Ha. 106.

(*h*) *Withington* v. *Withington*, 16 Sim. 104; *Re Harrison*, 22 L. J., Ch. 69; but see *Re Bignold*, L. R., 7 Ch. 223.

(*i*) *Mennard* v. *Welford*, 1 Sm. & G. 426. A mere temporary absence abroad would not unfit a trustee for the office. *Re Moravia Society*, 4 Jur., N. S. 703.

SUB-DIVISION VII.

The Protection and Relief accorded to Trustees.

Art. 56.—*Reimbursement of Expenses.*

Whether the settlement provides for the reimbursement of the trustee's expenses or not, he is entitled to be reimbursed all expenses which he has properly paid or incurred in the execution of the trust (*a*); and until they are paid he has a lien for them on the trust property (*b*). The question as to what expenses are, and what are not, properly incurred, depends upon the circumstances of each particular case (*c*).

Illust.—1. Thus, in *Bennett* v. *Wyndham* (*d*), a trustee in the due execution of his trust directed a bailiff employed on the trust property to have certain trees felled. The bailiff ordered the wood-cutters usually employed on the property to fell the trees, in doing which they negligently allowed a bough to fall on to a passer-by, who, being injured, recovered heavy **damages from the trustee** in a court of law. These damages were, however, allowed to the trustee out of the trust property, the Lord Justice Knight Bruce saying: "The trustee in this case seems to have meant well, to have acted with due diligence, and to have employed a proper agent to do an act, the directing which to be done was within the due discharge of his duty. The agent makes a mistake, the consequences of which subject the trustee to legal liability to a third party. I am

(*a*) *Worral* v. *Harford*, 8 V. 8; *Morrison* v. *Morrison*, 4 K. & J. 458.

(*b*) *Ex parte James*, 1 D. & C. 272; *Ex parte Chippendale*, 4 D.,

M. & G. 19; and see *Walters* v. *Woodbridge*, L. R., 7 Ch. Div. 504.

(*c*) *Leedham* v. *Chawner*, 4 K. & J. 458.

(*d*) 4 D., F. & J. 259.

of opinion that this liability ought, as between the trustee and the estate, to be borne by the estate."

2. So again, a trustee or executor will be allowed the amount of a **solicitor's bill** of costs which he has paid for services rendered in the matter of the trust (*e*).

3. But where a receiver (who is, of course, a constructive trustee) made several **journeys** to Paris, in order that he might be present at the hearing of a suit brought in the French courts in relation to the trust property, and it appeared that his presence was wholly needless, the whole question being one of French law, and not of fact, his travelling expenses were disallowed, on the ground that they were under the circumstances improperly incurred (*f*).

4. And so where trustees attempted, at the solicitation of their cestuis que trust, *some of whom were married women without power of anticipation*, to sell the trust property before the date named in the settlement, it was held that they were not entitled to be indemnified against the costs of an action for specific performance brought against them by the purchaser (*g*).

––––––

ART. 57.—*Protection against the Acts of Co-trustee.*

A trustee is not answerable for the receipts, acts, or defaults of his co-trustee (*a*), save only:—

α. Where he has *handed* the trust property to him without seeing to its proper application.

β. Where he allows him to *receive* the trust property without making due inquiry as to his dealing with it.

γ. Where he becomes aware of a breach of trust, either committed or meditated, and abstains from taking the needful steps to obtain restitution and redress, or to prevent the meditated wrong.

(*e*) *Macnamara* v. *Jones*, Dick. 587.

(*f*) *Malcolm* v. *O'Callaghan*, 3 M. & C. 62.

(*g*) *Leedham* v. *Chawner, sup.*

(*a*) *Dawson* v. *Clarke*, 18 V. 254; and as to settlements made since, see 22 & 23 Vict. c. 35, s. 31.

And even in these three cases he may, by express
declaration in the settlement, be made irresponsible (*b*).

ILLUST.—Thus in the case of *Wilkins* v. *Hogg* (*c*), which
now governs the subject, a testatrix, after appointing
three trustees, declared that each of them should be
answerable only for losses arising from his own default
and not for involuntary acts or for the acts or defaults of
his co-trustees, and particularly that any trustee who
should pay over to his co-trustees, or should do or concur
in any act enabling his co-trustees to receive any monies for
the general purposes of her will, should not be obliged to see
to the due application thereof, nor should such trustee be
subsequently rendered liable by any express notice or inti-
mation of the actual misapplication of the same monies. The
three trustees joined in signing and giving receipts to two
insurance companies for two sums of money paid by them,
but two of the trustees permitted their co-trustee to obtain
the money without ascertaining whether he had invested
it. This trustee having misapplied it, it was sought to
make his co-trustees responsible, but Lord Westbury held
that they were not; saying, "There are three modes in
which a trustee would become liable according to the
ordinary rules of law—first, where, being the recipient, he
hands over the money without securing its due application;
secondly, where he allows a co-trustee to receive money
without making due inquiry as to his dealing with it; and
thirdly, where he becomes aware of a breach of trust,
either committed or meditated, and abstains from taking
the needful steps to obtain restitution or redress. The
framer of the clause under examination knew these three
rules, and used words sufficient to meet all these cases.

(*b*) As to the whole of the article, see judgment of Westbury,
L. C., in *Wilkins* v. *Hogg*, 3 Giff.
116; 8 Jur., N. S. 25; and see

also *Dix* v. *Burford*, 19 B. 409;
Macklow v. *Fuller*, Jac.198; *Brumridge* v. *Brumridge*, 27 B. 5.
(*c*) *Supra*.

There remained therefore only personal misconduct, in respect of which a trustee acting under this will would be responsible. He would still be answerable for collusion if he handed over trust money to his co-trustee with reasonable ground for believing or suspicion that that trustee would commit a breach of trust; but no such case as this was made by the bill."

ART. 58.—*Trustee without Notice not bound to pay to Persons claiming through Cestui que trust.*

If the person who is really entitled to trust property is not the cestui que trust who appears on the face of the settlement, but some one who claims through him, and the trustees, having neither express nor constructive notice of such derivative title, pay upon the footing of the original title, they cannot be made to pay over again (*a*).

ILLUST.—Thus, in *Leslie* v. *Baillie* (*b*), a testator, who died and whose will was proved in England, bequeathed a legacy to a married woman, whose domicile, as well as that of her husband, was in Scotland. The husband died a few months after the testator, without having received the legacy. After his decease the executors of the testator, with knowledge of the before-mentioned circumstances of domicile, paid the legacy to the widow. It was proved that, according to the Scotch law, the payment should have been made to the husband's personal representatives. It was however held, that in the absence of proof that the executors of the settlor knew the Scotch law on the subject, the payment to the widow was a good payment.

(*a*) Lew. 579; *Cothay* v. *Sydenham*, 2 B. C. C. 391; *Leslie* v.   *Baillie*, 2 Y. & C. C. 91.
(*b*) *Supra.*

ART. 59.—*Concurrence of or Release by the Cestuis que trust.*

A cestui que trust who has assented to or concurred in a breach of trust (*a*), or who has subsequently released or confirmed it (*b*), cannot afterwards charge the trustees with it : Provided—

α. That the cestui que trust was sui juris at the date of such assent or release (*c*) ;

β. That he had full knowledge of the facts and knew what he was doing (*d*), and the legal effect thereof (*e*) ;

γ. That no undue influence was brought to bear upon him in order to extort the assent or release (*f*).

A cestui que trust, however, who is *not* sui juris, and who concurs in a breach of trust, may bind himself from afterwards charging the trustees if he employ fraud (*g*); save only where the cestui que trust is a married woman without power of alienation (*h*).

ILLUST.—1. Stock was settled on a married woman for her separate use for life, with a power of appointment by will. The trustees, at the instance of the husband, sold out the stock and paid the proceeds to him. The wife filed a bill to compel the trustees to replace the stock, and obtained a decree, under which the trustees transferred part

(*a*) *Brice* v. *Stokes*, 11 V. 319; *Wilkinson* v. *Parry*, 4 Russ. 272; *Nail* v. *Punter*, 5 Sim. 555; *Life Association of Scotland* v. *Siddal*, 3 De G. & J. 74; *Walker* v. *Symonds*, 3 Sw. 64.

(*b*) *French* v. *Hobson*, 9 V. 103; *Wilkinson* v. *Parry, sup.; Creswell* v. *Dewell*, 4 Giff. 465.

(*c*) *Underwood* v. *Stevens*, 1 Mer. 717; *Leach* v. *Leach*, 10 V. 517; *Lord Montford* v. *Cadogan*, 19 V. 9.

(*d*) *Buckeridge* v. *Glass*, 1 Cr. & Ph. 135; *Hughes* v. *Wills*, 9 Ha. 773; *Cockerill* v. *Cholmeley*, 1 R. & M. 425; *Strange* v. *Fooks*, 4 Giff. 408; *Murch* v. *Russell*, 3 M.

& C. 31; *Aveline* v. *Melhuish*, 2 D., J. & S. 614.

(*e*) *Cockerill* v. *Cholmeley, sup.; Marker* v. *Marker*, 9 Ha. 16; *Burrows* v. *Walls*, 5 D., M. & G. 254; *Stafford* v. *Stafford*, 1 D. & J. 202; *Strange* v. *Fooks, sup.*

(*f*) *Bowles* v. *Stewart*, 1 Sch. & Lef. 226; *Chesterfield* v. *Janssen*, 2 V. 158.

(*g*) *Lord Montford* v. *Cadogan, sup.; Sharpe* v. *Foy*, L. R., 4 Ch. 35; *Re Lush, ibid.* 591.

(*h*) *Arnold* v. *Woodhams*, L. R., 16 Eq. 33; *Stanley* v. *Stanley*, L. R., 7 Ch. Div. 589.

of the stock into court, and were allowed time to retransfer the remainder. The wife then died, having by her will appointed the stock to the husband. He then filed a bill against the trustees, claiming the stock under the appointment, and praying for the same relief as his wife might have had. It is needless to say that his claim was promptly rejected (*i*).

2. A formal release under seal, or an express confirmation, will of course estop a cestui que trust from instituting subsequent proceedings; and it would seem that any positive act or expression indicative of a clear intention to waive a breach of trust, will, *if supported by valuable consideration (however slight)*, be equivalent to a release (*k*).

3. An **infant or a feme covert** (unless in respect of her *separate estate* vested in her unreservedly (*l*)) cannot loose his or her right to relief, either by concurrence or release. And it has been considered that where a trust fund was settled upon trust for such persons as a feme covert should appoint, and in the meantime to her for her separate use for life, and she acquiesced in a breach of trust, her appointees could claim relief although she herself could not (*m*). It is, however, submitted that this case was wrongly decided, inasmuch as a feme covert, with a general power of appointment, is practically as much the absolute owner of the property as if it were conveyed to her absolutely; and indeed this latter view has been since adopted (*n*).

4. Where, however, property is settled upon a married woman simply, and not to her separate use, or where it is settled to her separate use, but she is restrained from

(*i*) *Nail* v. *Punter*. 5 Sim. 555.

(*k*) See *Stackhouse* v. *Barnston*, 10 V. 456; per Sir W. Grant and *Farrant* v. *Blanchford*, 11 W. R. 178; and Lew. 755.

(*l*) *Brewer* v. *Swirles*, 2 Sm. & G. 219; *Fletcher* v. *Green*, 33 B. 426; *Butler* v. *Compton*, L. R.. 7 Eq. 16; *Jones* v. *Higgins*, L. R.,

2 Eq. 538: *Taylor* v. *Cartwright*, L. R., 14 Eq. 175.

(*m*) *Kellaway* v. *Johnson*, 5 B. 319; *Vaughan* v. *Vanderstegen*, 2 Drew. 165.

(*n*) *Jones* v. *Higgins*, *supra*; and *Chartered Bank of Australia* v. *Lempriere*, L. R., 4 P. C. 596.

alienating or anticipating it (o), she is not competent to consent to or to release a breach of trust, and her concurrence or release will afford no protection to the trustee. For instance, where money is settled upon a husband for life, remainder to his wife for life or absolutely, her concurrence in a breach of trust during the life of her husband would have no effect. Neither would it if she were the tenant in possession to her separate use if she were restrained from anticipation; for, as was said by Vice-Chancellor Malins in *Stanley* v. *Stanley* (p), "In no case, and by no device whatever, can the restraint upon anticipation be evaded." The principle was very vigorously expressed by Lord Langdale in *Tyler* v. *Tyler* (q), in a passage which ought to be learnt by heart by every trustee. "We find," said his lordship, "a married woman throwing herself at the feet of the trustee, begging and entreating him to advance a sum of money out of the trust fund, to save her husband and her family from utter ruin, and making out a most plausible case for that purpose; his compassionate feelings are worked upon, he raises and advances the money, the object for which it was given entirely fails, the husband becomes bankrupt, and in a few months the very same woman who induced the trustee to do this, files a bill in the Court of Chancery to compel him to make good that loss to the trust. These are cases which, when they happen, shock everybody's feelings at the time; *but it is necessary that relief should be given in such cases, for if relief were not given, and if such rights were not strictly maintained, no such things as a trust could ever be preserved."*

5. A married woman is, however, legally responsible for a fraud, and *her ordinary* incapacity will not avail her; but if the property were settled upon her *without power of anticipation,* her fraud will not prejudice her (r). A settle-

(o) *Stanley* v. *Stanley,* L. R., 7 Ch. Div. 589.
(p) *Supra.*

(q) 3 B. 563.
(r) *Stanley* v. *Stanley, sup.*

ment was made on the marriage of a female infant,
whereby the husband covenanted to *induce* her to settle
her real estate upon attaining twenty-one, and to concur
in such settlement himself. He neglected to do so however, and they subsequently mortgaged the real estate, but
the mortgagee had no notice of the covenant until just
before the deed was acknowledged. It was held, that the
wife's fraud in not disclosing the existence of the settlement bound her estate, and bound her *not to consent* to the
settlement which the husband had covenanted that he
would induce her to settle (*s*).

ART. 60.—*Laches of the Cestuis que trust when a bar to
Relief.*

The Statutes of Limitation do not apply to declared
trusts (*a*) (except where they are created by way of
a *charge* on real estate, unconnected with a
duty (*b*)), nor to trusts which *on the face of a written
instrument* are resulting trusts (*c*), although they
are applicable to other constructive trusts (*d*) ; but
in taking an account for the purpose of charging a
trustee with personal liability, every fair allowance
ought to be made in his favour if it can be shown
that he acted bonâ fide, and that the claim sought
to be enforced is one which arose many years ago,
and one of the nature and particulars of which the
cestuis que trust was, at the time when it arose,
perfectly cognizant (*e*).

ILLUST.—1. If land be devised to a person upon trust to
receive the rents and thereout to pay certain annuities,
the surplus rents **result to the heir-at-law** upon the face of

(*s*) *Sharp* v. *Foy*, L. R., 4 Ch.
85; and see *Re Lush, ibid.* 591.
(*a*) 3 & 4 Will. 4, c. 27, s. 25.
(*b*) *Ib.* s. 40.
(*c*) Lew. 719; *Salter* v. *Cavanagh*, 1 Dr. & W. 668; *Matlow* v.
Bigg, L. R., 18 Eq. 246.

(*d*) *Beckford* v. *Wade*, 17 V. 97;
Petre v. *Petre*, 1 Dr. 371.
(*e*) See per Westbury, L. C.,
in *McDonnell* v. *White*, 11 H. L. C.
570; *Thompson* v. *Eastwood*, L. R.,
2 Ap. Ca. 215.

the instrument, and the heir-at-law is therefore not statute barred by any length of possession of the trustee (*f*).

2. But a resulting or other **constructive trust**, depending upon evidence *dehors* the written instrument, is within the statute (*g*); and so a tenant for life of leaseholds who renews in his own name (*h*), or a mortgagee in possession (even though the mortgage is in the *form* of a trust) (*i*), is entitled to the benefit of the statute.

3. **Simple charges** are, however, expressly provided for by the statutes (*k*). Where, however, a charge is so coupled with a trust as to be in reality a trust itself, the statutes do not apply. For instance, where a testator charges his property with payment of his debts, and imposes an obligation on the devisee to exert himself *actively* in paying the debts, the case will not fall within the statutes (*l*).

4. An estate is devised to A. and his heirs, charged with the payment of 500*l*. to B. and C. upon certain trusts. Here, as between A. and the two trustees, there is a mere charge; but as between the trustees and their cestuis que trust there is a trust (*m*).

5. As has been stated, even a cestui que trust of a declared trust may disentitle himself to relief by **great laches.** Thus A., being greatly in debt, executed a deed of trust for the benefit of his creditors, and among the property was the benefit of a lease for lives, renewable for ever, on which the rent reserved was a high rack rent. The tenant under this lease complained, and the trustee, with the knowledge, but without the consent, of A. (but with the consent and approbation of A.'s brother, who had the management of A.'s affairs), accepted a reduced rent. A. complained of the abatement, but took no steps to put an

(*f*) *Salter* v. *Cavanagh, sup.*
(*g*) See note (*d*), p. 160.
(*h*) *Petre* v. *Petre, sup.*
(*i*) *Locking* v. *Parker*, L. R.,
6 Ch. 30.

(*k*) 3 & 4 Will. 4, c. 27, s. 40.
(*l*) *Hunt* v. *Bateman*, 10 Ir. Rep. 360.
(*m*) Lew. 721.

end to it for some years. It was held that after the expiration of the trust, the trustee could not be called upon
to make up the deficiency (n). It would, however, seem
that a mere knowledge, without suing for a few years, as
for ten years, will not destroy the right (o), particularly
where the trustee has not acted bonâ fide.

6. So again, in *Jones* v. *Higgins* (p), it was declared in
a marriage settlement that a sum of money, then in the
hands of the lady's brother, should be held by three
trustees, one of whom was the brother, upon trust at the
request in writing of the lady to pay to her the whole or
any part absolutely, and until such request upon trust,
when and as the same should come into their hands, to
invest the same and pay the interest to the wife for life for
her separate use, and after her decease as she should by
will appoint, and in default of appointment to her husband. The money was allowed to remain for thirteen
years in the hands of the brother, who paid the interest
to the husband, and also paid him part of the principal,
with the wife's knowledge. The husband died, the brother
became insolvent, and the wife filed a bill against the
trustees ; but it was held, that although the trustees had
been guilty of a breach of trust, the wife was debarred
from relief on account of her long acquiescence.

7. So, wherever it is for the general **convenience** that a
suit in respect of a long dormant grievance should be disallowed, the court will refuse relief on the ground that
" Expedit reipublicæ ut sit finis litium" (q). For instance,
where a plaintiff seeks to set aside a purchase from him by
his solicitor, a delay of less than twenty years *may* bar
the right to relief, if it would be inconvenient to grant
it (r); or where, in an action for an account, the plaintiff
by lying by has rendered it impossible or greatly incon-

(n) *McDonnel* v. *White, sup.*   (q) Lew. 715.
(o) L. R., 2 Eq. 538.   (r) *Gresley* v. *Mousley,* 4 D. &
(p) *Tarrant* v. *Blanchford,* 11   J. 78.
W. R. 178.

venient for the defendant to render the account he calls for, he will get no relief (s).

_____

Art. 61.—*The Gainer by a Breach of Trust must pro tanto indemnify Trustee.*

As between the trustees and a third person who has reaped the benefit of a breach of trust, the latter must indemnify the former to the extent of the property actually received by him under the breach of trust (a); and where he is a cestui que trust the trustees will have a lien on his share for such amount (b).

Illust. 1.—Thus, personalty was bequeathed upon trust for **tenants for life**, with executory trusts in remainder, but without directions as to investment. The trustees, at the instance of the tenants for life, invested on mortgage of a precarious nature, in consequence of which the tenants for life received a far larger income; but the corpus of the estate was in the result greatly depreciated. The trustees having been ordered to refund the loss to the trust property, claimed to be generally indemnified by the tenants for life who had reaped the benefit of the breach; and their claim was allowed, but only to the extent of the property actually received by the trustees in consequence of the improper investment (c).

2. And so, if the trustees by mistake pay capital to the tenant for life, instead of income, they must of course make the loss good to the trust property; but they will, never-

_____

(s) See per Lord Alvanley, in *Pickering* v. *Stamford*, 2 V. 272; and see also *Clegg* v. *Edmonston*, 3 Jur., N. S. 299; *Tatam* v. *Williams*, 3 Ha. 347.

(a) Lew. 744; *Raby* v. *Ridehalgh*, 7 D. M. & G. 108; *Trafford* v. *Boehm*, 3 Atk. 440; *Lord*

Montford v. *Lord Cadogan*, 19 V. 639; *Brown* v. *Maunsell*, 5 Ir. Ch. R. 351; *Walsham* v. *Stainton*, 1 H. & M. 337.

(b) *Prime* v. *Savell*, W. N. 1867, p. 227; Lew. 746.

(c) *Raby* v. *Ridehalgh*, *sup.*

theless, be entitled to be recouped out of the life interest (x).

ART. 62.—*Trustee has a Right to Discharge on Completion of his Duties.*

Upon the completion of the trust a trustee is entitled to have his accounts examined and settled by the cestuis que trust, and either to have a formal discharge given to him or to have the accounts taken in court. He cannot, however, demand a release under seal (y).

ILLUST.—Thus, a trustee on finally transferring stock to a cestui que trust demanded from the latter a deed of release. The cestui que trust, however, refused to give him anything except a simple receipt for the amount of stock actually transferred, which, of course, left it open to him to say that that amount was not the amount to which he was entitled. The court held, that no *deed* was demandable ; the Vice-Chancellor saying : "But though it may not have been the right of the trustee to require a deed, I think that it was his right to require that his account should be settled ; that is to say, that he and his family should be delivered from the anxiety and misery attending unsettled accounts, and the possible ruin, which they who are acquainted with the affairs daily litigated in the Court of Chancery well know to be a frequent result of neglect in such a matter. . . . He was bound to give an account if demanded, but giving the accounts he was entitled (to use a familiar phrase) to have them wound up. It is true that the accounts, though settled, might be liable to be surcharged and falsified. That might or might not be, but still the trustee had a right to have his accounts gone through, executed, and settled. . . . . If the plaintiff was satisfied upon the accounts as sent in

---

(x) See *Barratt* v. *Wyatt*, 30 B. 442 ; *Davies* v. *Hodgson*, 25 B. 177 ; *Griffiths* v. *Porter*, ib. 236.

(y) *Chatley* v. *Heatley*, 2 Coll. 137 ; *Re Wright*, 3 K. & J. 421.

that nothing more was coming to him, he should have expressed his willingness to close the account. On the other hand, if he was dissatisfied with it, he should have asked to have the account taken " (*z*).

ART. 63.—*Advice of a Judge.*

A trustee may apply, by petition (*a*), to any judge of the Chancery Division of the High Court of Justice, for his opinion, advice, or direction on any such *present* (*b*) questions respecting the exercise of his discretion and the management of the trust property as are of minor importance (*c*) and do not include questions of detail, difficulty (*d*), or construction (*e*). The petition must be served on all such parties interested (*or* all such parties must attend the hearing) as the judge shall deem expedient. A trustee, bonâ fide stating the facts in such a petition, is indemnified against any loss which may occur from following the advice or direction given by the judge (*f*).

ILLUST.—1. The court will, upon such a petition, give advice as to investments (*g*), payment of debts (*h*), the propriety of the trustees consenting to a sale (*i*), the advancement of money for maintenance or repairs (*k*), as to leasing the trust property (*l*), and other matters of a like character.

(*z*) *Chadwick* v. *Heatley, sup.*

(*a*) The act gave the alternative of summons, but the court has decided that the application ought to be made on petition, *Re Dennis*, 5 Jur., N. S. 1383.

(*b*) 22 & 23 Vict. c. 35, s. 30 ; *Re Box*, 1 H. & M. 552 ; 11 W. R. 945.

(*c*) Lew. 413 ; *Re Muggeridge*, Johns. 15 ; *Re Mockett, ib.* 628 ; *Re Spiller*, 8 W. R. 333 ; *Re Jacob*, 9 W. R. 474.

(*d*) *Re Barrington*, 1 J. & H. 142 ; but see *Re Mockett, sup.;*

Marsh v. *Att.-Gen.*, 2 J. & H. 61.

(*e*) *Re Evans*, 30 B. 232 ; *Re Muggeridge, sup.; Re Hooper*, 29 B. 657 ; but see *Re Peyton*, 10 W. R. 515.

(*f*) 22 & 23 Vict. c. 35, s. 30.

(*g*) *Re Lorentz*, 1 Dr. & S. 401; *Re Knowles*, 18 L. T., N. S. 809.

(*h*) *Re Box, sup.*

(*i*) *Earl Paulett* v. *Hood*, L. R., 5 Eq. 115.

(*k*) *Re Hotham*, L. R., 12 Eq. 76; *Cuthbertson* v. *Wood*, 19 W. R. 265.

(*l*) *Re Shaw, ib.* 125.

2. But where trustees were authorized to invest trust monies in the purchase of lands, and they presented a petition asking the court for its advice as to the application of a further portion of the trust monies to the **permanent improvement** of the lands, the court, not having the requisite machinery for investigating the details, refused to give any advice (*m*).

3. Where the case is **hypothetical, and not present,**—as, for instance, where the question asked was as to the incidence of future calls which might be made on account of shares bequeathed—the court will give no advice, and will order the petition to stand over until the event happens(*n*).

ART. 64.—*Craving the administrative Assistance of the Court.*

Trustees (*o*) may relieve themselves of responsibility in the following cases, and to the following extent:
α. Where the trust property consists of money, or annuities, or stocks standing in their names at the Bank of England, or in the East India Company, or the South Sea Company, or in any government or parliamentary securities, the trustees, or the majority (*a*) of them, may, on filing an affidavit shortly describing the settlement according to the best of their knowledge and belief, and with the privity of the paymaster-general of the Chancery Division of the High Court, pay such money into the said bank to the account of the said paymaster-general, in the matter of the particular trust, or transfer or deposit such stocks or securities into or in the name of such paymaster-general,

(*m*) *Re Barrington*, 1 J. & H. 142; *Re Simson*, 1 J. & H. 89; *Marsh* v. *Att.-Gen.*, *sup.*

(*n*) *Re Box*, *sup.*

(*o*) It would seem that by the operation of sub-sect. 6 of sect. 25 of the Judicature Act, 1873, these provisions are extended to all constructive trustees, such as insurance companies, &c.; see *Re Haycock*, L. R., 1 Ch. Div. 611.

(*a*) 12 & 13 Vict. c. 74.

to attend the orders of the court. The receipt of one of the cashiers of the said bank for money, or, in the case of stocks or securities, the certificate of the proper officer, that they have been transferred or deposited, is a sufficient discharge to the trustees (*b*), who are thereby released from seeing to the future application of that particular fund, but are not released from the office of trustee (*c*);

β. Where the trust property is not of the kind aforesaid, *or* where the trustee wishes to be discharged from the *office of trustee*, he may institute a suit for the administration of the trust by the court (*d*).

Provided that where the equities are perfectly clear and unambiguous (*e*), or he merely craves to be released from caprice or laziness, or is otherwise not justified in the course he has pursued (*f*), he will have to pay all the costs; and even where he acts bonâ fide, but without any real cause, he will not be allowed his own costs (*g*). And where he brings a suit, when the same object might have been obtained by payment into the bank, he will not be allowed the extra costs occasioned thereby (*h*); and he will always appeal from an order of the court at his own risk (*i*).

ILLUST.—1. The only part of the article which requires illustrating is the proviso. A **trustee is justified** in paying

(*b*) Trustee Relief Act, 10 & 11 Vict. c. 96, s. 1.

(*c*) *Barker* v. *Peile*, 2 Dr. & S. 340; *Re Cox's Trusts*, 4 K. & J. 199; *Re Williams's Trusts, ib*. 87; *Re Bailey's Trusts*, 3 W. R. 31.

(*d*) *Talbot* v. *Earl Radnor*, 3 M. & C. 252; *Goodson* v. *Ellison*, 3 Russ. 583.

(*e*) *Re Knight*, 27 B. 145; *Lawson* v. *Copeland*, 2 B. C. C. 156; *Re Elliot*, L. R., 15 Eq. 194: *Re Foligno*, 32 B. 131; *Re Woodburn*, 1 D. & J. 333; *Beattie* v. *Curzon*,

L. R., 7 Eq. 194: *Re Hoskins*, L. R., 5 Ch. Div. 229.

(*f*) *Forshaw* v. *Higginson*, 20 B. 485; *Re Stokes*, L. R., 13 Eq. 333.

(*g*) *Re Leake*, 32 B. 135; *Re Heming*, 3 K. & J. 40; Morgan's Ch. Acts, 68.

(*h*) *Wells* v. *Malbon*, 31 B. 48; but see *Smallwood* v. *Rutter*, 9 Ha. 24.

(*i*) *Rowland* v. *Morgan*, 13 Jur. 23; *Tucker* v. *Horneman*, 4 D. M. & G. 395.

money into court where he cannot get a valid discharge ; as, for instance, where the cestuis que trust are infants (e) or lunatics (f).

2. So, where under a creditor's deed money was **claimed** both by the settlor and the creditors, the trustee was held to have been justified in paying the money into court (g).

3. So, a trustee may properly pay money into court where it is **claimed by the representative** of a cestui que trust; for non constat, but that the cestui que trust may have disposed of it (h). On the other hand, it has been said (i) that a trustee ought not to hesitate to pay the money to a cestui que trust who claims in default of appointment, if he has good reason to believe that the power has never been exercised; Jessel, M.R., saying : " If there had been no such case as *Re Wylly's Trusts* (k), and no such opinion as that referred to, I should probably have made the trustees pay the costs of the transfer of the fund into court. They had no notice of any appointment by the lady, and no ground for believing that any appointment had been made. The solicitor, who had acted for Mrs. Cull from the time of her marriage, wrote to say that there was not the slightest ground for supposing that she had made any appointment. The trustees had, therefore, fully discharged their duty, and I am of opinion that they could not have been made liable if they had then paid over the fund to the petitioner, even if an appointment had been subsequently discovered. In the case of *Re Wylly's Trusts* the late Master of the Rolls said : ' The trustees had a

(e) Re Cawthorne, 12 B. 56 ; Re Beauclerk, 11 W. R. 203; Re Coulson, 4 Jur., N. S. 6 ; Re Richards, L. R., 8 Eq. 119.

(f) Re Upfull, 3 M. & G. 281 ; Re Irby, 17 B. 334.

(g) Re Headington, 6 W. R. 7 ; but see Re Moseley, 18 W. R. 126.

(h) Re Lane, 24 L. T. 181;

King v. King, 1 D. & J. 663.

(i) Re Cull, L. R., 20 Eq. 561; but see and consider Re Wylly, 28 B. 458.

(k) Re Swan, 2 H. & M. 34 ; but see Re Roberts, 17 W. R. 639; Re Bendyshe, 5 W. R. 816 ; Re Wylley, 28 B. 458; Re Williams, 4 K. & J. 87.

right to satisfactory evidence that Mrs. Wylly had made no appointment of the funds, by which I understand him to mean such evidence as a conveyancer would require : a letter from the solicitor would in such a case be quite sufficient. ' "

4. Where the cestui que trust is a **married woman,** it has been held that the trustee may pay into court, in order that she may assert her equity to a settlement (*l*).

5. Again, where the trustee has a bonâ fide **doubt as to the law** (*m*), or has received a bonâ fide claim sanctioned by respectable solicitors (*n*), he may properly pay the fund into court.

6. But where a cestui que trust in reversion had gone to Australia, and had not been heard of for some years, suddenly reappeared, and there was **no reasonable doubt** as to his identity, it was held that the trustee was not entitled to pay the trust fund into court instead of paying it over to him; Malins, V.-C., saying : "At the time when the trustees were uncertain whether he was living or dead they might with propriety have paid the money into court, but they did not do so then ; on the contrary, they retained it in their possession until they were informed that a letter had been written by him from Australia, stating that he should return home immediately, and then they insisted upon paying the money into court, notwithstanding the representation made to them that they should wait until the petitioner's arrival in England. The petitioner left England when he was twenty-six years of age, and a man does not often change so much after that age that he cannot be easily recognized, and there was every reason to suppose that his identity would be at once proved, and that would have settled the question without expense. . . . I think these proceedings were perfectly unjustifiable ; and although it

(*l*) *Ante*, note (*k*), p. 168.   *Gunnell* v. *Whitear*, 18 W. R. 883.
(*m*) *King* v. *King*, 1 D. & J.   (*n*) *Re Maclean*, L. R., 19 Eq.
663 ; *Re Metcalfe*, D. J. & S. 122 ;   282.

is clear that the court will incline towards the payment of the costs of trustees when they act in a bonâ fide way, yet, on the other hand, it is most important that trustees should not incur unnecessary expenses for the purpose of relieving themselves of all liability, and particularly so when there is no reasonable doubt in their way." His honor, therefore, ordered the trustees to pay the costs *of all parties* (n).

7. Trustees may **properly institute a suit** where there is a dispute as to the interests of the cestuis que trust in real property; as, for instance, where the settlor was tenant in tail of the property, and disentailed it by an assurance, the validity of which is disputed (o).

8. And so it was said in *Goodson* v. *Ellison* (p), that a trustee under an old trust creating successive limitations of equitable interests, some of which had failed, was entitled, before he could be required to convey, to have the equitable title of those who called for a conveyance ascertained by inquiry, and to have the deed of conveyance settled by the proper officer of the court.

9. And again, where there was a voluntary settlement, and the trust property was an ascertained and undisputed fund which might have been paid into the bank without suit, but there were **divers disputes** as to the proper cestuis que trust, and out of such disputes several suits had sprung, to all of which the trustee was a necessary defendant; it was held that he was entitled to institute a suit to be relieved of the trouble and annoyance (q), V.-C. Malins saying: " It has been contended that it can signify nothing to a trustee whether he is discharged or not, for under the Trustee Relief Act, if he paid the money into court, he would be discharged from liability. But, in fact, the trustee is not in that way discharged from *being a trustee*.

(n) *Re Elliott*, L. R., 15 Eq. 194; *Re Foligno*, 32 B. 131; *Re Knight*, 27 B. 45; *Re Woodburn*, 1 D. & J. 333.

(o) *Talbot* v. *Earl Radnor*, 3 M. & K. 252.
(p) 3 Russ. 583.
(q) *Barker* v. *Peile*, 2 Dr. & S. 340.

If he brings the money into court under the act, he still remains a trustee, and though he would be under no liability quoad the fund brought in, he would not be discharged from liability quoad the past income, and, moreover, he must be served with notice of all proceedings under the act in relation to the fund, and this of necessity would compel him to incur some expense in employing a solicitor; and, moreover, it is within the range of possibility that the court might, under the powers given by the act, direct a suit to be instituted to determine the rights of the parties claiming the fund at some future time, to which he would be a necessary party, not having been discharged from being a trustee. I am of opinion that the Trustee Relief Act does not deprive the trustee of the right to come here and ask to be discharged, if the circumstances justify him in so doing, as they do here, and that he is, therefore, entitled to costs as between solicitor and client."

10. But where there is no dispute respecting the *amount* of a trust fund, and no justifiable ground for the trustee retiring from his office, the only doubt being as to the proper persons entitled; and the trustee, instead of paying the money into court under the Trustee Relief Act, institutes a suit for the purpose of having the rights of the cestuis que trust declared, he will be allowed such costs only as he would have been entitled to if he had paid the fund into court under the act (*r*).

(*r*) *Wells* v. *Malbon*, 31 B. 48.

Division IV.

THE CONSEQUENCES OF A BREACH OF TRUST.

SUB-DIVISION I.

THE LIABILITY OF THE TRUSTEE.

ART. 65.—*Loss by Breach of Trust generally a simple Contract Debt.*

A LOSS occasioned by a breach of trust is a simple contract equitable debt only (*a*), unless the settlement is so worded as to imply a covenant in law on the part of the trustee to perform the trust (*b*).

ILLUST.—1. A mere recital in a deed of the acceptance of the trusteeship is not sufficient to raise a covenant on the part of the trustee, and therefore will not render a loss incurred by a subsequent breach of trust a specialty debt (*c*).

2. But where it is "**declared and agreed**," or "declared" alone, that the property shall be held upon such and such trusts, and the trustee executes the deed, and subsequently commits a breach of trust, the loss will be considered as a specialty debt due from him to the estate (*d*).

ART. 66.—*The Liability where joint quâ Cestuis que trust may be distributable quâ Trustees.*

Each trustee is in general liable to the cestuis que trust for the whole loss when caused by the joint default of all the trustees (*a*). A decree against

(*a*) *Vernon* v. *Vaudrey*, 2 Atk. 119; *Ex parte Blencowe*, L. R., 1 Ch. 393.

(*b*) *Benson* v. *Benson*, 1 P. W. 131; *Wood* v. *Hardisty*, 2 Coll. 512; *Holland* v. *Holland*, L. R., 4 Ch. 449.

(*c*) *Isaacson* v. *Harwood*, L. R., 3 Ch. 225.

(*d*) *Westmoreland* v. *Tunnicliffe*, W. N. 1869, 182; *Richardson* v. *Jenkins*, 1 Dr. 477; and see generally, *Isaacson* v. *Harwood*, sup.

(*a*) *Wilson* v. *Moore*, 1 M. & K. 126; *Lyse* v. *Kingdom*, 1 Coll. 184; *Ex parte Norris*, L. R., 4 Ch. 280.

all may be enforced against one or more only (*b*).
But as between themselves, where all are equally
guilty of a breach of trust not amounting to actual
fraud (*c*), those who have had to refund the loss to
the trust will be entitled to contribution from the
others (*d*) ; and where one is more guilty than the
other or others, the whole loss may be thrown upon
him (*e*). The claim to contribution is a specialty
debt (*f*).

ILLUST.—1. A loss was suffered by the creditors of a
bankrupt through the joint default of the **assignees in
bankruptcy.** A decree was made against them, and one
of them had to make the loss good. Contribution was,
however, enforced against his co-assignees, and the objection that these latter acted only for conformity was disallowed. Sir W. Grant, M. R., said : " Where entire
damages are recovered against several defendants guilty of
a tort, a court of justice will not interfere to enforce contribution amongst wrongdoers ; but here there is nothing
but the non-performance of a civil obligation. The liability is not ex delicto unless every refusal to comply with a
legal obligation makes a party guilty of a delictum" (*g*).

2. So where a large balance was found to be due jointly
from a trustee and the representatives of a deceased co-
trustee, but costs were given to both out of the trust estate,
it being admitted that no part of the loss could be recovered from the estate of the deceased trustee, it was
held that the surviving trustee, upon paying the whole of
the loss, was entitled to a **lien for half** of it on the costs
awarded to the representatives of his deceased co-trustee (*h*).

(*b*) *Att.-Gen.* v. *Wilson*, Cr. &
Ph. 28 ; *Fletcher* v. *Green*, 33 B.
426.

(*c*) *Att.-Gen.* v. *Wilson*, *sup.* ;
see *Lingard* v. *Bromley*, 1 V. & B.
114 ; *Tarleton* v. *Hornby*, 1 Y. &
C. 336.

(*d*) *Lingard* v. *Bromley*, *sup.* ;
Birks v. *Micklethwaite*, 33 B. 409 ;

Att.-Gen. v. *Dangars*, *ib.* 624.

(*e*) *Featherstone* v. *West*, 6 Ir.
Rep. Eq. 86 ; Lew. 744.

(*f*) So made by 19 & 20 Vict.
c. 97 ; *Lockhart* v. *Reilly*, 1 D. &
J. 464.

(*g*) *Lingard* v. *Bromley*, *sup.*
(*h*) *Fletcher* v. *Green*, 33 B. 515.

3. H. W., as trustee of a marriage settlement, held a bond to secure 1,200*l.* J. W., his brother, who was a specialty creditor of the obligor, obtained possession of the obligor's assets and applied them in payment of his own debt and of simple contract debts before administration, which was afterwards granted to the obligor's widow (the sister of J. W.), who was entirely guided by his advice. Subsequently, J. W. represented to H. W. that only 600*l.* was forthcoming and available for the bond. H. W., acting on this statement, retired from the trust; and a memorandum was endorsed on the trust deed, signed by the administratrix and by the tenant for life of the trust fund, stating that 600*l.* only were available to pay the bond, and J. W. was appointed trustee of the marriage settlement in place of H. W. The assets of the obligor would have been, if properly administered, sufficient to pay the bond in full. Under these circumstances it was held that J. W. and H. W. were both liable to the full amount of the bond; but that J. W.'s assets (he having died) were **primarily answerable,** as he had received the trust fund (*i*).

ART. 67.—*The Measure of the Trustee's Responsibility.*

The general measure of a trustee's responsibility for a breach of trust is the amount by which the trust property has been depreciated without interest (*a*): Provided that—

    a. Where he has actually received interest, or ought to have received interest, he will be liable to account for what he has received in the one case (*b*), and for what he ought to have received in the

(*i*) *Featherstone* v. *West*, 6 Ir. Rep. Eq. 86.

(*a*) See *Att.-Gen.* v. *Alford*, 4 D. M. & G. 851; *Stafford* v. *Fiddon*, 23 B. 386; *Vyse* v. *Foster*, L. R., 8 Ch. 333; *Ex parte Ogle*, *ib.* 716; *Burdick* v. *Garrard*, L. R., 5 Ch. 233.

(*b*) *Ib.*, and see *Jones* v. *Foxall*, 15 B. 392.

other, which is, in the absence of express direction, 4 per cent. (c);

2. Where it is so fairly to be presumed that he did receive interest, that he ought to be estopped from denying that he did actually receive it, he will be liable to pay simple interest at 4 or 5 per cent. according to the circumstances. But where he has employed the trust property in trade or speculation, he will be liable to pay interest at 5 per cent. with yearly, or even half-yearly, rests, if he may reasonably be presumed to have made that amount, or (where he has *actively* employed it in trade or speculation), at the option of the cestuis que trust, to account for all the profits made by him (d). The circumstances which will raise such a presumption admit of no rule, but, in general, misconduct, which has had his own benefit as the end in view, will raise it (e).

ILLUST.—1. A trustee who is guilty of **unreasonable delay in investing** trust funds will be answerable to the cestuis que trust for simple interest at 4 per cent. during the continuance of such delay (f).

2. A trustee who without proper authority calls in trust property invested on mortgage at 5 per cent., would be liable for that rate of interest, for although he may not actually have received that rate, he **ought to have done so** (g).

3. A trustee retained trust funds uninvested for several years, and **mixed them with his own** private monies. The Vice-Chancellor held that 5 per cent. *compound* interest was chargeable; but on appeal this decision was reversed, Lord

(c) *Att.-Gen.* v. *Alford, sup.;* *Stafford* v. *Fiddon, sup.*

(d) See *Jones* v. *Foxall, sup.;* *Vyse* v. *Foster, sup.; Burdick* v. *Garrard, sup.*

(e) See and consider judgments, *Att.-Gen.* v. *Alford, sup.; Ex parte Ogle, sup.; Mayor of Ber-* wick v. *Murray,* 7 D. M. & G. 519; *Townend* v. *Townend,* 1 Gif. 212; *Burdick* v. *Garrard, sup.; Vyse* v. *Foster, sup.*

(f) *Stafford* v. *Fiddon, sup.*

(g) See judgment in *Jones* v. *Foxall, sup.*

Cranworth saying: "Generally speaking, every executor and trustee who holds money in his hands is bound to have that money forthcoming; he is, therefore, chargeable with interest, and is almost always to be charged with interest at 4 per cent. It is presumed that he must have made interest, and 4 per cent. is that rate of interest which this court has usually treated it as right to charge. . . . . In the present instance, I observe that one of the grounds of misconduct relied upon by the Vice-Chancellor is, that the defendant did not communicate the matter to the rector and churchwardens (the cestuis que trust). This was extremely improper conduct, no doubt, but not in itself such conduct as enables me to make any alteration in the mode in which he is to be dealt with in point of interest. *It is not misconduct that has benefited him*, unless indeed it can be taken as evidence that he kept the money fraudulently in his hands, meaning to appropriate it. In such a case, I think the court would be justified in dealing, in point of interest, very hardly with an executor, *because it might fairly infer that he used the money in speculation, by which he either did make 5 per cent., or ought to be estopped from saying that he did not.* The court would not inquire what had been the actual proceeds, but in application of the principle, in odium spoliatoris omnia præsumuntur, would assume that he did make the higher rate, *that is, if that were a reasonable presumption*" (h).

4. In *Burdick* v. *Garrard* (i), a **solicitor,** as the agent of the plaintiff, held a power of attorney from him, under the authority of which he received divers sums of money, and paid them into the bank to the credit of his (the solicitor's) firm. On a bill being filed by the client for an account, the Vice-Chancellor made a decree for payment of the principal with *compound interest ;* but the Court of Appeal reversed this decision, Lord Hatherley saying: "The Vice-Chancellor has directed interest to be charged at the rate

(h) *Att.-Gen.* v. *Alford, sup.*   (i) L. R., 5 Ch. 233.

of 5 per cent., which appears to me to be perfectly right, and for this reason, that the money was retained in the defendants' own hands, and was made use of by them. That being so, the court presumes the rate of interest made upon money to be the ordinary rate of interest, viz. 5 per cent. I cannot, however, think the decree correct in directing half-yearly rests, because the principle laid down in the case of *The Attorney-General* v. *Alford* appears to be the sound principle, namely, that the court does not proceed against an accounting party by way of punishing him for making use of the plaintiff's money, by directing rests, or payment of compound interest, but proceeds upon this principle, that either he has made, or has put himself into such a position that he is to be presumed to have made, 5 per cent., or compound interest, as the case may be. If the court finds it is stated in the bill, and proved, or possibly (and I guard myself on this point of the case) if it is not stated, but is admitted on the face of the answer without any statement in the bill, that the money received has been invested in an *ordinary* trade, the whole course of decision has tended to this, that the court presumes that the party against whom relief is sought has made that amount of profit which persons ordinarily do make in trade; and in those cases the court directs rests to be made. But how does the case stand here? . . . . It must not be forgotten that a solicitor's business is not such a business as I have described; it is not one in which half-yearly or yearly rests, as the case may be, would be made in making up the account. There is nothing like compound interest obtained upon the money employed by a solicitor. On the contrary, he is out of pocket for a considerable period by those moneys which he expends, and upon which he receives no interest for possibly three or four years. It appears to me, therefore, that no case arises here in which you could say that such a profit has been made, or necessarily is to be inferred."

5. In order to charge a trustee with compound interest, or with actual profits for employing the trust funds in trade, there must be **an active calling** in of the trust moneys for the purpose of embarking them in the trade or speculation. In *Vyse* v. *Foster* (k) the facts were as follows:—A testator was partner in a well-established and prosperous business, under articles, by which, on the death of any partner, his share was to be taken by the surviving partners, at a price to be ascertained from the last stock-taking, and to be paid by instalments extending over two years, with interest at 5*l.* per cent. per annum from his death. He appointed three executors, *one of whom was one of the partners* in his business, and another some years after his death became a partner; the third never was concerned in the business. The value of the testator's share was ascertained but not paid, the amount being allowed for some years to remain in the hands of the firm, who treated it in their books as a debt, and allowed interest on it at 5*l.* per cent. per annum, with yearly rests. One of the testator's residuary legatees, upon becoming entitled to payment of her share, refused to accept payment on the above footing, and filed her bill against the executors, claiming to be entitled to a share in the profits of the business arising from the use of the testator's capital. Upon these facts, it was held that the plaintiff was not entitled to any account of profits, the mere delay by executors in calling in a debt due to the testator from a firm of which some of the executors were members, not giving his estate any right to share in the profits. Lord Justice James said: "If an executor or trustee makes a profit by an improper dealing with the assets or the trust fund, that profit he must give up to the trust. If that improper dealing consists in embarking or investing the trust money in business, he must account for the profits made by him by such employment in such business, or at the option of

(k) L. R., 8 Ch. 309.

N 2

the cestuis que trust, or if it does not appear, or cannot be made to appear, what profits are attributable to such employment he must account for trade interest—that is to say, interest at 5 per cent. In this case the successive partnerships have charged themselves in their own accounts with interest at 5 per cent. and with annual rests, and the sum due on that footing has been paid. And the questions, therefore, are, whether the plaintiff is entitled to anything; and if anything, to what and from whom in respect of the surplus profits due to capital, and how are such surplus profits to be ascertained. In the first place, there is a clear breach of trust in not calling in the money. . . . But it is necessary to consider another aspect of the matter. . . . This court is not a court of penal jurisdiction. It compels restitution of property unconscientiously withheld; it gives full compensation for any loss or damage through failure of some equitable duty; but it has no power of punishing anyone. In fact, it is not by way of punishment that the court ever charges a trustee with more than he actually received or ought to have received and the appropriate interest thereon. It is simply on the ground that the court finds that he actually made more, constituting monies in his hands had and received to the use of the cestuis que trust (*l*). A trustee, for instance, lending money to his firm, is answerable for such money, with full interest, to the uttermost farthing; but to make him answerable for all the profits made of such money *by all the firm* would be simply a punishment. . . . Is the mere fact of the union of the three characters—debtor, executor, and trader —in the same person, sufficient to entitle the estate to an investigation into the trader's own business, because there has been some delay, or great delay, in paying off the debt? We have found no case in which this has been laid down, even in the case of a sole executor, sole debtor, sole trader.

(*l*) But see per the same learned judge in *Ex parte Ogle*, L. R., 8 Ch. 717.

There have been hundreds, probably thousands, of cases in which traders have been executors, and in which, on taking their accounts, balances, and large balances, have been found due from them; but in no case, so far as we are aware, has it ever been held, that (where there has been no active breach of trust in the getting in or selling out trust assets, but where there has been a mere balance on the account of receipts—legitimate receipts—and payments) the omission to invest the balance has made the executor liable to account for the profits of his own trade. But this case is far stronger than the case we have suggested; and if the rule as to profits were to apply to it, it would be difficult, if not impossible, to exclude from its application, cases where it would shock the common feelings of mankind."

ART. 68.—*Charge upon Property of the Trustee with which he has mixed the Trust Property.*

Where a trustee mixes the trust property with his own, so that the two cannot be separated with perfect accuracy, the equity of the cestuis que trust will attach on the entire fund for the whole of what is due to them (*a*).

ILLUST.—In *Cook* v. *Addison* (*b*), A. was one of the trustees under a settlement, and he was also, in his own right, the lessee of a house. This house he sublet to S., who covenanted to repair it. S. afterwards borrowed (legitimately) a sum of money from the trustees, and therewith purchased from A. the furniture in the house, and executed a mortgage of his underlease, and a bill of sale of the furniture to the trustees. S. getting into difficulties, A. put an end to the underlease and re-entered and took possession. He subsequently assigned the premises to F. at a rent of 310*l.*, and a premium of 100*l.* The

(*a*) *Lupton* v. *White*, 15 V. 432; 372.
Pennell v. *Deffell*, 4 D., M. & G. (*b*) L. R., 7 Eq. 471.

furniture was purchased by F. for 550*l.*, and he also paid 250*l.* towards repairs. A. invested a sum to make good the principal trust fund, but refused to pay the interest which had accrued due from S. It was held, however, that he had, by his conduct, mixed the trust funds with his own, and that the interest must be paid out of the sum received by him from F. for repairs; the Vice-Chancellor Stuart saying, "It is a well-established doctrine in this court, that if a trustee or agent mixes and confuses the property which he holds in a fiduciary character with his own property, so as that they cannot be separated with perfect accuracy, he is liable for the whole. In this case, it is impossible to say how much of the 250*l.* received by the defendant Addison from Fowler for repairs consisted of what was due under the covenant to repair in the under-lease. The consequence is, that the whole 250*l.* is liable to the demands of the cestuis que trust, so far as necessary to make up, with the other sums admitted to be part of the trust property, the full amount of the trust fund of 520*l.*, with interest at five per cent. per annum."

ART. 69.—*Property acquired by a Trustee out of Trust Funds becomes Trust Property.*

If a trustee has disposed of the trust property, and the money or other property which he has received or acquired out of the proceeds can be traced in his hands, or in those of his representatives, such property will be liable to the cestuis que trust, and will be burdened with the same trusts as the original trust property (*a*).

ILLUST.—1. Thus where **money is handed to a broker**

(*a*) *Taylor* v. *Plumer*, 3 M. & S. 562; *Chedworth* v. *Edwards*, 8 V. 46; *Frith* v. *Cartland*, 2 H. & M. 417; *Lench* v. *Lench*, 10 V. 517; *Hopper* v. *Conyers*, L. R., 2 Eq. 549; *Trench* v. *Harrison*, 17 Sim. 111; *Lane* v. *Dighton*, Amb. 409; *Scales* v. *Baker*, 28 B. 91; *Cook* v. *Addison*, L. R., 7 Eq. 466; *Ernest* v. *Croysdill*, 2 D., F. & J. 175.

for the purpose of purchasing stock, and he invests it in unauthorized stock, and absconds, the stock which he has purchased will belong to the principal, and not to the broker's assignee in bankruptcy. For a broker is a constructive trustee for his principal, and, as was said by Lord Ellenborough, "the property of a principal entrusted by him to his factor for any special purpose, belongs to the principal notwithstanding any change which that property may have undergone in form, so long as such property is capable of being identified and distinguished from all other property" (b).

2. Trustees had power, with the consent of the tenant for life, to sell the trust property, and they were directed to invest the purchase-money in the purchase of other real estate, to be settled on the like trusts. The trust property was sold under this power for 8,440l., and the tenant for life was allowed (wrongly) to keep the purchase-money. About the same time he **purchased another estate** for 17,400l., of which sum 8,124l. was part of the above-mentioned trust money. This estate was conveyed to him in fee simple. The tenant for life eventually became bankrupt, and it was held, that as against his assignees in bankruptcy, the original trustees of the settlement had a lien on the estate which he had purchased, to the extent of the moneys invested in its purchase (c).

3. So, in *Hopper* v. *Conyers* (d), a solicitor having in his possession the title deeds of an estate mortgaged to his client, deposited them with his own banker to secure an advance, which he applied in the purchase of an estate on his own behalf. When the mortgage to his client was paid off, he applied the money in **repaying the loan from his banker,** and informed his client that he had re-invested the mortgage money upon other good security, and his

(b) *Taylor* v. *Plumer, sup.;* and see also *Ex parte Cooke,* L. R., 4 Ch. Div. 123.

(c) *Price* v. *Blakemore,* 6 B. 507.
(d) L. R., 2 Eq. 549.

client thereupon executed a re-assignment of the mortgaged property. In fact the solicitor never re-invested the money upon other good security, although he continued to pay interest upon it until his death. Upon the true state of the transaction being discovered, the court held, that the client was entitled to a lien upon the estate purchased by the solicitor.

4. W. having entrusted P., his solicitor, with a sum of 7,700*l.* for investment on mortgage on his behalf, was informed by P.'s clerk, in conversation, that P. proposed to invest the money on mortgage of leasehold property at Camden Town at 5 per cent.; and subsequently received a letter from P., stating that "the money was put on 5 per cent. mortgage, as arranged by my clerk with you." On P.'s death, it was found that no mortgage existed in favour of W., but that P. had advanced 100,000*l.* to a firm of builders, on a mortgage of their leasehold property at Camden Town. It was held that P., and those claiming under him, were bound by the representation made by him, and were estopped from denying that the 7,700*l.* formed part of the 100,000*l.* so invested (*e*).

ART. 70.—*No Set-off allowed to the Trustee where Breaches are distinct.*

A trustee is only liable for the actual loss in each distinct and complete transaction which amounts to a breach of trust, and not for the loss in each particular item of it (*a*); but a loss in one transaction or fund is not compensated by a gain in another and distinct one (*b*).

ILLUST.—1. In *Vyse* v. *Foster* (*c*) a testator devised his real and personal estates upon common trusts for sale, making

(*e*) *Middleton* v. *Pollock*, L. R., 4 Ch. Div. 49.
(*a*) *Vyse* v. *Foster*, L. R., 8 Ch. 336.
(*b*) *Wiles* v. *Gresham*, 2 Drew. 258; *Dimes* v. *Scott*, 4 Russ. 195.
(*c*) *Supra.*

them *a mixed fund.* His trustees were advised, that a few
acres of freehold land which belonged to him might be
advantageously sold in lots for building purposes, and that
to develop their value, it was desirable to build a villa
upon part of them. They accordingly built one at a cost
of 1,600*l.* out of the testator's personal estate. The evidence
showed that the outlay had benefited the estate, but Vice-
Chancellor Bacon disallowed the 1,600*l.* to the trustees in
passing their accounts. The court of appeal, however,
reversed the Vice-Chancellor's decision, the Lord Justice
James saying, "As the real and personal estate *constituted
one fund,* we think it neither reasonable nor just to fix the
trustees with a sum, part of the estate, bonâ fide laid out
on other part of the estate, in the exercise of their judgment as the best means of increasing the value of the
whole. If they were mistaken in this, which does by no
means appear, the utmost they could be fairly chargeable
with would be the loss (if any) occasioned by the mistake
in judgment."

2. In *Wiles* v. *Gresham* (*d*), on the other hand, by the
negligence of the trustees of a marriage settlement a bond
debt for 2,000*l.* due from the husband was not got in, and
was totally lost. Certain other of the trust funds were
without proper authority invested in the purchase of land
upon the trusts of the settlement. The husband, out of
his own money, greatly added to the value of this land;
and upon a claim being made against the trustee for the
2,000*l.*, they endeavoured to set off against that loss the
gain which had accrued to the trust by the increased value
of the land, but their contention was disallowed, the two
transactions being separate and distinct.

3. Again: Trustees had kept invested on unauthorized
security a sum of money which they ought to have invested
in consols, and which was in consequence depreciated.

(*d*) *Supra.*

Eventually part of the money was invested in consols, at a far lower rate than it would have been if invested according to the directions in the will. The trustees claimed to set-off the gain against the loss, but were not allowed to do so; because "at whatever period the unauthorized security was realized, the estate was entitled to the whole of the consols that were then bought, and if it was sold at a later period than it ought to have been, the executor was not entitled to any accidental advantage thence accruing(e). This case is at first sight difficult to be distinguished from *Vyse* v. *Foster*, but it will be perceived that the loss and gain resulted from two distinct transactions. The loss resulted from a breach of trust in not realizing the securities; the gain arose from a particular kind of stock being at a lower market value than usual at the date at which the trustees bought it.

4. Where, however, trustees committed a breach of trust in lending trust moneys on mortgage, and upon a suit by them the mortgaged property was sold and the money paid into court and invested in consols pending the suit, and the consols rose in value, the trustees were allowed to set-off the gain in the value of the consols against the loss under the mortgage, for the gain and loss arose out of one transaction(f). It is, however, very difficult to reconcile this case with the last one, but it seems to be reasonable and in accordance with common sense.

Art. 71.—*Cestuis que trust may compel Performance of Duty or prevent Commission of Breach of Trust.*

Where the court is satisfied that trust property is in danger, either through the supineness (a) of, or a contemplated or probable active breach of duty (b)

(e) *Dimes* v. *Scott*, 4 Russ. 195.
(f) *Fletcher* v. *Green*, 33 B. 426.
(a) *Foley* v. *Burnell*, 1 B. C. C. 277; *Fletcher* v. *Fletcher*, 4 Ha. 78.

(b) *Talbot* v. *Scott*, 4 K. & J. 139; *Middleton* v. *Dodswell*, 13 V. 266; *Dance* v. *Goldingham*, L. R., 8 Ch. 902.

by, the trustees, or where the latter are residing out
of the jurisdiction of the court (*c*), an injunction
will be granted at the instance of any person with
an existing, vested or contingent interest (*d*), either
compelling the trustees to do their duty (*e*), or restraining them from interfering with the trust pro-
perty(*f*), as the case may require; and if expedient
a receiver will be appointed (*g*).

ILLUST.—1. Thus, if one commits some trespass upon
lands in the possession of the trustee, and the latter
refuses to sue him, the court will oblige him to lend his
name for that purpose, on receiving a proper indemnity
from the cestuis que trust (*h*).

2. And so if a tenant for life **refuses to renew leaseholds,** the court will compel him to do so, and a receiver
of the income of the trust property will be appointed to
collect sufficient to pay the renewal fine (*i*).

3. In *Earl Talbot* v. *Scott* (*k*), lands were vested in trustees
by act of parliament, upon trust for sale, and subject thereto,
upon trusts inalienably annexing the rents to the Earldom
of Shrewsbury. The Earl of Shrewsbury attempted to
disentail (which of course he could not do effectually), and
devised the lands to the same trustees, upon trust for a
particular claimant of the title. The trustees accepted this
trust, and claimed to receive the rents in that character,
pending proceedings by the plaintiff to establish his claim
to the earldom. A receiver of the rents was however
appointed on his application, upon the ground that the
trusts of the will were **in conflict with the prior trusts**
upon which they held the estate.

(*c*) *Noad* v. *Backhouse,* 2 Y. C. C.
529.
(*d*) Lew. 697; *Scott* v. *Becher,*
4 Pr. 346; and compare *Davis* v.
Angel, 10 W. R. 723, with *Re
Shepherd,* 4 D., F. & J. 423.
(*e*) See cases in note (*a*).
(*f*) See cases in note (*b*).
(*g*) See cases in note (*b*); and
Bennett v. *Colley,* 5 Sim. 192.
(*h*) *Foley* v. *Burnell, sup.*
(*i*) See *Bennett* v. *Colley, sup.;*
and Lew. 696.
(*k*) *Supra.*

4. So in *Evans* v. *Coventry* (*l*), a bill was filed by a plaintiff insured in a society whose funds were liable to pay the insurance money, on behalf of himself and other persons so insured, charging a loss of the funds through the **negligence of the directors.** The answers and affidavits showed that the secretary had absconded with part of the funds, and that some of the directors were in needy circumstances, and the court granted an injunction restraining the directors from touching the funds, and appointed a receiver of them. Lord Justice Knight Bruce saying, "The application before the court is founded on the common right of persons who are interested in property which is in danger to apply for its protection. . . . . In my judgment the objections which have been urged against this application might be urged with as much reason, as much force, and as much effect, if this were an application to restrain the felling of timber in a case of waste, partly perpetrated and partly imminent."

5. On similar grounds the court will appoint a receiver and grant an injunction where from the **character or condition of the trustee** he is not a fit person to have the control of the trust property; as, for instance, where he is insolvent (*m*), or about to become a bankrupt (*n*), or is a person of dissolute habits, or dishonest (*o*).

6. Again, the court will grant an injunction to restrain a sale by trustees at an **under value** (*p*), although this was at one time doubted (*q*).

(*l*) 5 D., M. & G. 911.
(*m*) *Mansfield* v. *Shaw*, 3 Mad. 100; *Gladdon* v. *Stoneman*, 1 Mad. 143, n.
(*n*) *Re H.'s Estate*, L. R., 1 Ch. Div. 276.
(*o*) See *Everett* v. *Prythergch*, 12 Sim. 365.

(*p*) *Anon.*, 6 Mad. 10; and see *Webb* v. *Earl of Shaftesbury*, 7 V. 488; *Milligan* v. *Mitchell*, 1 M. & K. 416; *Dance* v. *Goldingham*, L. R., 8 Ch. 902.
(*q*) *Pechel* v. *Fowler*, 2 Anst. 519.

ART. 72.—*Fraudulent Breach of Trust a Crime.*

A trustee who fraudulently appropriates or disposes of the trust property, in any manner inconsistent with the trust, is guilty of a misdemeanor, and is liable to be kept in penal servitude for not more than seven and not less than five years, or to be imprisoned, with or without hard labour, for not more than two years: Provided, that no criminal proceedings can be instituted without the sanction of the Attorney-General, or of the Solicitor-General, or (if civil proceedings have been commenced) of the judge of the court wherein they have been commenced (*a*). The fact, that a breach of trust is a crime, does not affect the validity of any civil proceeding, nor any agreement for restoration of the trust property (*b*).

(*a*) 24 & 25 Vict. c. 96, s. 80.   (*b*) *Ibid.*, s. 86.

SUB-DIVISION II.

LIABILITY OF PARTIES OTHER THAN THE TRUSTEES.

ART. 73.—*Liability of Cestui que trust who is Party to
a Breach of Trust.*

WHERE one of several cestuis que trust has joined in
a breach of trust, his whole equitable interest
under the settlement (*a*) (except where he also has
the legal estate (*b*)) may be stopped by his co-
cestuis que trust as against him and all persons
claiming under him, except purchasers for value
without notice (*c*), until the whole loss has been so
compensated: Provided that this article does not
apply where the guilty cestui que trust is a feme
covert *without power of anticipation* (*d*).

ILLUST.—1. A trustee in breach of trust lent the trust
fund to A. B., the tenant for life. The trustee afterwards
concurred in a creditors' deed, by which A. B.'s life interest was to be applied in payment of his debts, and the
trustee received thereunder a debt due to him from A. B.
Before the other creditors had been paid, the trustee retained the life income to make good the breach of trust.
It was held, upon a bill filed by those claiming under the
creditors' deed, that the court would not restrain the
trustee from making good the breach of trust out of the

(*a*) *Woodyatt* v. *Gresley*, 8 Sim.
180; *Fuller* v. *Knight*, 6 B. 205;
M'Gachen v. *Dew*, 15 B. 84;
Vaughton v. *Noble*, 30 B. 34;
Jacubs v. *Rylance*, L. R., 17 Eq.
341.
(*b*) *Egbert* v. *Butter*, 21 B. 560;
Fox v. *Buckley*, L. R., 3 Ch. Div.
508; but see *Woodyatt* v. *Gresley*,
sup.

(*c*) *Williams* v. *Allen No.* 2, 32
B. 650; *Kilworth* v. *Mounteashel*,
15 Ir. Ch. R. 565; *Jacubs* v.
Rylance, sup.; Ex parte Turpin,
1 D. & C. 120; *Woodyatt* v. *Gresley, sup.; Cole* v. *Muddle*, 10 Ha.
186.
(*d*) Lew. 744; and see *Stanley*
v. *Stanley*, L. R., 7 Ch. Div.   .

life income, for although the trustee, being a creditor and
party to the deed, had, quâ himself, no right to retain the
life interest, yet, as representing the cestuis que trust, he
was justified in doing so. And the Master of the Rolls
said: "This bill, proposing to leave nothing but the personal liability of Knight (the trustee) for the reparation of
the breach of trust, seeks to withdraw the liability of the
life estate, and thus materially diminish the security of the
cestuis que trust. . . . I cannot reconcile myself to
the notion, that this is a course which this court could
pursue"(e).

2. In *Woodyatt* v. *Gresley* (f), the facts were as follows.
On the marriage of Sir N. and Lady Gresley two settlements were executed: by one, a sum of stock and estates
in W. (the lady's property) were conveyed to trustees in
trust for her for life, with remainder in trust for the children of the marriage; and by the other, Sir N. granted out
of his estates a rent-charge to Lady G. for life. She, after
her husband's death, fraudulently obtained a transfer of
the stock, and sold it out; and afterwards she assigned her
life interest in the estates in W. and the rent-charge to A.
for valuable consideration, *but with notice of the fraud.* It
was held, that the rents of the estates in W. and the rent-
charge were liable to be applied to replace the stock, and
a receiver of them was appointed for that purpose.

3. But where a testator devised certain real estate for
life to one of his executors and trustees, and the devisee
afterwards committed a breach of trust and filed his petition for liquidation, it was held, that as against the trustee
in liquidation the other cestuis que trust had no lien on
the interest of the trustee, the Lord Justice James saying,
"The estate of a *legal* devisee is, under no circumstances,
under the control of the court"(g).

(e) *Fuller* v. *Knight, sup.*   (g) *Fox* v. *Buckley*, L. R., 3
(f) 8 Sim. 180.   Ch. Div. 511.

ART. 74.—*Liability of Third Parties privy to a fraudulent Breach of Trust.*

All persons who are parties to a fraudulent breach of trust render themselves equally liable with the trustees, and the Statute of Limitations will not run in their favour until the fraud is known to the persons affected by it (*a*).

ILLUST.—1. A testator bequeathed a sum of 600*l*., which he described as being in the hands of one Gregory (to whom he had lent the same on the security of his note of hand), to his son-in-law Rolfe, upon trust to invest the same and pay the dividends and interest to his daughter, the wife of Rolfe, for life, for her separate use; and after her death, upon trust for Rolfe for life, with remainder to their children. On the death of the testator, Rolfe the trustee became indebted to Gregory, and in order to discharge part of that debt he delivered to Gregory the note of hand for 600*l*. It was held that as Gregory had information of the manner of the bequest he was a party to the fraudulent abstraction of the trust property, and liable to refund the amount, and that being founded on fraud the Statute of Limitations did not apply (*b*).

2. So where a fund was standing to the account of two trustees in the books of some bankers, who had notice that it was a trust fund, and by the direction of the tenant for life only they transferred it to his account, and thereby obtained payment of a debt due from him to them. It was held that the trustees might sue the bankers to have the trust fund replaced, and that the Statute of Limitations was not applicable (*c*).

3. In *Eaves* v. *Hickson* (*d*), trustees had paid over trust

(*a*) *Rolfe* v. *Gregory*, 11 Jur., N. S. 98; *Bridgeman* v. *Gill*, 24 B. 302; *Eaves* v. *Hickson*, 30 B. 136; and see per Malins, V.-C., *Morgan* v. *Elford*, L. R., 4 Ch. Div. 352.

(*b*) *Rolfe* v. *Gregory*, sup.
(*c*) *Bridgeman* v. *Gill*, 24 B. 302.
(*d*) 30 B. 136.

funds bequeathed to the children of one William Knibb, upon the faith of a forged marriage certificate, which *William Knibb produced to them*, from which it appeared that certain illegitimate children of his were legitimate. It was held that William Knibb, who had produced the certificate, must be made responsible for the money as well as the trustees. ——

ART. 75.—*Following Trust Property into the Hands of Third Parties.*

If trust property comes into the hands of any person inconsistently with the trust, then—

α. If such person has got the *legal* estate, he will be a mere trustee for the persons entitled under the trust; unless he, or some person through whom he claims (*a*), has bonâ fide purchased the property for valuable consideration, and without receiving notice of the existence of the trust before completion of the purchase, *and* before payment of the purchase-money (*b*);

β. If he has not got the legal estate (*c*), or if the property is a mere chose in action (*d*), he will be a mere trustee, notwithstanding that he purchased it bonâ fide for value and without notice; unless (being a chose in action) the property consists of a negotiable instrument (*e*), or an instrument which was intended by the parties to it to be transferable free from all equities attaching to it (*f*).

ILLUST.—1. Thus in *Boursot* v. *Savage* (*g*), A., one of

(*a*) *Harrison* v. *Forth*, Pr. Ch. 51; *Martins* v. *Joliffe*, Amb. 313; *M'Queen* v. *Farquhar*, 11 V. 478.

(*b*) *Bassett* v. *Nosworthy*, 2 L. C. 1; *Boursot* v. *Savage*, L. R., 2 Eq. 134; *Mackreth* v. *Symmons*, 15 V. 349; *Pilcher* v. *Rawlins*, L. R., 7 Ch. 259; and as to the time at which the notice is effectual, *Lady Bodmin* v. *Vanderbendz*, 1 Ver. 179; *Jones* v. *Thomas*, 3 P. W. 243; *Attorney-General* v. *Gower*, 2 Eq. Ca. Ab. 685, pl. 11;

More v. *Mahow*, 1 Ch. Ca. 34.

(*c*) See per Lord Westbury, *Phillips* v. *Phillips*, 4 D., F. & J. 208.

(*d*) *Turton* v. *Benson*, 1 P. W. 496; *Ord* v. *White*, 3 B. 357; *Mangles* v. *Dixon*, 3 H. L. Cas. 702.

(*e*) *Anon.*, Com. Rep. 43.

(*f*) *Re Blakeley Co.*, L. R., 3 Ch. 154; *Re General Estates Co.*, ibid. 758; *Crouch* v. *Crédit Foncier*, L. R., 8 Q. B. 374; and see Judicature Act, 1873, s. 25.

(*g*) L. R., 2 Eq. 134.

U.T.   O

three trustees, executed an assignment of leasehold property, held by them jointly, to a purchaser, and forged the
signatures of his two co-trustees, and also the requisite
assent of his cestui que trust to the sale.   A. was a solicitor,
and acted as such for the purchaser.   It was held, that in
accordance with the maxim *Qui facit per alium, facit per se*,
the purchaser had constructive notice by his solicitor of the
existence of the trust, and that although the execution by
one of three joint tenants was a valid assignment of the
legal interest in one-third of the property to the purchaser,
yet the constructive notice of the trust disentitled him from
taking any beneficial interest.

2. So where there is a **lien for unpaid purchase-money**
(which, as we have seen, burdens the estate with a trust
pro tanto), a subsequent purchaser, with notice of the lien
(such, for instance, as that which is constructively afforded
by the absence of an indorsed receipt on the conveyance (*h*)), will take the estate subject to it (*i*).

3. If an alienee is a **volunteer**, then the estate will remain burdened with the trust, whether he had notice of
the trust (*k*) or not (*l*); for a volunteer has no equity as
against a true owner.

4. But where one purchased lands from a devisee of
them bonâ fide, and without notice of any defect in the
will, and afterwards the heir of the testator filed a bill,
alleging that the testator had revoked his will, it was held
that the purchaser was entitled, whether the will was revoked or not (*m*).

5. In *Thorndike* v. *Hunt* (*n*), a trustee of two different
settlements having applied to his own use funds subject
to one of the settlements, replaced them by funds which,

(*h*) 2 Prest. Conv. 429.
(*i*) *Mackreth* v. *Symmons*, 15 V.
349.
(*k*) *Mansell* v. *Mansell*, 2 P. W.
678.
(*l*) *Ibid.; Spurgeon* v. *Collier*, 1

Ed. 55.
(*m*) *Bassett* v. *Nosworthy*, 2 L.
C. 1.
(*n*) 3 D. & J. 56; and see *Case*
v. *James*, 3 D., F. & J. 256; and
Dawson v. *Prince*, 2 D. & J. 41.

under a power of attorney from his co-trustee under the other, he transferred into the names of himself and his co-trustee in the former. In a suit in respect of breaches of trust of the former settlement, the trustees of it **transferred the fund** thus replaced **into court,** and it was held by the Court of Appeal, that the transfer into court was equivalent to an alienation for value without notice, and that the cestuis que trust under the other settlement could not follow the trust fund.

6. The trustees of a settlement advanced the trust money on the security of real property which was conveyed to them by the mortgagor, the mortgage deed noticing the trust. The surviving trustee of the settlement afterwards reconveyed part of the property to the mortgagor on payment of part of the mortgage money, which he forthwith appropriated. The mortgagor then conveyed that part of the property to new mortgagees, concealing, with the connivance of the trustee, both the prior mortgage and the reconveyance. When the fraud was discovered the cestui que trust under the settlement filed a bill against the new mortgagees, claiming priority; but the court refused to interfere, Lord Justice James saying, "I propose to apply myself to the case of a purchaser for valuable consideration without notice, obtaining on the occasion of his purchase, and by means of his purchase deed, some legal estate, some legal right, some legal advantage; and according to my view of the established law of this court, such a purchaser's plea of a purchase for valuable consideration without notice, is an absolute, unqualified, unanswerable plea to the jurisdiction of this court. . . . In such a case a purchaser is entitled to hold that which, without breach of duty, he has had conveyed to him"(o).

7. It would seem that a bonâ fide purchaser for value would not be bound by **notice of a very doubtful equity;**

(o) *Pilcher* v. *Rawlins,* L. R., 7 Ch. 259.

for instance, where the construction of a trust is ambiguous or equivocal (*p*); but where he is ignorant of any well-understood doctrine of equity, such, for instance, as that relating to the separate estate of married women (*q*), he will not be excused.

8. A purchaser with notice from a purchaser without notice is safe; for if not, an innocent purchaser for value would be incapable of ever alienating the property which he had acquired without breach of duty, and such a restraint on alienation would necessarily create that stagnation against which the law has always set its face (*r*).

9. Where a trustee, holding a mortgage, **deposits the deeds** with another to secure an advance to himself, the lender will have no equity against the cestuis que trust, however bonâ fide he may have acted, and however free he may have been of notice of the trustee's fraud, for he has not got the legal estate, and therefore his equity, being no stronger than that of the cestuis que trust, the maxim *Qui prior in tempore, potior in jure est* applies (*s*).

10. It is upon this principle that **choses in action** are generally taken, subject to all equities affecting them. Thus in *Turton* v. *Benson* (*t*), a son on his marriage was to have from his mother, as a portion, a sum equal to that with which his intended father-in-law should endow the intended wife. The son, in order to induce the mother to give him a larger portion, entered into a collusive arrangement with the father-in-law, whereby, in consideration of the latter nominally endowing his daughter with 3,000*l.*, the son gave him a bond to repay him 1,000*l.*, part of it. This bond, being made upon a fraudulent consideration, was void in the hands of the father-in-law, and it was held,

---

(*p*) *Hardy* v. *Reeves*, 5 V. 426; *Cordwell* v. *Mackrill*, Amb. 516; *Warwick* v. *Warwick*, 3 At. 291; but see and consider per Lord St. Leonards, *Thompson* v. *Simpson*, 1 Dr. & War. 491.

(*q*) *Parker* v. *Brooke*, 9 V. 583.
(*r*) See cases cited note (*a*), *sup.*
(*s*) *Newton* v. *Newton*, L. R., 4 Ch. 143; and *Joyce* v. *De Moleyns*, 2 J. & L. 374.
(*t*) 1 P. W. 496.

that being a chose in action, he could not confer a better title upon his assignee.

11. The bonâ fide purchaser of an equitable interest without notice of an express trust, cannot defend his position by subsequently, and after notice, getting in an outstanding legal estate *from the trustee;* for by so doing he would be guilty of taking part in a new breach of trust (*u*). But it would seem that if he can perfect his legal title without being a party to a new breach of trust (as, for instance, by registering a transfer of shares which have been actually transferred before notice), he may legitimately do so (*r*).

ART. 76.—*Liability of Persons paying Money burdened with a Trust to see to its Application.*

Where a person purchases trust property under a
   trust for sale with notice of the trust, or pays
   money owing to the trust estate with like notice,
   he is bound to see to the application of money
   paid by him (*a*), except in the following cases,
   namely:—

   α. Where the settlement expressly exempts him
   from doing so;

   β. Where the settlement is dated subsequently
   to the 28th August, 1860, and the duty is not
   expressly cast upon him by the settlement (*b*);

   γ. Where the trusts of the money are not simple

(*u*) *Saunders* v. *Dehew*, 2 Ver. 271; *Collier* v. *McBean*, 34 B. 426; *Sharples* v. *Adams*, 32 B. 213; *Carter* v. *Carter*, 3 K. & J. 617.

(*r*) *Dodds* v. *Hills*, 2 H. & M. 424.

(*a*) Dart, 596, 5th ed.; *Elliott* v. *Merryman*, 1 L. C. 64.

(*b*) 23 & 24 Vict. c. 145, s. 12. This statute is the only one which can be relied on. Lord St. Leonards' Act, 22 & 23 Vict. c. 35, s. 23, which was intended to have the same effect, seems to

have begged the question, inasmuch as it states that the purchaser shall be discharged by "the receipt of any person to whom any purchase or mortgage money *shall be payable* upon any express or implied trust," whereas the whole question is, whether the purchase-money *is* payable to the trustee or to the cestuis que trust. In addition to which it only applies to purchasers and mortgagees.

trusts (*c*), or being simple trusts it is gathered from
the settlement that the settlor *contemplated* the possibility of any of the cestuis que trust being under
disability at the date of the sale or payment (*d*), or
in any other case where an intention to impose the
duty on the purchaser or person paying cannot
reasonably be inferred (*e*).

ILLUST.—1. Sub-article γ is the only part of the foregoing article which requires illustration. Where the trust
is for **payment of general debts** either alone or in priority
to specified debts or legacies, the purchaser is discharged
from seeing to the application of the purchase-money;
because the trustee has to ascertain and test the validity
of all debts which may be alleged to be due, and therefore the trusts of the purchase-money are not simple
trusts (*f*); and a simple exemption holds where the purchase-money is to be applied in the purchase of other
lands (*g*), or on other special trusts. But where the trusts
of the purchase-money are **to pay certain specified debts**
or specified legacies, so that the parties entitled are clearly
ascertained by the settlement, and if there is no other evidence of the intention of the settlor to exempt the purchaser
from seeing to the application of the purchase-money, he
will be bound to do so. For in equity the cestuis que
trust are the absolute owners, and the trustee is a mere
instrument or agent, and therefore the cestuis que trust
are the persons to receive the purchase-money, and to give
a valid receipt for it (*h*). It is, however, humbly conceived

(*c*) See Story, § 1134, and cases
cited as illustrations, *infra*.

(*d*) Dart, 597, 5th ed.; *Sowarsby*
v. *Lacey*, 4 Mad. 142; *Lavender*
v. *Stanton*, 6 *ibid*. 46; *Balfour* v.
Welland, 16 V. 151; *Breedon* v.
Breedon, 1 R. & M. 413.

(*e*) Dart, 596, 5th ed.; and see
generally *Elliott* v. *Merryman, sup*.

(*f*) *Elliott* v. *Merryman, sup.;*
Johnson v. *Kennett*, 3 M. & K.
624; *Eland* v. *Eland*, 4 M. & C.

420; *Forbes* v. *Peacock*, 1 Ph. 717;
Robinson v. *Lowater*, 5 D., M. &
G. 372; *Re Langmead*, 7 D., M. &
G. 353.

(*g*) *Doran* v. *Wiltshire*, 3 Sw.
699.

(*h*) *Wetherby* v. *St. Giorgio*, 2
Ha. 624; *Johnson* v. *Kennett, sup.;*
Horn v. *Horn*, 2 Sim. & St. 448;
Lloyd v. *Baldwin*, 1 V. sen. 173;
Ithell v. *Beane*, *ibid*. 215; *Binks*
v. *Lord Rokeby*, 2 Mad. 238.

that if the doctrine that a power to give valid discharges is to be implied where the trustee has some unascertained duty to perform with the purchase-money before paying it over to the cestuis que trust were carried to its logical conclusion, it would apply to cases in which the purchase-money is to be distributed among specified persons; but the trustee is directed to first *pay thereout all expenses of the sale.* For it does not seem reasonable to suppose that the settlor intended to impose on the purchaser the duty of ascertaining that the costs deducted were properly incurred at all, or if properly incurred were properly taxed before payment. It is difficult to see wherein such a case differs from a general charge of debts, inasmuch as the ascertainment of the expenses of the sale would require quite as much circumspection and trouble on the part of the purchaser as an investigation into the settlor's general debts. However, I am not aware that the doctrine has ever been pushed to this extent; and it is not considered very probable that the court would do so now.

2. Where the trust was to pay certain specified sums and then to invest the residue, it was held that the purchaser was bound to see to the payment of the specified sums.

3. But where a testator devised certain land unto his children, "the same to be sold when the executors and trustees of this my last will shall see proper to dispose of it, and the money arising out of my said lands and tenements to be equally and severally divided among my above named children," **some of whom were infants,** it was held that the trustees could give valid receipts, the Vice-Chancellor saying: "It is plain the testator intended that the trustees should have an *immediate* power of sale. Some of the children were infants, and not capable of signing receipts. I must, therefore, infer that the testator meant to give to the trustees the power to sign receipts, being an authority necessary for the execution of his declared purpose"(i).

(i) *Sowarsby* v. *Lacey, sup.*

4. On the other hand, where the intention on the part of the testator cannot be implied, as for instance, where he contemplates that all the cestuis que trust will be **sui juris at the date** of sale, but in fact one or more of them labour under some disability (as, for instance, if one dies and his representative is an infant) at that date, the purchaser will have to see to the application of the purchase-money; for the rule of law depends upon construction or intention, and not convenience (*k*).

5. As the rule depends upon implied intention, an implied power to give valid discharges is not taken away by the fact that, at the actual date of sale, the status of the parties interested is such as would have rebutted the presumption had the settlor had such status in his contemplation at the date of the settlement (*l*). For instance, where a testator devises property to trustees upon trust to sell and pay debts generally, and subject thereto upon trust for A. B., the non-existence of debts at the time of sale is, in general, immaterial; for the testator contemplated that there would be some, and therefore intended to give the trustees power to give valid discharges (*m*). But if the *sole* object of the trust was to pay debts, and the purchaser knew that there were none, or that they had been paid, he will of course not be justified in paying the purchase-money to the trustee, for the sale would in such case be itself a breach of trust, and the purchaser taking with notice would of course be responsible under Article 75 (*n*).

6. It may here be mentioned that on similar principles where there is a *charge* of debts and a power of sale in the event of the personal estate proving deficient, the purchaser need not concern himself to ascertain whether there is a deficiency in the personal estate (*o*).

(*k*) Dart, 597 and 599, 5th ed.
(*l*) Ibid. 600.
(*m*) Forbes v. Peacock, 1 Ph. 721; Sabin v. Heape, 27 B. 553; Balfour v. Welland, 16 V. 151.

(*n*) Watkins v. Cheek, 2 S. & S. 199; Eland v. Eland, sup.
(*o*) Greatham v. Cotton, 13 W. R. 1009; Bird v. Fox, 11 Ha. 40; but see Pierce v. Scott, 1 Y. & C. Ex. 257.

INDEX.

———◆———

ABROAD, trustee residing, may be removed, 149.

ACCELERATION of a trust for sale, breach of trust, 119.

ACCEPTANCE OF A TRUST, 88 *et seq.*
prior agreement not equivalent to, 87.
taking out probate equivalent to, 88.
interfering with trust property generally equivalent to, 88, 89.

ACCOUNTS, trustee should be ready with, 125.
trustee entitled to have his, gone through and settled or impeached, 164.

ACCUMULATION. *See* PERPETUITIES.
direction for, until a given age generally futile, 142.

ACQUIESCENCE. *See* CONCURRENCE *and* LACHES.
in voluntary trust after learning its true nature, 45.

ACTIONS, trustee the proper plaintiff in, regarding the trust property, 101.

ACTS of the settlor, when admissible to rebut presumption of trust, 26, 74.

ADVANCEMENT of infants, 134. *And see* RESULTING TRUST (3).

ADVANTAGE, trustee must not gain any, from trust, 127 *et seq.*

ADVERSE TITLE. *See* JUS TERTII.

ADVICE, trustee committing breach of trust in [pursuance of legal, not indemnified, 104.
of judge, trustee may get, 165.
under what circumstances given, *ib.*

AGE, attempt to restrain enjoyment of property until a given, generally futile, 142.

AGENT is a constructive trustee, 79.
when trustee may employ an, 112 *et seq.*
how far trustee liable for defaults of, *ib.*

ALIEN may be a cestui que trust, 43.
may be a trustee, 85.

ALIENATION. *See* ANTICIPATION.

ALLOWANCE. *See* SALARY *and* REIMBURSEMENT.

ANNUITY, person for whom an, is directed to be purchased may claim money, 143.
even though anticipation be restrained on pain of forfeiture, *ib.*

ANTICIPATION, restraint on, generally void, 33—140.
aliter, in case of pay, pensions or property inalienable by statute, 28, 29.
aliter, in case of married woman during coverture, *ib.*
married woman restrained from, cannot release a breach of trust, 157.
not liable for fraud, 190.
may nevertheless bar estate tail, 141.

APPEAL by trustee is at his own risk, 167.

APPORTIONMENT of purchase-money on a joint sale, 113.

ARTICLES, marriage, construed liberally. *See* EXECUTORY TRUSTS.

ATTORNEY. *See* SOLICITOR.

AUTHORITY of trustee. *See* POWERS.
of cestui que trust. *See* CESTUI QUE TRUST.

BANK ANNUITIES. *See* INVESTMENT.

BANKER, when trustee, liable for failure of, 116.
trustees may remit money through, 117.

BANKRUPT TRUSTEE may be removed, 148.

BANKRUPTCY, trust for personal enjoyment notwithstanding, is illegal, 32.
trust until, and then over, good, 33.
a voluntary settlor cannot settle upon himself until, and then over, *ib.*
what settlements are void against the settlor's creditors in, 53.
of trustee, 100.
  trust property not divisible amongst his creditors, if recognizable, *ib.*
  aliter, where it cannot be identified, 101.
of agent or factor, money of principal not divisible among creditors, 100.

BARRING ENTAIL, married woman restrained from anticipation is capable of, 141.

BILL IN PARLIAMENT, trustee may oppose, 132.

FORMALITIES unnecessary where trust based on value, 19.
necessary where trust is voluntary, 20.

FRAUD of settlor. *See* RESULTING TRUST (2) *and* VALIDITY.
whereby a settlor is induced not to make a will or not to comply
with Statute of Frauds, 40.
converts a wrongdoer into a trustee, 82.
a secret agreement to share expectant legacies is not a, 28.
of trustee's solicitor, whether trustee liable for, 113, 115.
infants and married women are liable for, 85, 157, 159.
aliter, where married woman is restrained from anticipation, 157,
159.

FRAUDS, STATUTE OF. *See* WRITING.

FRAUDULENT breach of trust a crime, 188.
intention of settlor does not estop him claiming a resulting trust.
See RESULTING TRUST (2).

GAINER by breach of trust must pro tanto indemnify the trustee, 163.

GIFT, imperfect voluntary, is not equivalent to a declaration of trust,
24 *et seq.*
voluntary when it raises a resulting trust. *See* RESULTING TRUST
(1) *and* (3).

GUARDIAN, undue influence of, 44.

HEIR. *See* RESULTING TRUST.
of last surviving trustee, when he may execute a special trust, 146.

"HOPES." *See* LANGUAGE.

HUSBAND of woman to whom property is given for her separate
use is a trustee, 19.

IGNORANCE. *See* VALIDITY.

ILLEGAL TRUST, 30 *et seq; and see* PERPETUITIES; THELLUSSON ACT;
BANKRUPTCY; ANTICIPATION; ILLEGITIMATE CHILDREN; *and* RESULT-
ING TRUSTS.

ILLEGITIMATE CHILDREN, trusts by deed or will for another's
future, are illegal, 33.
trusts by deed for settlor's own future, are illegal, *ib.*
trusts by will for settlor's own future, are valid, 34.

ILLUSORY TRUSTS, 17.

IMMORAL TRUSTS. *See* ILLEGITIMATE CHILDREN.

IMPERATIVE, words when sufficiently. *See* LANGUAGE.

IMPLIED TRUSTS, 4, n. (*f*).

U.T.   P

P 2

U.T.   Q

VALIDITY OF A TRUST, as to object. *See* ILLEGAL TRUST.
(1) *As against the settlor*, 44 *et seq.*
    fraud, 44, 47.
    undue influence, 44.
        of clergyman, 46.
        of father, *ib.*
        of guardian, 44.
        of legal adviser, *ib.*
        of doctor, *ib.*
        of trustee, *ib.*
    ignorance of the effect of the settlement, *ib.*
        illness, 46.
        inexperience, 45.
        old age and infirmity, 47.
        mistake, *ib.*
        even where value given, *ib.*
    subsequent acquiescence validates, 45.
    onus of proving validity of a voluntary settlement, *ib.*
    power of revocation in voluntary settlements not essential to, *ib.*
(2) *As against creditors*, 47 *et seq.*
    direct intention to defraud, 49, 50.
        settlement to avoid execution, 50.
        settlement on self until bankruptcy, 51.
    where no direct intention to defraud, but the necessary consequence of settlement would be to do so, *ib.*
    assignee for value, how far bound by notice of the effect of his purchase, *ib.*
(3) *As against creditors in bankruptcy*, 53.
(4) *As against subsequent purchasers*, 54 *et seq.*
    direct intention to defraud, *ib.*
    voluntary settlements always bad in the hands of cestuis que trust against, *ib.*
    very small consideration sufficient to protect cestuis que trust, 55.
    power of revocation always makes settlement bad as against, 54.
    notice to purchaser immaterial, *ib.*
    collusion between settlor and purchaser, 56.
    cestuis que trust have no equity to the purchase-money, *ib.*
    purchasers from the cestuis que trust are protected, 55.
    such settlements are only void pro tanto, 56.

VALUABLE CONSIDERATION, what trusts are based on, 4.
    where there is, formalities are immaterial, 19.
    where there is not. *See* VOLUNTARY TRUST.
    marriage is a, 5.
    what limitations in a marriage settlement are not based on, *ib.*
    limitations in favour of children of a former marriage are based on, 7.

VENDOR, constructive trustee for purchaser, 80.
    must take reasonable care of estate before completion, 110.

VESTING property in new trustees, 150.

VOLUNTARY TRUST. *See* VALUABLE CONSIDERATION.
    when primâ facie valid, 20 *et seq.*
        must be an executed trust, 20.
        imperfect gift not enforceable, 23, 24, 25.
        mere covenant to settle not enforceable, 21.
        when settlor has done all in his power to create an executed
           trust, 22.
        conflict of authorities, 24.
    when invalid from something attending its inception. *See* VALI-
        DITY (1).
    when invalid as against creditors. *See* VALIDITY (2).
    when invalid as against creditors in bankruptcy, 53.
    when invalid as against subsequent purchasers. *See* VALIDITY (4).

VOLUNTEER, 20 *et seq.*
    assignee of a lease cannot be a, 5.
    donee of trust property under a breach of trust cannot retain it, 194.
    See also VOLUNTARY TRUST *and* VALUABLE CONSIDERATION.

WAIVER of breach of trust, what amounts to, 158.

"WELL KNOWS." *See* LANGUAGE.

WORDS. *See* LANGUAGE.

WRITING, necessity of, in declarations of trust of real estate and
    leaseholds, 37.
            aliter, in personal property, *ib.*
    what the writing must show, 38, 39.
    where fraud handwriting unnecessary, 40.
    resulting trust, where declared trust was not reduced into, 65.

London : Printed by C. F. Roworth, Bream's Buildings, Chancery Lane.

www.ingramcontent.com/pod-product-compliance
Lightning Source LLC
Chambersburg PA
CBHW030403270326
41926CB00009B/1250